TEN LANTERNS

Light Your Way—Lighten Your Pain

EVAGORAS EVAGOROU

BALBOA.PRESS

A DIVISION OF HAY HOUSE

Balboa Press books may be ordered through booksellers or by contacting:

Balboa Press
A Division of Hay House
1663 Liberty Drive
Bloomington, IN 47403
www.balboapress.com
844-682-1282

Because of the dynamic nature of the Internet, any web addresses or links contained in this book may have changed since publication and may no longer be valid. The views expressed in this work are solely those of the author and do not necessarily reflect the views of the publisher, and the publisher hereby disclaims any responsibility for them.

The author of this book does not dispense medical advice or prescribe the use of any technique as a form of treatment for physical, emotional, or medical problems without the advice of a physician, either directly or indirectly. The intent of the author is only to offer information of a general nature to help you in your quest for emotional and spiritual well-being. In the event you use any of the information in this book for yourself, which is your constitutional right, the author and the publisher assume no responsibility for your actions.

Any people depicted in stock imagery provided by Getty Images are models, and such images are being used for illustrative purposes only. Certain stock imagery © Getty Images.

Print information available on the last page.

ISBN: 979-8-7652-3727-4 (sc)
ISBN: 979-8-7652-3728-1 (hc)
ISBN: 979-8-7652-3729-8 (e)

Library of Congress Control Number: 2023907638

Balboa Press rev. date: 07/07/2023

Life has many stories.
Not all of them are pleasant so
I chose the most beautiful one to tell you!

Ten Lanterns

Light Your Way—Lighten Your Pain

An experiential story that will help you pursue the happy life you deserve.

A spiritual map and compass to guide you on your journey of personal fulfillment.

Dedicated to the sender and the custodian

Contents

Introduction

It is important to mention from the beginning some points that are fundamental to a full understanding of the meaning of my book.

I use the word *pain* to refer to physical and emotional pain. In addition, the use of the word also reflects sadness, melancholy, panic, fear, anguish, loneliness, anxiety, despair, and all other emotions that, in life, cause us great pain.

The practices you'll find in the book will help you face pain head on, not avoid it. Pain needs systematic management, not ostrichism. You will encounter several times the expression, *Let pain come but not be welcome!* Obviously, I am referring to immediate, active, and drastic management of pain. Pain must be removed for satisfaction to follow.

I use the terms *spirit* and *soul* without making a distinction, while understanding the conceptual difference that may exist. By using these words, I am referring to the perennial incorporeal essence of a living being. I, therefore, use the terms *spiritual map* and *spiritual compass* frequently.

The *spiritual map* refers to the daily predetermined and well-thought-out plans you must make to help you understand and appreciate your own, personal, unique entity and reality. This clairvoyance—your insight—is the map you use to move forward in every direction of space and time. If the map you hold is correct, then you know where you were, where you are, and where you want to go. Therefore, the mapping you do is extremely important and requires a great deal of effort to craft.

The *spiritual compass* refers to all the aids, tools, practices, values, and perceptions you will have at your disposal to make your journey, safely and successfully. It will be everything that potentially will get you back on track when you stray off course. Consequently, a spiritual compass can also be another person holding a lantern—or more, to light your way and bring you back to the *Great Road!*

Note to the Reader

I write to you every day.

I write until my eyes get misty.

I write until my hands are numb.

I write to you as fast as I can because I have discovered that time is one of the most precious things in the world.

To free your body and soul from pain requires a journey to the illuminating stations of your life. To do this, you must break the boundaries of time and space. If the regressions from the back-and-forth journey make you dizzy or confused, please be patient until we reach the last station. There, I promise you, the *last route* will light the way, and all will become crystal clear.

I welcome you to the distinguished seats of the first carriage to continue the journey of the quest together—the invitation is mine, and the choice is yours.

May the words infuse the spirit and encourage the desperate, awaken the asleep, welcome the lost, and, above all, comfort all those in pain. May the journey provide each passenger with inexhaustible strength for personal development and transformation. May the luggage we carry be as light as a feather.

"Story or fairytale, truth or fantasy, possible or impossible?" the mind asks curiously.

"What difference does it make? What really matters is what has been awakened inside you and what you are going to do about it," the heart replies.

Enjoy our choiceful journey to a successful life!

Preparation

The starting point of all achievement is Desire. Keep
this constantly in mind. Weak desire brings weak results,
just as a small fire makes a small amount of heat!
—Napoleon Hill

September. What a blessing!

The executives return from their summer holidays with batteries
fully charged and an appetite to change everything in one day. It is
the month that marks the end of the holidays and the beginning of
another challenging corporate year. Young students usually call it *the
first school meeting,* and older students call it *the kick-off meeting.*

It doesn't matter if you are young or old. The best student always
anticipates the kick-off by taking time during the summer vacation
to make the necessary preparations—to finally read the best-selling
book on leadership that was gathering dust; to exchange business
cards at the first opportunity; to discuss investment opportunities
while playing golf with two stockbrokers; or finally to spend some
time with the family.

A major shipping company based in Greece also wanted to start
the new business year in the best possible way. Invitations for the kick-
off meeting were sent to management during the last week of August.

This year will begin with a bang! The kick-off meeting is to take
place in a five-star hotel on the second weekend of September at

seven o'clock in the evening, rather than in the large reception hall of their headquarters at seven on a Monday morning. The second bang will be when a guest speaker takes the stage and presents something completely different and unexpected, unlike previous years when the captain has told the same old stories. Assuredly, this year's event will be quite different from all previous ones.

The owner and CEO of the shipping company, the so-called captain, sought to meet me a year ago when I toured Greece to promote my book. He contacted my publisher's PR department, leaving a request for my personal mobile number, claiming that it was "urgent and important" that he speak with me. Perhaps that's the most favored expression used by executives when they send their requests back and forth; it's all urgent and it's all important, which often results in a dozen or so people crippling themselves to get the job done.

His last name—synonymous with the name of the shipping company—triggered the alarm at the offices of my publishing house. It didn't take long to track me down; I was enjoying the traditional dishes in a Greek taverna. They secured my permission to give my cell phone number to the captain. After all, it was urgent and important!

Later that evening, I found myself chatting on the phone with one of Europe's most successful shipowners and accepting an invitation to a get-to-know-you lunch on his yacht, moored at Flisvos Marina. I could have never refused an invitation that would give me the opportunity to meet a shipping legend and, at the same time, board a spectacular yacht for the first time. As a child, I would gaze at the boats in the marinas and dream that one day I would have one of my own. When I got older and wiser, I just got a model boat and put it on the library shelf to remind me of my illusory dream.

The dream of being on board a real yacht, however, would be fulfilled, with a condition the captain gave to me—to sign ten copies of my book with a special dedication: "I wish you a fair wind and smooth sailing until you reach the destination your captain desires!" According to him, he would give these books to the group's ten general managers, who control a company of more than five thousand employees and associates.

I have Captain Legend—that's what his colleagues call him—in sight for the first time, and I immediately understand how he acquired that nickname. It is obviously associated with his various achievements and adventures over seven decades, but the association with his physical appearance and his dynamic attitude is obvious. He is full of youthful vigor and endless energy, with eyes that sparkle with the flames of good living. His broad shoulders and well-toned arms confirm the five miles of swimming he boasts of doing every morning, summer and winter. Despite the divine dishes I spot on the table, his lean body is a testament to a man who takes care of his diet, health, and appearance.

An upbeat, unstoppable seventy-three-year-old "teenager" looks at me with admiration while welcoming me aboard his ship with a naval salute. His one-ninety height inspired him to name his yacht *L90*; the *L* is from the word Legend, and *90* is for the size of his custom-built yacht. It is, in his words, only ninety feet long! What an introduction with just one handshake!

After many enlightening conversations, I realize that he is a man of spiritual wisdom and abundant knowledge. The smile I detect behind his long white beard, combined with the deep bass tones of his voice, inspire a sense of awe in me. The reflection of the sun peeking out from behind him, the white linen clothing that dances lightly with the air, and the smoke wreathing his face from his Cuban cigar cause my imagination to run wild. The fleeting thought crosses my mind that I should write a book of his stories and adventures at sea. I shall call it *A Legend among Us*.

At some point, he mentions that, without exception, he wears only white garments. A white tuxedo with a white tie is enough for a formal dinner, and white jeans with a white shirt is more than enough for a quick visit to the office. The company's headquarters are in Palaio Faliro, a stone's throw from the marina, which is why a chauffeur is always on standby near the mega-yacht platform; for the most part, he works remotely from his yacht's office, located on the third deck, where the view is beyond revealing. These are some of the new words I learn from our very first meeting: a *platform* is the hydraulic bridge that takes you up to the yacht; a *mega-yacht* is a boat that is as large as his *L90*; *deck* refers to the boat's floors; and *knots* is how the cruising speed is controlled. As for the view from the third deck, I'll limit myself to one word: magnificent!

Magnificent is not only the view and the boat itself but also our meeting. The hospitality is exceptional, and the philosophical conversation is illuminating. I soak up all the knowledge and wisdom he generously shares, as I inhale the ozone from the sea breezes.

Finally, I'm ready to say goodbye with the utmost gratitude. Before that happens, I sign the ten books I had promised him in advance. I now stand across from him, extending my hand for the customary farewell handshake. He arches his eyebrows, gently pushes my hand to the side, and gathers me into his arms. The final highlight of the day are the words he whispers in my ear: "Thank you for opening my heart!"

To disguise his obvious emotions, he clears his voice and says stoically, "I want you to know that the day you received my call and accepted my invitation, I instructed the HR Department to order one thousand copies of your book from the publishing house. To begin with, I will make sure they go to everyone who has supervisory duties in my company and some other sleepers I have in mind. The ten signed ones will go to the executives, and we'll see from there. God has plans for everyone!"

It is my turn to return the hug and say a humble and genuine, "Thank you!"

Before we part, he tells me that he will save my mobile phone number and contact me again very soon.

Leaving the marina on this starry evening, I take with me a little coolness from being in the shadow of a true legend and a huge dose of satisfaction. It is a confirmation that my book is useful, even to a seasoned seafarer who has seen and experienced it all.

Countdown

Start by doing what's necessary; then do what's
possible. And suddenly you are doing the impossible!
—Francis of Assisi

August. What a blessing!

My birthday heralds my favorite month and the beginning of my summer holidays. And what an amazing coincidence that an invitation to the Great Britain Hotel in Syntagma Square in Athens arrives while I am on my summer holiday in Great Britain, finally visiting friends at their lovely house in the Elmbridge area of Surrey.

On a cool Tuesday afternoon, while enjoying cocktails in the back garden overlooking the River Thames, my phone rings. The screen shows Captain Legend, and my soul travels at supersonic speed, taking me back on board his yacht. Rising abruptly from doing some sun therapy, I find a quiet spot for some psychotherapy. The pool area is a noisy cacophony of friends' children and their guests, who set the neighborhood on fire with their shouting and laughter.

Sitting on the grass, under the shade of a century-old oak tree, I answer the phone in a very summery mood. "At your command, Captain Legend!"

"How is my great teacher doing?"

"He is drinking cocktails in England and is ready to dive into the pool if he ever wants a great body like yours. I'll swim five miles for you and five for me. Will it be enough?"

"Do you have a lifeguard? Drinking and swimming is supposedly a dangerous combination. I don't want to lose you, now that I've found you."

The small talk continues, enhanced with our private jokes, not forgetting the standard joke we always share: his asking how I managed to become a bestselling author at age forty-three and my asking how he managed to become a legend at age seventy-three. Then comes our laughter and the discussion about whether I would agree to swap our duties. He plays a dishonest game every time because he tempts me by transferring the ownership of the *L90* to my name if I accept to lift the burden off his shoulders.

Detecting voices in the background, I pluck up the courage to ask him directly, with a little bit of humor, "Don't tell me you're having a party on my yacht, and I'm not invited!"

"You're not missing anything at all. I'm sailing the Ionian Sea with about twenty friends and colleagues. We left Kefalonia and are heading to my beloved Ithaca in amazing weather! We don't get more than twenty knots as a fair wind is serving us. It looks like your wish has come true."

"How glad I am to hear that! But what are you doing speaking with me on the phone? You should be clinking glasses and drinking champagne. Isn't that what you boat owners do all summer?"

"Something like that, assuming you have good company, good mood, good manners, and good intentions, and your journey has good progress—basic choices if you want to create good memories. As you see, I have memorized the first choices from your book. I am a good student, after all!"

"The best! How can I help you create even better memories?"

"Here's what I thought. I've been thinking about it for days, and now, I've made up my mind. Since your wish for a fair wind has been granted, and I am enjoying the calmest sea I have ever sailed on with my boat, we will offer the same possibilities to my group. Please open your diary and check your availability for the second weekend in September."

Struggling for a while to keep the line open and at the same time open the calendar on my mobile phone, I check the busy month of September. To my surprise the aforesaid weekend is completely empty and available.

"It looks fine to me. Surprisingly, I have absolutely nothing planned for then. Will you take me on the boat trip you promised me?"

"Book the whole weekend, and don't ask too many questions! If you want to, try to come earlier. And don't you dare book a hotel and buy a ticket, or I'll drown you in the pool myself! I'll tell Frida to take care of everything, and she'll update your PA. Is that understood?"

I note the stern tone in his voice.

"Can I say no to Captain Legend? But at least tell me what you have in mind so I can sleep on it."

"This year's kick-off meeting has been planned and invitations have been sent out already. Don't envision too many people—about three hundred in all. This year, I decided to take them to the Hotel Grande Bretagne. And much to their surprise, instead of putting them to sleep with my speech, which features the same stories of daring every year, you will pop up, take the stage, and rouse them!"

"Where did that idea come from?"

"I have realized that over the years, I have invested tens of thousands in the training and development of my staff without ever questioning the benefits of this investment. When I first asked for a breakdown from Mark, the general manager of HR, he proudly informed me that we spent almost half a million on technical seminars in the last period. He was very embarrassed when I asked him how much we have invested in soft-skills seminars, as he likes to call them. All he managed to achieve with this answer was to raise my blood pressure sky high, for two reasons. First, he has not invested a single cent in soft-skills seminars, and second, he has not learned over the years that there is nothing soft about this huge and important area of work. I told him to start looking for a job if he fails this year to invest the same amount of money in people skills, as I like to refer to them. What do you say?"

"I say that you never cease to amaze me!"

"All those who meet you a month from today will also be amazed, my dear friend. No doubt they've already got a big buzz from seeing your name in gold letters on their invitation. When I told you about my preference for white, you told me that your favorite color is gold, right? Anyway, they all received a copy of your book long ago, but I am not sure how many of them have read it already. Once they get to know you, though, I'm sure they will swallow it in a day's bite, as I did that summer on Hvar Island in Croatia. That was the only day that I didn't swim, since you had me drowning in thoughts, my great teacher!"

"You are always so generous, my captain! But tell me something. What do you mean, they're already excited to meet me? We only talked about it a moment ago. Don't tell me you announced me before we even discussed it."

"Stop grumbling like a first-grader who doesn't like his teacher! Please forward my best regards and thanks to your personal assistant for her discretion. Sweet girl! She managed to clear your entire three-day weekend in just five minutes without asking me much of anything. Keep an eye on her, or I'll steal her from you one day. My PA, Frida, is constantly capricious and jittery. I must remember to give her a copy of your book. You will not encourage her with fair winds and mumbo-jumbo. Your focus is strictly confined to the need to obey her captain. And if that doesn't work, then God help me with her!"

"Since you conspired with the diary boss, I'll pass. Thank you very much for the invitation, which I am very honored to receive and accept. I'll see you a month from today. Fortunately, I'm in the best country in the world when it comes to shopping. Tomorrow, I will go hunting for a suit!"

"Do not get a gold one! We'll be irreparably exposed, King Midas!"

"I'll buy your next favorite color—navy blue."

"You got it! Thank you. You go dive in the pool, and I'll go drown my boredom in champagne. Over and out!"

● ● ●

It's *over and out* for the summer holidays too, and here I am again, facing the biggest challenge of my life—packing my suitcase!

I must have made fifty trips in the last ten years and have yet to come to terms with this challenging process. Packing always irritates me, and as a result, it bores me to death. I leave everything to the last minute, and the outcome is always a disaster. There is no way I ever succeed in gathering all the necessities together, and there is no trip where I don't get frustrated with my shortcomings. The end result is that I am forever enriching my collections. I have so far managed to collect thirteen toothbrushes, twenty nail clippers, seven mobile phone chargers, ten electricity adapters, and nine pairs of reading glasses, as well as many other assorted items. Not to mention the waterproof jackets I buy every time I visit rainy cities and—surprise, surprise—realize once again that I haven't packed a raincoat. I am the proud owner of one in every color!

For some reason, this time I have a completely different feeling. The day is Thursday, one day before the trip to Greece, and my sweet PA has made sure to schedule no meetings or obligations beyond noon. The whole afternoon in my calendar is highlighted in yellow, with PACKING written in capital letters, in case it could possibly escape my attention. When I left the office, she wished me a safe journey and good luck. She did not forget to ask me to extend her heartfelt regards to the "sweet gentleman" with whom she conspired on the phone.

The next day's flight is at seven in the morning, and I want to get an early night to give me the energy and enthusiasm I'll need for the intensive weekend ahead. My wife awaits me at home and has my favorite meal in the oven: stuffed vegetables with rice and minced meat—delicious dolmades!

"Finally, we can have a meal together," she says as I enter the kitchen, and it's not long before she continues her complaint that she isn't coming with me to Greece. Once again, I explain that she will be hopelessly lonely because Captain Legend has filled my Sunday with focus groups and personal coaching sessions. She ends her protest relatively effortlessly, once I promise we'll visit Greece together as soon as possible.

The food needs another twenty minutes before serving, and we agree to eat after I finish my packing. Taking strength from the divine smells coming from the kitchen, I head to our room. The empty suitcase is waiting, and I do hand stretches to prepare my body for yet another packing battle. My wife, as usual, brings me the clothes and other essentials at the speed of a bee.

I start putting things into the bag, including all the items for my morning preparation: hair cream, shaving cream, eye cream, neck cream, hand cream.

"Have mercy on me, oh God! You have turned me into a cream freak!" I yell at my wife in desperation and burst out laughing.

"Don't forget your allergy cream," she calls as she descends the stairs, heading to the kitchen, leaving me on the battlefield. After all, she has collected almost everything together for me. She even chose the shirt and tie that perfectly match the suit she picked out in London. I had only chosen the color, navy blue.

Luckily, this time I find everything ready except for the black leather shoulder bag that I invariably carry to every presentation. In it, I gather all the items I want to display to my audience. I have found this process to be extremely effective for the Doubting Thomases who sometimes attend speeches only to claim their disbelief in miracles. Happily, it doesn't happen often—in fact, hardly ever. The one time it did happen, however, was enough to give birth to the idea of having a black leather shoulder bag containing all the material I need for a compelling presentation.

The evidence and documents are in place from the previous trip, but my ritual never changes. I empty the entire contents onto my bed, and, one by one, with love and affection, I place them back into the black bag. To the audience, they are mere artifacts, but to me, they are priceless acquisitions. These are my treasures from my journey of discovery that began in 1993 at my grandfather's mountain mansion. One by one, I pick up each item and examine it closely. I still have the urge to give each item a kiss, to say a thank-you, or to offer a kind word before I carefully place them all back in the bag.

I was ecstatic the first time I saw this bag hanging for sale at a Christmas bazaar in Vienna. It had exactly the internal dividers I was looking for, but most paradoxically, it had a gold-colored buckle with my initials on the outside! I couldn't believe my eyes and asked to buy a pair so I could have a spare! I held it tightly in my hands as soon as the vendor, who also happened to be the maker, mentioned that it was the only one in the world with those initials, as he never uses the same buckle on another bag. In this way, he wants his unique bags to end up with unique customers. Unbelievable! The bag with my initials was in Austria, waiting patiently for me to possess it and feel truly special. This was indeed as unbelievable as the *apfelstrudel* that shortly followed at Café Mozart.

The bag is now open, awaiting its treasures. I start with the pink magic stick and continue with the laminated referral letter from the doctor, my friend's first-edition book, the special shot glass, the thirty-three amber rosary beads, and many other unique items. In the past, I had many more documents with me. These are now safely housed in my office safe, as I only ever show the scanned copies on the giant screens now.

With all these technological advances, I carry only my electronic stick to help me advance the slides on the screens. The stick also has the ability to emit a red laser beam, but I have not yet found the appropriate opportunity to use this option. It's been years since I used the beam in my seminars, "Positive Communication and Inspirational Leadership," to corner the *naughty students* in the class. Lectures are quite a different event.

The suitcase is ready, and the black leather bag is full of treasures. The tickets and accommodation documents are also ready in an envelope organized by our assistants. I check for a third time that my passport and driver's license are also in the bag. This time, I don't forget to take the necessary reinforcements. I have chosen the book *The 3ʳᵈ Alternative* by Dr. Stephen R. Covey to keep me alert during the stultifying hours at the airport and on the plane. I have been wanting to read this masterpiece for a long time, but until now, I have not had the chance. I had taken it with me to London, but my wife made sure I didn't get the slightest opportunity to open it. Stowaway it traveled, and stowaway it came back!

Finally, I am ready! After a cooling bath, down the stairs I go to the main living room and kitchen, happily whistling the tune to "Summertime [and the living is easy]." I have built up much strength from my summer vacation, as well as an incredible appetite for dolmades and a desire to chat with my wife before I go to bed. Opening the fridge, I gaze at some treats that challenge me beyond belief. In the end, I choose to stay true to the diet I've started to kill the sins of summer. I just grab a glass bottle of water and close the fridge. And then—it happens!

The pain has chosen to visit me again. It never crossed my mind that the nightmare I buried twenty-two years ago would come back into my life once more. A sharp, unbearable pain starts in the back of my neck, and, like a bolt of lightning, it descends throughout my body in an instant. It cuts off my breath and forces me to fold over and fall to the floor in the fetal position.

This happens if the lung wall is pierced or an opening occurs, allowing air to invade the chest cavity. The air takes over most of the cavity that the lung needs in order to expand, squeezing the lung into a corner, unable to make any movement. In this case, as it was back then, I am blessed that the other lung is working normally, although it's becoming exhausted with trying to compensate for the functional gap left by the decommissioned lung.

As the glass bottle falls, shattering on the floor, along with the fragments of my soul, I know exactly what is happening to me. Years ago, I had the misfortune of experiencing this torment over and over again—a collapsed lung from spontaneous pneumothorax!

I had talked about this matter with my wife when we first met. Being innocent enough, she had asked me about the scars I have on both sides of my chest. Occasionally, the subject of my health would surface, giving me the opportunity to remind her that if anything like this ever happened again, every minute that passes would be extremely critical to my life.

The guidelines we laid out are clear. If a lung episode happens on a weekday, when emergency services are usually chaotic, we would take our car and drive as fast as possible. If it happens on a weekend, then it's wiser to call for an ambulance.

Our emergency plan is in place, and she is holding my hand tightly while driving like crazy to the Emergency Department at the American Medical Center, all the time saying, "Please, take another breath for me ... another breath for your mom ... another breath for your dad ... another breath for your sister ... another one for your godson!"

She has unconsciously found the best way to encourage me to take another breath—not for me but for my dearest loved ones. By torturously doing as she asks, I ultimately am preventing myself from passing out from lack of oxygen and unbearable pain.

At the entrance of the emergency department, I am collected by the nurses, as my wife speaks over the phone with my personal doctor, who knows my medical history. As I am wheeled inside, I keep my eyes fixed on my wife's face until the automatic doors close our visual connection. She barely has the time to put her palm to her mouth and blow me a kiss, as she is now isolated on the outside of the ER. I hear a loud, "Goodbye, my love!"

We stop for a few minutes in the Intensive Care Unit to have the IVs inserted in my arm and to take the necessary chest x-ray. A few minutes later, the anesthesiologist arrives, wanting to make sure my last meal was at least seven hours ago. He is delighted to hear that the last thing I ate was a banana at eleven in the morning, and he calls my doctor on his mobile phone. I realize that the process is already underway.

"We're ready! The x-ray confirms compressive collapse of the entire right lung, and we've been fasting since morning. Should I do a presedation and take him to the theater?" the anesthesiologist asks my doctor.

Hopes and wishful thinking during our drive are now over. It's now clear that I'm about to go into surgery once more. Memory brings back details of the events of the year 2000, when I first became acquainted with the lung syndrome and its pain. I remember also the postoperative pain that continued for months, the mental pain that never went away, and the pain I caused my family every time.

I let the tears roll from my eyes and think of nothing but the automatic door that closed a moment ago, leaving my wife and my dreams behind it.

I am naked underneath a navy-blue surgical gown, immediately reminding me of my trip to Greece, but that no longer matters. I close my eyes and imagine my wife informing my office of the unexpected development. My PA will act on everything, informing first my publishing house, then the shipping company. All appointments will have to be canceled for the next four months, and she will have to reply to the hundreds of unanswered emails from my readers, accumulated over the summer period. I like to answer all of them personally, no matter how many, so I want to at least let them know that there will be a slight delay on my behalf.

Despite the fact that the surgical theater is at subzero temperature, a warm hand touches my face, and I open my eyes.

"You're in good hands. Don't worry about a thing."

Her words are spoken affectionately, and I sink into her green eyes for reassurance. After all, that's all I can see above the mask, gloves, and surgical gown.

"I have been given this promise before, and look where I am now!"

"Please don't be pessimistic. I have studied your file, and I know your medical case. You shouldn't compare what happened years ago with today. Treatment has transformed since then. And don't forget the most important thing—you've got the best surgeon in the country with the most beautiful nurses!"

The humor and the attempt to raise my morale is not working, as fear and cold have seeped into my soul and body. "It's very cold in here," I say. "I can't feel my legs."

She hurries to take care of me with another blanket, then transfixes me with her bright green eyes.

"It's time to rest for a while, don't you think? You're constantly traveling and lecturing. You've been helping the whole world; now we're going to help you. When you wake up, I'll be the first person you see. And I'll want a book dedication for my son, who adores you! OK?"

I nod and use the last few moments to say a prayer, choosing a wish that evidently has proven effective only on my recently happy past. "I hope that tonight the wind is fair and that the captain, who will have my life in his hands, manages to tie me safely in my harbor. Lord Jesus Christ, have mercy on me!"

I barely finish my prayer before the green-eyed nurse appears once again. This time, she is not alone. Inside the operating theater are five others, positioned in various spots. They are obviously feeling good and chatting among themselves about their summer adventures. Indeed, the first and last face I see is that of the nurse with the green eyes—this time, with no goodbyes.

"I'm going to bring the respirator close to your mouth, and I want you to count down from ten. Start the countdown, please."

"OK. Ten, nine, eight, seven …"

And the clock stopped at exactly seven o'clock at night.

Station 10

The First Meetings

> I will persist until I succeed. Always will I take
> another step. If that is of no avail, I will take
> another, and yet another. In truth, one step at a
> time is not too difficult. I know that small attempts,
> repeated, will complete any undertaking!
> —Og Mandino

July. What a blessing!

The phone rings nonstop, but I have no desire to get out of bed. I shall ignore it completely, as the chances of its being for me are only 25 percent. In my parents' house, there are two landline phones and three roommates. One device is in the "good living room," access to which is allowed only on special occasions. The other device is in the kitchen. It is always awkward, chatting with my girlfriend while roommate number one—my dad—sits there enjoying his favorite snack, at the same time relishing my embarrassment. Happily, it doesn't take long for my favorite roommate number two—my mom—to intervene, and the kitchen clears in seconds. Only then do I feel free to respond, "I love you too, my dear Grace," and the conversation ends in the nicest possible way.

Grace was introduced to my family soon after we celebrated our six-month anniversary. Within a few more months, she had secured a place in my heart, a seat at our table, and a secret collaboration; incoming calls are handled by roommate number three—my sister— with absolute secrecy and discretion. Whenever another girl calls for me, my sister changes her voice and says that the girl has the wrong number. Furthermore, to ensure that her mission is carried out effectively, she states that the line belongs to an embassy and the caller will be reported if she uses it again! The result is that Grace sleeps soundly at night, while I sleep restlessly, as I have no other contacts. This "conspiracy" culminates with a rumor circulating at school that my father is an ambassador, and I run around trying to explain my sister's wild fantasies!

I'm pleased to say that my suffering regarding my incoming calls will soon be over. My beloved grandfather informs me that my Christmas present will be my first mobile phone! And, even better, the signal in the kitchen is not strong, no matter how much I raise the antenna, which is my perfect excuse to isolate myself in my room, away from the unwanted stares of the "Doberman." It turns out, though, that my sister also has enhanced hearing abilities. She sticks her ear to the door of my room and doesn't miss a word. As a result, Grace still enjoys her live streaming and updates around the clock.

More ringing from the phone curtails my musings. It is seven in the evening, and I am alone in the house. My sister is at her private English classes, and just a few minutes ago, Mom took the car to go and collect her. Dad, during these hours, is always at the restaurant, getting ready for the evening shift. Under normal circumstances, I would enjoy the luxury of exclusive time at home, but I am still confined to bed with postoperative pain. The insistent ringing, however, forces me to struggle from my bed and make my way slowly to the kitchen. The determination of the caller frustrates me, and I am geared up for a fight. At this hour, I reflect, it either will be somebody looking to sell something or, worse, another telephone survey for the upcoming May 27, 2001, parliamentary election.

Answering the phone, I recognize the voice of Ms. Mary, leaving me open-mouthed and with my heart fluttering; her call causes me the same palpitations as my first date with Grace. Even my ensuing concerns are the same: what will I wear on my first date? What will my first words be? How will I make a good first impression? A thousand positive thoughts and reflections! This is because a few minutes ago, Ms. Mary informed me of my good luck: "We will be able to reschedule the appointment due to a cancellation!" I pressed my luck by sending a message with the right subject: "Urgent and Important!"

From: MyEmail1977
Sent: July 7, 2000, 12:57
To: Coach
Subject: Urgent and Important

My dear Coach,

Your book has sustained me over a series of lung surgeries. Indeed, I couldn't have had a better mentor than you, since you went through a similar experience. Your book has helped me deal with my physical pain, but more importantly, it has helped me to deal with my mental pain: all the negative memories that circulate in my mind, even to this day. I am only twenty-three years old, and I feel incapable of leaving the nightmare behind me and moving on with my life; of being like all other people of my age. The first available appointment to visit you is three months from today, but I urgently need your guidance, especially now that I am recovering at home. I realize how many people need your help, but I hope to meet you in person as soon as possible because I need help! Thank you very much!

"Well, young man, Coach will be able to see you on Friday at seven o'clock in the evening. Do you think you'll be able to come?"

Her insistent tone expected an immediate answer—as if there was ever a chance to refuse such an invitation! Apparently, my coach had arranged to advance my appointment after reading my email. At last, I'd meet my *bodyguard* in person. Mom nicknamed him that, as every time I talked about him and his book, the pain would magically disappear from my hospital room. I have archived a copy of my email in the binder under the title, "Meetings with My Bodyguard," along with several scattered pages containing various quotes from his book—positive thoughts that helped me lighten the pain on a daily basis. Picking up the book, I gaze for quite some time at his photograph on the back. Transfixed by his smile, I mentally begin further conversations with him, totally lost in his eyes, and I contemplate, "From painful to painless with the right choices!"

All my previous chats with my coach were long distance. This one was no different. In hospital, when I was in pain and the nurse told me that the next pain relief medication was not due for two hours, I would practice the first choice suggested in his book: "Choose to have good company."

Choose to have good company.

I vividly remember the dawn pain waking me up once again—such disappointment when I realize that I am not in my cozy bed at home but in a hospital bed. The pain is determined to interact once again. It is desperate to spend time with me before the sun comes up. I press the red panic button, and as soon as the nurse arrives, I try to negotiate yet more analgesic.

The battle is lost; the next redemptive dose is due at seven with my breakfast. The suggestion arrives: "Try to take your mind somewhere else," while she arranges the blanket that had fallen to the floor during my restless sleep.

That was it!

"Choose to have good company!" I say quite loudly. Picking up his book, my coach is summoned, as I really need him right now. I can't be left alone with the pain, and I desperately need reinforcements.

I'm browsing the pages, heading to my favorite chapter, in which Coach and his young friend are enjoying cocktails at an event. As the pain stubbornly continues its intensity, I close my eyes and mentally find myself at the same venue. I have a conversation with my coach, enjoying a cocktail at the same time. The conversation soon turns to the football derby and our different views about a last-minute disputed penalty.

"Red card for a horrid tackle and a clear penalty!" he exclaims with certainty, as I try in vain to change his mind. He may be negative about my opinion of the game, but in my own game, there are positive developments. The intensity of the pain recedes because I don't give "him" the attention "he" seeks. Still closely observing our arguments about the game, pain now seems distant and bored and ready to abandon the fight against me.

"Good thing he doesn't like football," I whisper in Coach's ear, and we burst out laughing. Pain doesn't like that at all, clearly understanding that he is indeed unwelcome. When the argument about the game escalates, pain is finally completely fed up and leaves the room. It's time to say goodbye to Coach as well, as I am finally soporific and want to continue my sleep. I close the book, put it next to the photo of Saint Paisios, and at last close my eyes. It's the first time I've ever been able to fool the pain, and I am so happy about it.

But the cheater always returns! He'll complain that I didn't enjoy his company the last time, and he will boost his intensity. Although I am not in physical pain, he has chosen to engage on another level: taking over my mind, disrupting my positive thoughts, and shaking my psyche. He has chosen to hurt me mentally, as he knows there is no medication for that. He has made it clear that I will not easily escape him, and he has not failed to remind me that my prolonged postoperative absence will not be appreciated by the bank that has only recently employed me. He further enlightens me that even when I'm discharged, I will remain stagnant, while my colleagues will continue unabated on their learning and development paths and progress. He also reminds me that the rest of my peers are continuing their summer vacation while I continue my hospitalization. He has even brought me a mirror so that I can enjoy a sorry sight—all that's left is skin and bones, a scruffy face, and a chest punctured by thoracic drainage tubes.

My heart is broken into a thousand pieces. I return the mirror to him at once, no longer able to bear the pitiful sight of my own reflection. As he takes the mirror back, I catch him looking proudly at his own reflection, a huge smile of satisfaction on his face, knowing that he has once again accomplished his mission to the fullest. This time, he has managed to fool me, and I am so sad about that.

I have no choice but to call the nurse and lie about my pain levels. Any pain measurement above eight on a scale of ten indicates a desperate situation, and a half dose of additional medication follows. I now hold a shot glass full of liquid analgesic, and, despite its horrible taste, it's my turn to have a huge smile on my face. In just a few minutes, the drug will work its miracle, and I will try to fool the pain for a second time. And I am so excited about that.

I turn my attention back to the legal drama I've been trying to watch on TV, but it is completely boring. The judge is too strict for my taste, so I turn off the TV. In just a few minutes, the medicine will have kicked in, and I'll finally be free—unlike Ben, who has been arrested for petty theft, and the judge did not have the courtesy to take into account the mitigating circumstances of the ragged father of four. He sent him unceremoniously to Central Prison.

While I am convinced that I picked up the remote control and turned off the television about twenty minutes ago, the voice of the heartless judge still echoes in my ears. Agonizingly opening my left eye, the judge is now staring at me, banging the wooden hammer on the bench so loudly that my eyes open wide.

"It is now time for the prosecution to address my court. Please be as brief as possible and straight to the point!" says the judge in a forceful tone, addressing the public prosecutor, who is none other than my well-known and ruthless friend, Mr. Pain!

He stands up, buttoning his jacket, and takes his first steps into the courtroom, approaching the judge's bench. Raising his head, he begins his boastful argument about my situation.

"Your Honor, here we are with a case in hand of clear injustice. We have a young man of twenty-three, who, for two weeks now, has been hospitalized after a lung operation that lasted five hours. The lobes of both lungs have been removed, and he has lost a part of his respiratory system. He will need two months of intensive physiotherapy, and if all goes well, he should be able to return to work in four months. This is unfair, to say the least, Your Honor, as here is a young man who is highly active and energetic. He has already been banned indefinitely from the activities he loves, such as the gym, scuba diving, and running marathons. He also has been deprived of his right to work for the coming few months. If you ask me, ladies and gentlemen, it would not be too much to say that he has been deprived of the right to a carefree life—or at least, a life as he would like it to be. And I respectfully ask the following four questions, Your Honor: (1) How will he be able to live with it? (2) How will he be able to find the strength to overcome it? (3) How will he live with the syndrome knocking on the door? (4) Why did this happen to him at this wonderful age? I expect the court to understand the seriousness of the case and to exonerate the accused, who has chosen to remain depressed, scared, and angry after all he has been through. It is his choice, and I cannot understand what else the defense counsel can present to us. I will make sure, as a responsive prosecutor, to visit him as often as possible and remind him of all the injustices that he has endured, which give him the well-earned right to feel depressed, scared, and angry. It is his choice and his right, and no one can condemn him for it. Thank you."

Clearly troubled, the judge casts a grim look to our side and passes to my defense.

"Thank you, Prosecuting Counsel, for your opening statement. The defense now has the floor."

My own bodyguard, acting as a defense counselor, first turns his eyes to me before standing up for the response. He whispers in my ear, "I will do my best to represent us!"

He stands in the middle of the room and begins stoically. "Your Honor, I have been counseling for twenty years, and I must admit that this case is indeed tough. Although it will sound like an oxymoron, the young age should not be considered as a mitigating factor. Let me explain to you straightaway what I mean by this assertion. My client is fully aware of his condition and fully understands the seriousness of his health situation. When surgery was chosen as an urgent and important action, it was not a decision in the heat of the moment but a premeditated and well-organized one. My client consulted the best doctors and spent countless hours studying the syndrome he was enduring. In addition to this, he equipped his psyche by reading self-help books. Moreover, during his hospitalization, he made sure that he was fully cooperative with the doctors and other medical staff. Accordingly, there is no evidence to suggest or justify the conclusion that this man's choice is to remain in a state of pain, with its accompanying depression, fear, and anger. The only firm conclusion that can be drawn is that this young man needs proper guidance to help him get out of the pain prison and leave depression, fear, and anger behind."

"Please conclude!"

"Certainly, Your Honor. No man deserves to remain in this state forever. Depression, fear, and anger is the worst combination and will lead you into a dark prison. We all know very well how difficult— not to say impossible—it is to escape the shackles of pain. I would agree with my honorable colleague that the court should understand the seriousness of the case. Nevertheless, the solution lies in proper guidance and assistance so that he can be freed from his depression, fear, and anger and live the rest of his life in normality. I will make sure, as a counselor, to help him lighten the pain, deal with his negative emotions, and find again his lost hope and passion for life. His choice is clear—the right to live a pain-free life. Thank you very much."

As he returns to our bench with a smile of satisfaction on his face, Mr. Pain takes up his firing position. He stands in complete silence for a whole minute, giving the subconscious signal that he is about to reveal something extremely important. Clearing his voice, he picks up the pace.

"Your Honor, what my good colleague has conspicuously avoided stating to the court is the total number of surgeries required to treat the condition. He has, in my view, deliberately avoided commenting on the total time frame of suffering and misery. Allow me to enlighten the court as to the time that has been lost—two years, ladies and gentlemen! For two years, this young man has been in and out of operating theaters while others of his age have been in and out of cafeterias and discotheques. Therefore, I cannot understand to what normal life my colleague is referring for this young man to continue enjoying freely. Four, Your Honor—yes, you heard me right—four operations in two years! Not one, not two, not three, but four open-chest surgeries, each with a postoperative recovery period of four months. While there were assurances that the first two operations were completely successful and would prevent similar problems in the future, unfortunately, again and again, recurrences have driven him to the same hospital. In conclusion, who can criticize this young man's decision to remain depressed, scared, and angry after this prolonged nightmare? Thank you again."

He returns triumphantly to his seat, glancing disdainfully to our side. The judge is making notes. We remain frozen in our seats. Finally, the judge deigns to nod his head. It is time for more defense from my counselor.

"Your Honor, please allow me to read a short extract from the book I hold. It is called *The Greatest Salesman in the World* and is by the well-known author Og Mandino. As I have already mentioned, my client's stay in the hospital was beneficial because of the positive attitude he chose to have. He took advantage of the dead time by reading books on counseling and guidance, which leads us to safely assume that his intention is to put the pain behind him. From the whole book, the following paragraph has been selected, and at his request, I shall read it to you:

> I will always go one step further. And if that's useless, I'll do another and another. Really, one step at a time is not that hard. I will persevere until I succeed. Henceforth I shall regard each day's effort as a single tap with my ax on the trunk of a mighty oak tree. The first blow will not shake the wood, nor the second, nor the third. Each blow alone can be of no consequence, of no consequence at all. And yet from childish blows the oak will slowly fall. The same will be true of my efforts today. I will be like the raindrop that strips the mountain bare. Like the insect that devours the tiger. The star that lights up the earth. The slave who builds the pyramid. I will build my castle one brick at a time, for I know that small efforts, when repeated, will finish any work. I will persevere until I succeed!

"It is my belief, Your Honor, that this man seeks help and guidance rather than approval to remain in a state of seeming hibernation that will sink him even deeper. This is a young man who, before these terrible events took place, was the life and soul of the party."

"That is a hearsay allegation, Your Honor! I object on the basis of relevance!" Mr. Pain interjects forcefully.

The judge gives him a stern nod to sit silently in his seat and then gives a signal to my counselor to continue.

"Please be patient, Mr. Pain, and it will all become clearer, even to you! He was known throughout his school for his sociability and friendliness. As a result, his classmates voted him class president. But this is just one small fact among many others. I find it equally useful to mention the Ethos and Personality Award he received from the minister of education in 1995, witnessed and applauded by hundreds of students and many teachers. I should also mention that he stood in front of fifty members of parliament in November 1994 and demanded the right for schoolgirls to wear trousers, rather than skirts, during the freezing winter months. He later served in one of the most elite corps of the army—the military police—where he again managed to stand out with his personality. He was appointed as personal driver to the corps commander. Many of his admirable achievements are recorded at the university."

"Your Honor, will this monologue take much longer?" Mr. Pain comments.

"I will allow it, as it is important evidence concerning the personality and the intentions of the accused. Please continue."

"Thank you very much, Your Honor. He became the first freshman ever to be elected as student body president. He then demanded that the Dean's Council accept his recommendation that a small portion of student tuition fees go into a special fund. From this fund, hundreds of needy students have made their dreams come true as they studied on scholarship. For this alone, his name was included in the Dean's Honor List. If, by the way, you are wondering whether his vigorous social activities ever affected his academic progress, it is worth mentioning that he received his master's degree with summa cum laude, an honor that is awarded to the best graduating student of the year."

"What data do you have of his activities following university, Counselor?"

"His overall actions have not gone unnoticed by the government, which chose him to go to Israel for a reconciliation conference between Greek and Turkish Cypriots that lasted two months. He took part in a social experiment in which Greeks and Turks worked, cooperated, and lived together in a vast kibbutz in the Negev Desert of Israel. This young man led the delegation, and at the end, he wrote the progress report together with his Turkish counterpart. The report was handed to the United Nations and the other participating states. I will stop here, although his list of achievements continues on the next page of my notes."

"What about work experience?"

"Thank you for encouraging me to continue, Your Honor. He has been employed by the largest bank in our country, working in the Human Resources Department. Although his absences from work have been frequent due to the four operations and the ensuing long postoperative periods, the bank has not replaced him and patiently awaits his return. Therefore, there is not the slightest doubt that depression, fear, and anger have not and will never play a defining role in the life of this brilliant young man. I presume that they are merely temporary residuals, arising from his temporary condition and not from his overall standing over the years. Thank you very much."

My counselor sits down on our bench without so much as a glance at me, attempting to hide his emotions.

The judge, unperturbed, says, "Today's session is adjourned due to the late hour. I am scheduling the next court date two weeks from today, when we will conclude with the defendant's confession."

The judge's wooden hammer bangs vigorously, and my eyes open abruptly. It takes me a few moments to realize where I am and what is happening. The sudden transition from courtroom to hospital room is emotionally unsettling. The sedative, however, has done its job, and I managed to lighten my pain, even for only one episode.

Station 9

The Flights

I am not a product of my circumstances. I am a
product of my decisions. I am what I am today
because of the choices I made yesterday!
—Stephen R. Covey

April. What a blessing!

The rain has been nonstop since morning, and lightning illuminates the dark hospital room. The nurse places my meal tray on the overbed table, rolling it as close to me as possible.

"Bon appétit! And you know what comes after this," says the nice girl in the white uniform, winking at me cheekily.

"The best time of the day," I exclaim with joy because after my lunch will come the "magic shot."

The evening-shift nurse and I have so named the small clear plastic cup of pain-relief medicine because it transforms me, just like magic, taking effect in just twenty minutes. It starts with a numbness in my legs; then my whole body begins to relax until my mind finally surrenders to its power. From there, I take over as the pilot. I can fly to any destination and to any time in my life that I wish. Time and space no longer have limits—no restrictions whatsoever. I think about it, and it's done.

On every trip I have the choice to determine my mood. There are three buttons in the cockpit. The red one is labeled "Bad Mood," the green one is "Good Mood," and the orange button has a capital A ("Alpha"), which will activate the autopilot. I do not need approval from the control tower for takeoff, nor is a pilot's license required to navigate my personal airplane. All I need to do is select my mood and my destination, then press the orange button and let Captain Alpha fly me away!

If I choose the green button, I will make my journey in a joyful, positive mood. As I look down from above, I will see only the beautiful landscapes. I will choose to see the green fields that soothe me, the vastness of the sea that refreshes me, the sun that warms me, the birds that fly by my side, and all the wonders accompanying me on my flight. By selecting the red button, I will enter an area of intense turbulence. In choosing "Bad Mood," I will ignore all the beautiful factors in my journey, picking at, dwelling on, and criticizing all the bad things that happen to me, unaware that I myself am ultimately the architect of my landscape.

I have a client at the bank, an architect by profession, who is unable to see that he is the architect of his own misery. Mr. Black predetermines the tone of the upcoming day from first thing in the morning.

According to him, the story never changes: "I put on my black shirt. I take my coffee black with black sugar. I drive my black car. I wear my black glasses, and I am prepared for another blackout at work." Every morning, Mr. Black selects a black mood, making him unable to remove his black sunglasses to locate the green button. Choosing green for a change would mean he possibly might detect, for the first time, the green field that is right next to his gray parking spot. But no! He always chooses the red button, so he never allows the sun to penetrate his black sunglasses and warm his eyes. Mr. Black will continue to be a miserable pilot until he decides to lose the glasses, open his eyes, and dial the correct coordinates into his navigation system each morning.

Good or bad mood, green or red button—the only thing that never changes when flight Morphine 727 is over is the usual jet lag, dizziness, and nausea.

"It's probably just turbulence," I always try to console myself. Such trips are the norm to me during these difficult times; therefore, I eat my dinner at breakneck speed, grasp the magic shot, select my coordinates, and finally hit the green button.

"Cheers," I say aloud as I rinse my throat with liquid analgesic.

These flights have a duration of nearly five hours, and I don't want to miss a minute. I fasten my seat belt, start the aircraft's engines, and hit the orange button. On this trip, the final destination is my desire to rebuild my shattered patience.

Grandpa Takis sits comfortably and contentedly in a front-row seat, enjoying the welcoming drink brought by the flight attendant. He is the most suitable VIP passenger for Patience Island, as everything he has achieved in his life is the result of his inexhaustible powers of restraint. He is proud to share his secret with everyone: "In all my years of running my restaurant, I have fed what seems to be the whole country, and every customer has gone away happy and satisfied. My secret ingredient is my endless patience!"

Grandma Vasia, on the flip side, is seated at the very back of the plane, complaining about the cold food, the uncomfortable seat, the heat, and the unacceptable hygiene standards and generally harassing the flight attendants over everything. Since she opted for "Bad Mood"—as usual—she has rejected the welcoming drink, as the glass is too small for her liking.

Flying above the clouds, I use my intercom to welcome all the passengers and prepare their entertainment. I dim the cabin lights, invite them to enjoy the movie, and press the PLAY button.

The opening title on their individual screens—"A true story dating back to 1980"—piques the passengers' interest positively and encourages them to don their headphones. The introductory music lulls them for a while before I take on the role of narrator and awaken everyone with the passion in my voice. Captain Alpha takes over the activity required for a safe journey, while I concentrate on my storytelling:

"Ladies and gentlemen and dear children, good evening and welcome to this flight to Patience Island. I hope you are sitting comfortably, for your journey is about to begin.

Once upon a time, well hidden in the heart of a green forest, there was a restaurant. To enjoy a meal at Grandpa Takis's restaurant, you have to overcome two major obstacles—first, to find out whether a table is available, and second, to have a navigation system in your car.

The first obstacle has a relatively easy solution. Simply call the five-digit telephone number, 21410, and Grandma Vasia will answer abruptly, "Takis's Delis!" If she had ever had the opportunity of meeting Alexander Graham Bell, who invented the telephone, she would have hung him up along with the tablecloths when doing the morning laundry. In her life were two things she hated more than any others: the incessant incoming calls from customers and the smell of charcoal on Grandpa Takis's clothes late at night, when he had finished work.

The second obstacle has to do with the location of the restaurant. God created a small paradise in the middle of nowhere, and this is where Takis decided to build his little Eden. Exactly how he had managed to convince Vasia to leave her parents' coastal villa and live with him in the capital remains a total mystery.

Back in the day, before the days of satnav and GPS, customers calling for directions were at the mercy of Grandma Vasia's mood. If you caught her in a good mood, it took about seventeen minutes from the city center to the restaurant, driving the "city road," as she called the main asphalt road. However, if she was really not in the mood to give any kind of service whatsoever or if she considered that the customer had used an inappropriate tone, then add to his bill a worn tire or a damaged shock absorber, as she would have directed him via the rocky "country road" in retribution.

The renaming of the restaurant that shortly followed was no coincidence. The original name, Takis's Delis, mostly had customers who were family members, neighbors, and the kittens that partied with the leftovers. It became obvious that the restaurant's location had not been properly analyzed in Grandpa Takis's business plan, and drastic improvements needed to be made. A solution came with the ten lanterns he placed around the perimeter of the restaurant, which stood out like fireflies in a bush. From then on, Grandma Vasia's task became easier and more efficient, as she brought everyone in from the city road with instructions to head for the ten lanterns. Customers got used to saying, "Let's go to the ten lanterns." Soon enough, Takis's Delis became a distant, delicious memory, and the restaurant was renamed Ten Lanterns.

Grandpa's reputation grew swiftly enough, and soon he had gained enthusiastic fans arriving from every city for his gastronomic creations. It became a must-do dining venue for celebrities, businessmen, politicians, and all food lovers who appreciated an extravagant meze that included artichokes with eggs, grilled snails, frog legs au gratin, chicken wings with French cheese, filet mignon with wild mushroom, and, of course, the complimentary final treat of sweet halvah that was served together with the bill. If the customer was totally replete, this dessert would be packaged to be taken home. Not surprisingly, the aroma of the syrup prompted most customers to eat it in the car!

Grandpa Takis, despite the accumulated exhaustion of the week, made sure that every Sunday, he gathered his whole family around the table. It was a family ritual, and the meal was not the main course but simply the excuse to bring us all together. Sunday's special dishes were the loud giggles of Grandpa while teasing Grandma Vasia, the singing contest that our cousin Viki always won, the piano concert by Maria, the joke of the day told by my godfather Fionos, the pecan pie that godmother Kika provided—and on and on we go! Of course, the caprices of Grandma Vasia were also enjoyed, as she insisted that the chicken wings were overcooked, or she complained that we didn't honor her spaghetti.

Sadly, not everyone had a good ending to these Sundays. When it was time to clear the table and wash the dishes, Grandpa Takis was already in seventh heaven with his brandy, the grandchildren had been excused from chores, and the sons-in-law were already in front of the TV for the Sunday football match. As you can imagine, Grandma Vasia's grim gaze would fall on her two daughters, who, having no other choice, would begin their duties without argument.

Now let's go back a little. When Grandpa Takis became financially solvent, he bought the land adjacent to the restaurant. His purpose was clear—he had no intention of expanding the business, only of expanding the family accommodation. As a truly traditional Greek father, he built two houses right next to his own house and restaurant. The reasons are obvious: to continue his close guardianship of his beautiful unmarried daughters and, at the same time, to have the first say in all upcoming developments. It didn't take long for him to grant approval to the first suitor who passed the "family exams" with flying colors; he bestowed his blessings on the marriage of his elder daughter. The prospective groom was an accountant, and, truth be told, Grandpa didn't fare too well with monetary issues. No matter how much he made as a restaurateur, Grandma Vasia was masterful at spending as much. Killing two birds with one stone, Grandpa Takis welcomed both a new family member and a competent accountant. Checkmate!

Within a year, Fionos was managing all the finances with great success, but all this came at a heavy price. Grandma Vasia added him to her blacklist, along with Mr. Bell. Fionos was blackballed; she now visited her once-daily hairdresser just once a week, and Renos started spreading rumors at his coffeehouse that the Takis family was in a tight spot! My dear Mr. Renos, you need to take off your black sunglasses to see the light. It's simply that the family has gained a skillful accountant, and wealth management is now the order of the day.

Grandpa Takis's intention of offering his younger daughter to the highest bidder resulted in innumerable interviews. Do not misunderstand his plans; Grandpa Takis always has the best of intentions. He might have given the impression that he would find the highest bidder for her hand, but eventually, he surrendered to the tallest bidder, as his daughter gave him no choice. One meter eighty-seven centimeters in height, a sporty two-seater car, a house by the sea, and eloquence that politicians would envy—not to mention a two-week hunger strike by his daughter—encouraged Grandpa Takis to give in.

My mother had become skin and bones before Grandpa finally threw in the towel and approved my future father. Even given this, I remain convinced that Grandpa Takis still weighed his options carefully before giving his final approval. He realized that luck had smiled on him again. He had another pawn on his chessboard. The first had brought about a financial miracle, and the new one could well be the PR star he was looking for. The hiring process was successfully completed, and the restaurant now had a marketing director and my mother had her prince. Checkmate!

The Ten Lanterns restaurant provided a comfortable life for the whole family for half a century. The tasks, chores, difficulties, and pros and cons of the family business were always on the agenda, but Grandpa Takis always had the right attitude and the good manners to deal with everything with patience and kindness. The grandchildren enjoyed their own super-privileges, which kept us oblivious of the troubles that Grandpa and the others faced on a daily basis.

"Eat, read, and play is your only job. My job is to tell you the rest when you're old enough"—that was Grandpa's favorite saying.

I am the only boy in the family compound, and I enjoy my own super-privileges and responsibilities. Big decisions that potentially will affect my life going forward always go through a family meeting on

Saturdays before being presented on Sunday to the higher authority—Grandpa Takis—for final approval.

"We'll see about that next Monday" is the answer to my complex requests, which included my wanting to buy a motorcycle at the age of fifteen. For some mysterious reason, I can't find these Mondays marked on the calendar. All the protagonists are missing except for me, who fervently needs their consent.

It is a beautiful Sunday afternoon as I inform my grandpa that I must update my school with my choice of courses before the summer vacations. I boldly announce to him my desire to do the finance courses, as this would prepare me for studies in business management. On hearing news that was not to his taste, he always has the same reaction: taking off his brown bone glasses and throwing them forcefully down on the table. This is a coded message for "I neither want to hear nor see!"

I try in vain to list the advantages of my becoming a corporate manager. He is not convinced by the argument that one day I could take over our family business.

"Those who have management issues, my sweet boy, should learn how to manage their eating habits and then everything will be fine." That is his first comment. Hopelessly romantic and stubborn, he has a habit of quoting parables and tips based on food and Greek cuisine.

His initial statement leaves little room for negotiation, and then he adds artfully, "Why don't you take a walk to the restaurant entrance and check the sign on the front desk?"

Strange instruction, I think, as I had memorized the sign over my many years of entering and exiting the restaurant.

I can't see the purpose of this conversation. I reply straight away,

"The sign says, 'Choose to have a good mood, or choose to leave right now,' and I've seen it a hundred times. I don't have to go all the way over there to read it again."

Choose to have a good mood.

"You are right, my boy! If you can explain to me the meaning of the sign, I might reconsider and let you become a business manager. If you can't, then you must listen to your grandfather and become a soul manager— a psychologist. Then I will feed their bodies, and you will feed their minds."

At this age, I am still too young to understand his intentions and expectations. It's easy to understand the literal meaning of the sign, which I now present with the persuasiveness of a lawyer but overlook the metaphorical meaning, which is vastly more important.

"Listen, son, I'd encourage you to go off and study psychiatry, but your mother's soul would wither away until the day you finish your studies and come back to her. Being a psychologist and mastering the science of the soul—that is, the study of people's thoughts and behavior—will, in fact, help you acquire deep judgment and rational thinking. Understanding people's behavior will make you able to guide and help them until their wants are noble and honest."

"What do I care what other people want or need, Grandpa?"

"If you help them to choose to have a good mood, then we will successfully change the world and make it a better place. If their wants and needs are driven by bad moods, then the world will become more and more unpleasant. I don't want my grandchildren and the rest of my family to live in a world like that. Therefore, being a soul manager will be much more fruitful than being a business manager!"

"What exactly are you expecting from me, Grandpa? Do you really believe that I can change the world? Who do you think I am?"

"Are you or are you not my chosen boy?"

"I am your chosen boy but not a magic boy."

"And what if I tell you that you can be both?"

"What do you mean?"

"I will prepare you to give your best self every day; you will then go the extra mile, and you will finally have a choiceful journey toward a successful life. I'm sure that our family's heritage will help you to change and grow along the way. And it may even help you to change and save the whole world."

"Save the world? Who, me? Oh, God!"

"Watch what you say because your mind listens and complies. My chosen boy, when your mind is suffused by unsettling thoughts that you cannot deal with, the best thing to do is prepare and enjoy a light supper and then go to sleep with your idea or problem. Sleep on it! In the morning, you will find the solution you seek right there on your breakfast plate. I guarantee this is the most effective problem-solving process. Now stop doubting yourself, and sleep on it."

"Grandpa, can we please go back to the discussion regarding my future?"

"This is exactly what we are doing right now."

"Grandpa, do you realize that in order to study psychology, I have to follow the classics courses and skip the business classes?"

"So what? You are a bright student and a diligent young man in everything you do."

"That's not the problem. The classics courses are not for me. To give you an idea, in each class, you'll find twenty girls and only one boy."

"What's the problem? Sounds like an advantage to me."

"Oh Grandpa, you and I are not going to get along today."

I sink into his black leather couch, and my dreams sink with me. With a sorrowful expression on my face and my eyes fixed to the floor, I await a sign of retreat from my opponent. This is a game of manipulation at which I am usually the master; I always take advantage of his love for me. But he is not done yet.

Speaking quietly and slowly, while continuing to search my face for confirmation, he intones, "I think it's time to tell you the rest." He pauses to see if I have grasped his meaning.

"So, we are done eating, studying, and playing," comes my cheeky reply, and I notice the joy on his face. This is the verification he has been seeking regarding his statement, "Eat, read, and play is your only job. My job is to tell you the rest when you're old enough," which has been delivered like a dose of antibiotics—three times a day.

"My boy, if you stop eating, the body will starve. If you stop reading, your mind will starve, and if you stop playing, your soul will also starve. You will not stop doing any of these three because they are the basic ingredients in your recipe for success. We'll just need to add some spicy condiments and new dishes occasionally to stimulate your palate because it's pointless to eat the same dish every day, even if it is our favorite."

"What do you mean, Chef Takis? We seem to be getting rather lost in translation today."

"My chosen boy, over the years, we've been preparing your body and mind. How about we start exercising your soul?"

"And how is that possible?"

"Let's make a deal. Since the Easter holidays are coming up and you'll have all the time in the world, how about the two of us spending a few days at our mansion in the mountains?"

"A few days!" This is probably the first time Grandpa Takis has been willing to leave the restaurant for such an extended period. Unreal! The family joke has always been that if his daughters decided to get married on a Saturday night, Grandpa would miss the wedding because he'd choose to work that night. He's never made such a compromise for anyone—such a long absence from the restaurant. "If you want me at your child's baptism, then make sure you change it to a Sunday night," was always the answer to the ignorant relatives who dared to organize an event on a Saturday and had the audacity to invite Chef Takis.

"Yes! A few days, my dear child. If you do me this favor, then I will give you the greatest gift that you have ever received from me. The only sure thing is that on this trip, you will finally understand the meaning of those words on our entrance sign."

His words both astonish and intrigue me. A gift from Grandpa Takis is a big deal, as he is committed to giving me gifts of great value. Since this would be the biggest one, I convince myself that applied science of the soul isn't such a bad idea after all. It is my turn to throw in the towel. I respond positively, even though a *bras de fer* for my future is about to take place in the mountain mansion.

We schedule our date for the following Saturday. Shaking hands completes the formalization of our agreement, and I'm sent off imperatively. The time already is seven o'clock, meaning we are late for our evening meal.

As I leave, a breeze slams the door, and my eyes open.

"What do you prefer for dinner? Pumpkin soup or chicken breast with grilled vegetables?"

I am looking at the nurse in confusion and wondering why she isn't wearing the proper uniform. The flight attendant brought me my coffee in the cockpit just ten minutes ago, so when did the uniform swap occur?

Once I recover my senses, having landed somewhat randomly in my hospital room, I realize that I need to pause my fairy tale for a while.

I close my eyes again and mentally address Grandpa Takis: *Our appointment stands. See you next weekend!*

Station 8

The Mountain Mansion

We fail because we give up, and we give up
because we never had a plan in the first place.
Planning is as natural to the process of success
as its absence is to the process of failure.
—Robin Sieger

The pumpkin soup smells delicious and will be just right for a winter's night. I don't have the pleasure of having my favorite nurse bring me the dinner tray, and I don't detect any actual appetite for conversation from the new face in the white uniform. I want to make sure, however, that the tray also bears the special shot, so I don't hesitate to ask her directly.

She limits herself to a terse reply: "You better watch out, young man. Do not get too comfortable with these powerful drugs!"

I knew from the first moment I saw her that we would not get along. She drops the tray on the table, and almost half the soup spills from the bowl.

You, ma'am, do not have the right to deprive me of my flights, I think as I watch her write her notes on the patient report sheet that hangs at the end of my bed. No more words are exchanged, no more glances. I just want her to get out of my room. I'm eager to continue my journey with Grandpa Takis.

I eat all my food like a good boy, turn off the lights, and hold the shot glass in my hand. I want to make sure the coordinates are correct, so I bring Grandpa Takis vividly to mind. Under no circumstances do I want the autopilot to take over and take me wherever he wants. I select the green button, set the necessary coordinates, and stay to watch the raindrops sliding down the windowpane. In a few minutes, my eyes grow heavy, and just before I surrender to sleep, I have time to whisper, "Grandpa, start the engine!"

The annoying beeps from the monitor above my head echo throughout the room, disturbing my sleep at five in the morning—beep, beep, beep, beep, beep—and suddenly, a prolonged beeeeeeeep startles me, interrupting my sleep completely.

"Where are you going in the middle of the road, mister? Open your eyes, and stay on course," Grandpa shouts, literally hanging out of the side window of the two-meter-wide gray Cadillac. In order to drive comfortably, Grandpa always needs both lanes of the road, while other drivers fall into the ditches so that Chef Takis can pass.

I also open my eyes as Grandpa performs a nervous maneuver to avoid the oncoming car. It takes me a few moments to recover, as I am still trying to figure out exactly where I am. We seem to be out of town and going uphill at low speed toward the mountains. He makes fun of me because my rise-and-shine early morning wake-up has knocked me out and made me miss half the journey. He doesn't miss the opportunity to point out that if I ever want to succeed in life, I should make peace with early wake-ups.

Realizing that I am not yet particularly talkative, Grandpa pushes his favorite tape of Greek folk songs into the cassette player. With one hand on the steering wheel and the other hanging out the window, he commands me to change the gears using the stick behind his steering wheel. After a short distance, he turns down the music, slows his speed, and clears his voice. He's ready to impart some important information.

"My mountain fellow, at the mansion we have five simple rules.

The first rule has to do with our *beginning*—the starting point of our day. Our morning uprising and our morning meal. The command for getting out of bed is given by Alanis, our rooster. Once he starts his yelling, we too begin our day."

He gives me a quick look, as he is sure I will want to debate this. I negotiate for two or three extra hours of sleep as I refuse to be at the mercy of Mr. Alanis's biological clock. Unfortunately, it seems the rules are not up for discussion but for digestion, and I give up loading my guns.

"When you wake up, you'll order whatever you want for breakfast and what you want your day to be like. You can say, 'Good morning, Grandpa! Today is a great day,' or 'I don't want to get out of bed. Today is a tough day.' It's your choice, but be careful what you order. It's exactly the same when ordering your breakfast. If you order a dynamic breakfast, you'll have the strength and energy to last the rest of the day. If you order just a black coffee with black sugar, then I am afraid you will be crawling around all day like a black snake. We must always make sure we eat right and order right. Got it?"

I remain silent and sleepy while Grandpa continues his speech.

"Take, for example, the menu in our restaurant. We offer thirty-three different options, and we don't serve up whatever comes to mind. We write down the customer's order carefully and execute it accurately. The same goes in our lives. Execution upon request! Your day will evolve based on your morning choice. Your week will be completed based on your daily choices. Is that understood?"

I nod my head in silent agreement and continue to listen without interrupting.

"The second rule is *planning*! Here, you will have increased duties, those of the secretary general. As we discuss the pending tasks, you will prepare a list, prioritizing the tasks that need to be accomplished. We will begin with the most important ones, such as starting the generator that will provide life to the mansion with its electricity. Then, we will relentlessly proceed with the digging, watering, fertilizing, pruning, and so on. With each task completed, the secretary will have the pleasure of taking his pencil and crossing it off the list. Understood?"

I nod, wondering how much longer this torture will last. "We're going to the mansion, not a military camp," I muse.

"The third rule is *cooperating*! Our combined actions! The word *cooperate* prevails over the word *operate* because the prefix *co* means combine. It's a composed task with added value. Therefore, together we will do all the jobs, whether we like them or not. For every task, we will evaluate the result, and for every collaboration, we will gather together all the positive factors—that is to say, what you bring to the table and what I bring to the table so we'll have the ingredients for a rich meal. Now that I mention the table, I am reminded that our synergy includes cooking. We will prepare the evening meal together, and as we enjoy our dinner, we will also evaluate the overall outcome of the day, always referring to the secretary's list. Do you have anything to comment?"

"Thank God you are going to feed me, Grandpa," I mutter with a little sarcasm.

Ignoring my subdued mood, he continues unabashedly. "The last two elements, perhaps the most important of all, have nothing to do with specific rules. They are essential ingredients that enhance the realization of the optimal result. Simply put, they are not rules like the first one that talks about the *beginning*, the second one that talks about *planning*, or the third one that talks about *cooperating*. The last two elements are values. These are the roots that drive our actions, improve our reactions, and lead to satisfaction. Action, reaction, satisfaction! Got it?"

"I'm trying, Grandpa, I'm trying. It's seven o'clock in the morning, and I haven't even had my coffee yet!"

He ignores me again. "The fourth rule—the fourth value—is *desiring*. It is the intensity of passion and the thrill you get from your action that fuels your every reaction, and then comes the satisfaction. Recall the song 'Thalassa, Thalassa' that we enjoyed earlier. Why you turn up the volume? Why do you close your eyes and sing along with passion? Why do your eyes get wet during the refrain? Why do you enjoy this song so much? Why do you listen to it repeatedly?"

"I don't know, Grandpa, but I'm sure you have all the answers!"

"The answer to all these questions is as simple as the lyrics of the song. Every desire that is reinforced by passion, longing, intensity, and energy stimulates our minds and our souls. Once this irrepressible desire is born in your mind, you must immediately bring it into the light through your actions. Give flesh and blood to your noble and sincere desires! And when your passionate, noble, and sincere desires lead you to good *actions*, the responses from others will pleasantly surprise you. The *reaction* from everyone will be positive and will support you on your journey to mutual *satisfaction*. Action. Reaction. Satisfaction!"

"Got it. And what's in it for me?"

"Your efforts will be appreciated by the young, the old, the knowledgeable, the ignorant, the happy, and the doleful. Then, any collective positive reaction will help both you and your fellow passengers make a wonderful journey happen. Everyone will be satisfied, and no one will blame your aspirations, as long as your desires are pure and your actions are passionate. Your fellow passengers will not only enjoy the journey but will ardently wish to be with you, time and time again, with the same intensity, with the same tears, and with the same calm and luminous expression that I saw on your face as you sang the song. They will come to desire what you desire, and you will all be as one. You will be like a magnet, attracting those who have the same ardent desire. Finally, because we'll arrive soon, I need to tell you about the fifth rule—the value of *respecting*. If your desires are pure and your actions are passionate, then the reaction—the result—will be beneficial to all. Your fellow passengers should first taste the fruits of your good deeds so that they thereafter acknowledge their good fortune in knowing you."

"Can you please give me an example?"

"Sure! If you are the train driver—the captain—and you manage to provide a safe and comfortable journey for your passengers, then this action represents the greatest tribute to respect. You offer care, comfort, affection, safety, and joy to your passengers throughout the journey. You meet your passengers' basic needs, and you are willing to go the extra mile to make sure they have a satisfactory trip. You do this not for yourself but because you wish to take good care of the others. As the captain, you will perform this task without expecting a gratuity, using the mind map of *values, action, reaction, satisfaction* to meet other people's wants, needs, and feelings favorably. And then, when you least expect it, someone will knock on your door and say, 'Thank you for this beautiful journey,' or 'It was the best experience of my life,' or even 'When shall we travel again?'—or even better, 'Thank you for saving my life!' And suddenly, when you weren't expecting or demanding a gratuity, their warm words and their acknowledgment will be the most valuable bonus in the world, simply because you have learned to give without expectation. This quote by Buddha sums it up precisely: 'When we stop expecting, we will have it all.' If you make the mistake of giving something good because you expect something greater, I'm afraid you will live a life full of disappointment. If you despair at the beginning because the gratuity was inadequate, you run the risk of the next deserving customer being left disappointed and starved—and, by extension, yourself again being left without a hefty tip. You will end up becoming the victim of your self-fulfilling prophecy."

"Translation, please!"

"Let me put this in simple mansion terms. Before we go to bed, we secure all doors and windows for our own safety, right? Well, we must do the same for all those who depend on us. We'll lock Alanis and his hens in their cage so the foxes don't get them. We'll put the kittens in their little house so they won't get cold. Then we'll shut down the noisy generator so the place will be quiet for us to sleep."

"And what about the electricity?"

"We don't need it while we are asleep, and we don't want to burn petrol unnecessarily. Just as we need and seek care, love, safety, and rest, so do all living creatures on earth, whether they are reptiles, flies, insects, humans, or our planet itself."

"Even the snakes?"

"Every form of life has its own mission and reason for existence. The world was not created just for humans. Our presence, especially our behavior toward all other living creatures, should not offend or threaten their existence. Think of how many beings live on earth—under the ground, on the ground, in the sky, and in the depths of the oceans. We coexist with numerous living creatures every day, each fighting their own battle to survive, each struggling to ensure the safety of their families and to protect their very existence."

"I never thought of it that way."

"The world was not created for our own satisfaction. It was not created for our pleasure, any more than it was created for the snake that crawls and shows its fangs, the lion that runs and roars, the falcon that flies and snatches with its claws. God placed us under the same heaven and on the same earth with the purpose of living in harmony and each contributing in a unique way—one with a purpose, all serving the One. Not one another but all together serving the One. God takes pleasure when we live in peace. Since we share the world with others, then we all have the right to the good life. There must be respect for everyone and everything. Seek to do good, and good will come to you.

It is your choice to have good manners. Remember our credo; good manners were, are, and will always be in fashion!"

Choose to have good manners.

"Got it! Stay in fashion!"

"Whatever you want to do with your life, whatever you want to achieve in your life, the Gardener's Five Rules will be the deep roots that will keep the oak tree safe. Let the earthquake and the storm come; nothing will bring down a deep-rooted tree. Please start thinking about the five rules: beginning, planning, cooperating, desiring, and respecting. Then we will soon see it in practice. And this is just to start with—my so-called foundations. Soon, I will tell you the rest."

"I'm sure of that."

"My chosen boy, always remember that the seed must be planted in fertile soil to have a chance in life. Only then will it root and grow. After planting the seed, you should have enough patience to wait until the sapling appears. After that, you will need water, fertilizer, and pruning. The One and almighty God will provide the light. For years, I've been preparing the fertile ground in your soul to not only accept the seed you will receive today but also to carry out the heavy task that has been patiently waiting for you for hundreds of years. I promised you that I would finally tell you everything on this journey. Until now, the instructions have consisted of eating, reading, and playing, right? That's no different from watering, fertilizing, and pruning. I've been preparing your fertile ground since you were seven years old."

"What do you mean, Grandpa?"

"Do you remember the fairy tale 'The King and the Cook'?"

"The story you used to tell me as we sat in front of the fire, after we had waited for Grandma Vasia to fall asleep?"

"Exactly!"

"Oh my God! I still have the smell of the olive logs burning in the fireplace and the sensation of your warm breath on my face as you told me that tale. Why did you stop? It's your fault I don't remember it anymore."

"Your mind may not remember it, but your soul recorded it the very first time you heard it. But why are you complaining? We agreed that on this trip, we'll talk about everything! Are you ready?"

"Ready! But can we listen to my favorite song one more time? The mansion is on our left, just after the narrow bridge."

"Find the song and turn up the volume, my chosen boy. We'll sing 'Thalassa, Thalassa'[1] with Nikos Nomikos so loudly that our voices will echo across the whole mountainside!"

Oh sea, my sea, what have you done to me!

---

[1] If you want to find us in the Asynchronous Zone of Today, search for the song on the internet, and enjoy it with us right now.

I lost every port for you.
And I am since then a sailor and tomorrow I set sail
again alone.

The mansion welcomes us with a cooling breeze. A calmness flows everywhere as soon as we park the Cadillac's sixty horses in the garage. The only sounds are the rustling of leaves and the chickens complaining about Grandpa's long absence. It seems to me that Alanis winks at me, warning me that countryside early morning wake-up calls will be a difficult task.

We put our luggage down and organize our supplies, don the appropriate gardening uniforms, and, with our wooden spears in hand, we head down the path leading to the small house that hosts the generator. To be perfectly honest, this place scares me a little. The huge machine is so loud when it starts up that it takes ten minutes for my hearing to return to normal.

The process of bringing the sleeping beast to life is relatively easy, considering the mammoth constructive task it performs of supplying electricity to a huge mansion. We flip a dozen or so switches on the electric panel and attach the pump to the generator's seized-up body. With much exertion, we turn the crank handle, which sets the flywheel in motion and starts the combustion process that powers the black rubber belt that keeps the pump going. Many times, my grandfather doesn't give the necessary intensity and passion to the pump's motion. After about twenty or so failed attempts, the generator finally kicks in, after first throwing out a blast of black smoke that takes our breath away. Despite the annoying constant noise, especially when the door is open, electricity is available for every need of the mansion.

We have a family joke about it—Grandpa Takis makes fun of Grandma Vasia for being just like the mansion's generator. Despite the noise she makes with her mumbling, she provides for all the needs of both the family home and the restaurant. Grandma has never realized that this is actually a wonderful compliment. As a result, she responds to him with various impolite expressions.

After waking up the generator, we then inspect the irrigation system to make sure that each tree and vegetable patch is getting a fair share of water. This important task takes us about three hours, and the chickens have started protesting, reminding us to feed them, clean them, and give them fresh water. This, of course, comes with the appropriate reward— fresh eggs to be scrambled for tomorrow's breakfast.

The cooking process is a ritual for Grandpa and a pleasure for anyone who watches him closely. He never starts cooking unless he first has properly prepared the cooking area—he sharpens knives, lines up seasonings, and washes vegetables arranged by category. Of course, his favorite brandy always is in a metal drinking vessel.

"It keeps my brandy cold and my heart warmer," he declares to justify pouring himself another.

My mission is to set the table with all the requirements. "Knife on the right, and fork on the left," he shouts from the kitchen. I don't know how many times I will have to hear this instruction in my life to make up for the mistake of that fateful day when Chef Takis's grandson made the tragic mistake of arranging them in reverse.

"Go get changed as soon as you're done setting the table. I'm not serving you in those clothes in my restaurant, mister! This outfit is only for gardening. Put your best clothes on, and come to eat. Chef Takis will be serving in ten minutes, so don't be late!"

I run to my room and open my suitcase, at once thinking of my mother, as the care she has put into packing is unparalleled. She has arranged everything with so much love. Shuffling through my clothes, I find a sealed envelope hidden inside my favorite T-shirt. I sit on the bed, and as I open it, I immediately recognize her calligraphic writing.

> My beloved son,
>
> Since I am not invited to the mansion, I managed to sneak into your things and come as a stowaway. Ha-ha-ha! This is the first time you've been away on a journey with your grandfather for so many days, and I'm convinced that your Easter holidays will be

unforgettable. I know the purpose of this journey, and I'm excited that upon your return, you will have co-decided your future plans and more. Please have your ears open to understand and your heart open to appreciate. You may feel somewhat disappointed that Grandpa has different plans in mind for you, but don't forget that you are the chosen boy. I kindly ask you to have all the patience in the world, as much as I've practiced in raising you. As I write this letter asking you to be patient, I recall another letter—a manuscript I prepared for you on the first day you started at elementary school. I don't know why I never gave it to you. Perhaps you didn't give me a reason to give it to you, as you grew up to be the most well-mannered and well-meaning boy in the world. Anyway, I found it, and I'm giving it away. It's yours anyway. I want you to know that I love you dearly and think of you every minute of every day. Take care of your grandfather, my kind boy, just like you take care of me and your sister every night when your father is working at the restaurant. I am confident that you'll take care of yourself too! Give Grandpa lots of kisses, and tell him that today I am finally delivering the best student in the world, as promised!

Kisses,
Your Mommy
PS: Now read my letter carefully

September 1983

You can't imagine my joy today, seeing you dressed up in your elementary school uniform for the first time. You're not even on the school bus yet, and I feel like I miss you already. I am so blessed to have you in my life, and I will arm myself with all the patience in the world to wait for you every time you leave our house. After all, I've been patient since the moment I knew that you had decided to come into our lives. After nine months, twenty extra pounds, and a week in the hospital, I was able to welcome you, strong and healthy, into my world. I patiently held you in my arms for the entire night, and I didn't want you to be taken from me. When I first looked into your little eyes and held your tiny fingers, I felt what love really means for the first time. All the hardship I had gone through in my life, up until that moment when I first held you, was a prologue of patience. And one strong emotion after another crafted a soft blanket that I used to wrap you tightly so that you wouldn't get cold or be hurt. I have never felt similar emotions, at least with such intensity, even though I had only known you for a few minutes. Then I began the process of becoming the best mother I could be. I was borne of a mother, but I wasn't born a mother, so I never thought I knew everything. I was ready to challenge all my beliefs and habits, no matter how deep-rooted they may have been, and become a primary school student like you. I immediately sought the opinions of experts, read quite a few relevant books, and kept a determined eye on becoming the mother you deserve to properly prepare you for the mission that awaits you. I recall a particular time when you were just three years old, and I owe you a sincere apology! Sometimes, I would purposely let you cry until you learned that crying doesn't win you anything, despite the fact that it broke my heart when it happened. There were times, despite the judgmental stares of others, when I left you on the floor until you found the courage to get up on your own. I had to arm myself with all the patience in the world—on one hand, to guide you properly, and on the other hand, to avoid saying yes to everything you wanted. I want you to know that I had the purest of intentions and the greatest passion to raise you the right way and make you a capable human being. When you asked me for things and I said no, and then you frowned and your eyes filled with tears, a little piece of my heart would turn to stone. The easiest thing would have been to always pamper you. But if I'd done that, you'd never know that you wouldn't always get your way in life or know that no one else will offer you the same patience and love that your parents offer. I had to figure out the mechanics and rules to prepare you. I had to teach you to be self-sufficient and strong until you had your own supply of patience. As you grew older, you needed me less and less. Even though in my eyes and in my soul, you will always be my baby, I can only raise you right and love you with all my heart. I will never get tired of telling you how much I love you, as you are the greatest miracle in my world. I will arm myself with all the patience it takes to await your return home, and once you are asleep at night, I will sneak into your room like a stowaway to kiss your forehead, just as I did when I first took you in my arms and have continued to do throughout all the years that followed. Despite whatever difficulties or problems cause me pain, physical or mental, I have the ability to lighten my pain because you light my way. You are my greatest miracle! What you don't know today, as you leave for elementary school, is that you are my greatest teacher! You teach me more every day than I teach you. I am so grateful to you, my son. You are my brightest teacher because, through the patience I learned in raising you, I have become a better person.

With love,

Your mom

I immediately lock the door and let the tears of pure happiness flow from my eyes. I have witnessed again the most powerful love —motherly love! How could I not cry tears of joy and gratitude for a mother who is always present, even when she is not physically there, making me feel important even in my smallest steps, creating and elevating my confidence, helping me join society without fear, and training me to love what I have so that I can have what I love—a special mother who crafted a loving blanket to cover me every night.

What strikes me most as I read the letter for the second time is her use of the word *patience*. It is in almost every sentence. It seems as if she wrote it back then for me to read today, when I am in need of a ton of patience.

I am interrupted by Grandpa as he knocks discreetly on the door of my room. I hastily wipe my eyes and open the door, hiding my face behind it.

"Dinner has been served, young man," he announces in a butler's tone and heads back to the kitchen. He does not ask why I am late or why my eyes are wet.

Station 7

The Fairy Tale

You must attach yourself spiritually to what
you have placed in your imagination as a future
fact, and never allow anyone, anything, any
circumstance, no matter how persuasive their
case, to alter what you know to be your destiny.
—Wayne W. Dyer

I step out of the room, leaving my soul inside. As the house has not
warmed up sufficiently, I put a large log on the fire. It must be a
pine log because it throws up lots of bright sparks. The red fireballs
transport me at supersonic speed to Eantos Street and into the good
living room of my parents' house. At this time of year, the room is
finally open and decorated in keeping with the Greek Easter tradition.
The centerpiece is the Easter tree—a one-meter-tall plastic tree, each
branch with a ring socket attached at its tip, where the family's Easter
eggs are placed. In our case, these are the magic red eggs!

Mom takes Easter traditions to a whole different level with her
rituals. Since her marriage, every Holy Thursday, as custom dictates,
she dyes the Easter eggs red. From the annual batch, she selects the
largest egg and, with a black marker, writes the date and the most
significant event of that year. Obviously, each year's magic egg will not

be eaten at the Easter Sunday feast but will be saved, and the following year, another special egg will be added to the collection.

To me, the most precious egg is the one inscribed "1976—my marriage," and the inscription that touches me most is "1977—my son." Of course, I can't resist playing a prank on my sister by taking the red egg with the message "1981—my sweet girl" and pretending to drop it!

Along the way, and to our great interest, we learned that the eggs dyed red on Holy Thursday are indeed holy! These eggs don't become rotten as the years go by. Instead, they shrink, their shells become increasingly brittle, the white part disappears, and the yolk turns into a little red ball called amber.

To date, we have collected seventeen magic eggs—the one from Mom's wedding and sixteen others, from the day I was born. Mom has even put a timeline on this ritual. We will stop saving red eggs when we have thirty-three, that being the years of Christ's life. As soon as they all perform their little miracle and turn into amber, we will take them to Grandma Vasia's jeweler and ask him to make a rosary with thirty-three amber beads.

While I am physically sitting in front of the fireplace, I am mentally with my family. But it doesn't take long for Grandpa to bring me hurtling back to the mansion as, with his untrained voice, he attempts to sing his favorite Greek *rebetiko* song. Chef Takis is a multitalented man, but he needs to give up singing!

Pouring his third or fourth—or probably fifth—glass of his favorite brandy into the tin mug, he approaches, full of joy and giddiness. He patiently waits for me to explain what happened in my room, yet I continue to sit silently before the fire.

"I assume you found a hidden note from your mom?"

"How do you know? Did you also conspire to do this?"

"Of course not! She's been doing the same thing for years.

Choose to have good intentions.

This fine woman, from the day she was born, has good intentions toward everyone. This hidden-messages ritual is not a new thing to me."

"What do you mean?"

"She leaves her messages everywhere. A yellow Post-it note on my coffee cup—'Daddy, don't forget your morning vitamin'—or a message hidden in my wallet—'Mom's birthday tomorrow, so don't forget the present or else.' A sticky note on my steering wheel—'Daddy, don't speed'—and various smiley faces wishing me good morning or good night, hidden in the restaurant kitchen. Sometimes even inside the fridge!"

"Did she put a note in your suitcase as well, Grandpa?"

"Yes, she did!"

"Do you want to tell me what she wrote to you?"

"I'll tell you if you tell me."

"Come on, we don't have to negotiate everything,"

"I agree, but you have to play fair. I have no problem reading mine to you. At least you could give me a synopsis of what she wrote to you."

"OK! Go get your letter, and we'll see."

As Grandpa goes to his room, I pop into my parents' living room for a last visit. Picking up the egg inscribed "1977—my son," I feel like the most important person in the world. A letter and an egg remind me of the true value of family; likewise, the value I have within my family. This feeling that I have value as a human being is very important to my mental health. This value is given primarily through parental love and the support of our own people. Since I was blessed enough to be valued during my childhood, then no pain will be able to break my spirit throughout my adult life. It needs no explanation that if I consider myself a truly valuable commodity, this confidence will always protect me from pain. As I contemplate all this, a fireball pops up and warms my heart, just as Grandpa returns from the room, holding a small piece of paper.

"Oh, dear! Is that tiny note the message you were referring to? Just to let you know, she left me two lengthy pages, so you'd better think again if you want us have supper on time."

He ignores my warning, puts on his brown bone glasses, and clears his throat. He wants an attentive audience.

"Dear Dad, the chosen boy is finally ready! I did everything I promised you in 1977 when we were alone in the maternity room, and you revealed to me our family's great mission. The student is ready, so I proudly hand him over to his teacher. However, I want to warn you that, at times, the roles might reverse, and you'll find yourself being the student, so please be patient and understanding. To the rest of the world, you are Chef Takis, but to him, you are his whole world. I realize that the spiritual burden you have carried all these years has made you anxious, so please be gentle in how you transfer it to him. Make sure that the transmission of this remarkable spiritual heritage is done in the best possible way. I humbly believe that the tenth receiver has grown up to be a loving and caring person. With the same love and care, I am sure he will continue his special mission. Good luck!

Your daughter, the custodian."

"What is this, Grandpa? I don't understand what she's saying! What's the special mission all about? Who is the tenth receiver, and who are the other nine? What is the spiritual heritage she is referring to? Why did Mom call herself the *custodian*? Grandpa, you're scaring me!"

"My boy, when you threw that log onto the fire and were surrounded by fireballs, were you afraid you would be burned?"

"Of course not!"

"Well, now that I'll be throwing you my own bright balls, fear has no place in our company. Throw your fear into the fire, and let my words warm you. Let my story enlighten your mind and fill your spirit."

"OK, but I just can't understand a word of Mom's note. You, on the other hand, seem quite familiar with the terminology. You are not surprised at all!"

"Tonight, my chosen boy, is the night that I will finally tell you all about it. I only request patience of you until we reach the *last station*, when your path will be lit and all your doubts resolved. It doesn't matter how long you've been in the dark; a single match is enough to light up a dark room that hasn't seen light for seventeen long years. The match will fuel the branch, the branch will ignite the log, and the fire will heat the room and our hearts. The same has already happened for us both today. We found a cold mansion that had been closed for a whole month. It was impossible to warm it up just like that. It took patience and time for the fire to do its magic."

"And what is your magic show for tonight?"

"A hungry bear won't dance, so I suggest we enjoy our meal, and then we'll have plenty of time to continue our chat."

I drag my numb feet to the dining table and sink my troublesome questions in the first glass of red wine, saving the second and last glass that I am allowed to have for later, as I am sure the rest of the evening will be full of surprises.

It is by far the quietest meal I have ever had with Grandpa. It's as if we are conserving our strength for the main event. The table is clear, the dishes are washed, and the stadium is now ready to host the grand finale.

Grandpa goes to turn off the generator as I light the candles dotted around the living room. As soon as I hear the generator's last tired breath, the trembling light from the lamps slowly fades. A sudden silence takes over—an absolute silence filled with magical acoustic tones. A symphony of dissimilar sounds contributes a wonderful musical harmony—a coexistence of sound! The old clock above the fireplace shows seven in the evening and ticks vigorously. There come the moans and whistles of the wind from outside, the crackling of pine logs on the fire, the hissing of warm air within the chimney, tweets and hums from the night birds roosting in the heart of the oak tree, the rustling of small nocturnal insects that have begun their night shift, and other indefinable small sounds that the human ear catches only under the mountain stars. The scenery is now completely changed, and the protagonists are the sounds and the shadows. Undulating forms thrown by the candles dance on the walls, and vivid red tongues of fire emit flickering reflections of light, giving life to the family photos on the shelves. I stare at the hundreds of books on the wooden bookshelves to the left and right of the stone-built fireplace. This is a place for eating, reading, and playing only, which is why no TV set is allowed in the mansion.

It's so quiet that I can hear Grandpa's footfalls as he walks back up the path to the house. He didn't take his black storm lantern with him, as a full moon illuminates the entire landscape. I glance around the room, and I am mentally transported to the time when people lived without electricity. Unknowingly, this is an eerie preparation for the story to follow—to a time past, set in 1470.

Grandpa hurriedly closes the door, commenting that it is getting chilly outside. He hangs up his coat and cap and heads for the bottle of brandy, pouring it without skimping. He then sits comfortably in his armchair, pulling the wooden lever on the side in order to stretch his legs out on the footrest. The "throne," as he likes to call his dark-brown leather armchair, is a place no one dares to sit, as it's where Grandpa Takis finally rests his tired body after a hard day's work. I sit on the couch to his left and observe his face as he watches the dancing flames of the fire. The way his seat is positioned leaves the left side of his face completely illuminated by the fire, while the right side is in darkness. I immediately have the impression that the most important person in my life, after Mom and Dad, ultimately has two faces: the face I've known all these years—that of the best grandfather in the world—and a darker, more mysterious one that will be revealed to me in a very short while.

"Grandpa, let's begin from the point where you said that tonight I'll be the student, and you'll be the teacher."

"Learn from your experiences to become wise. Learn from others to become wiser. Ignore learning to remain a fool!"

"Good thing I'm not a fool, right, Grandpa?"

"You are my *chosen boy*! Therefore, why do you need my confirmation?"

"Good to hear! Then how do we start tonight?"

"With me telling you a fairy tale!"

"Oh, how nice! Please tell me the story of 'The King and the Cook'!"

"Once upon a time, there were two completely different and distant worlds that were destined to become one. Distant worlds from us too, so synchronize your watch to travel back in time to Florence and to the year 1470.

The cook lives happily with his two daughters. He has his tavern in the heart of the forest and offers hospitality and good food to every traveler and wanderer in the area. He is famous for a creamy minced-meat pasta that he makes. He often boasts that the pasta is made by using a secret family recipe that he never reveals to anyone. The cook's only heartache is that he lost his wife to smallpox a year after the birth of their second daughter. But he never lost his courage, as he never wanted to deprive his girls of anything. To cheer them up when they speak of their mother, he always tells them, "Your mother opened a small box and gave me two angels, and then she got the smallpox and went to the heavenly angels."

On the other side of the world, we meet a king who is famous for his kindness, cheerfulness, vitality, and endless pleasure in helping the needy. The feasts he holds in the palace courtyard are open to all passersby. He makes sure there is plenty of food, fun, dancing, and singing into the early hours. He spends a lot of his time trying to be a fair king. At the same time, he makes sure that on holidays, he engages in his favorite hobby—hunting. His only sorrow is that his beautiful queen has yet to deliver the most precious thing in the world—a child who will become his heir. But he never loses hope.

The cook, over the years, has become very famous, and the reputation of the tavern has grown. At the same time, his daughters have been growing up, and before he knows it, he finds himself blessing his elder daughter in marriage. A young gold dealer has stolen her heart during a short visit to their village. The cook rubs his hands in satisfaction, as the merchant seems destined to become an ideal son-in-law and a good business partner. He sponsors the renovation of the tavern, turning it into a lodge. With the new layout, travelers now have the option of not only enjoying the magical Pasta a la Crème but also of resting in one of the ten sanctuaries offered by the cook on the first floor.

The year ends on a high note, as the two goals set by the king are achieved. The wheat crops fill the warehouses with two years' worth of stock, and the construction of protective stone walls is finally complete. Both the king and his people feel a pervasive sense of security that turns to joy and happiness. It is as if the king has the ability to transmit his own bliss to his kingdom surroundings. He decides that he deserves a new adventure and commands his governor to organize a hunt in the deepest forest, wherever it may be, no matter how far away. He informs the king regent to take over his duties, as the hunting group will be absent for a long time.

The king, his horses and dogs, and his fellow hunters, after traveling over mountains and seas, finally set up their tents in a valley called Casentino. The long journey had been exhausting, and as a result, they sleep for an entire day. The following day, they make a pilgrimage to St. Anthony's Abbey and beg the saint to provide them with good hunting and a great adventure. For the king's safety, the governor suggests wearing clothes with no royal insignia, which might give away their identity. They look like an ordinary group of seven hunters, ten horses, and fourteen dogs. The captain and the sailors are left behind to look after the ship, and they complain about missing all the action.

Meanwhile, the cook has his own complaint. The merchant has arranged his own long journey to the Persian Gulf, as he has a very important meeting with an Arab trader of gold and rare emeralds. The journey will last several months, and obviously, he will be accompanied by his wife. For the first time, the cook will not see his daughter for a long period. He limits his involvement to preparing some food for their journey, giving them his blessing, and wishing them good luck.

Out in the forest, the dogs are stirring up the whole area with their barking as they run around excitedly, picking up the game as it falls from the sky. The king, despite his love of hunting, has total respect for nature and all its creations. Killing is not the purpose; it's only to fulfill the need for food—and perhaps a need to have a good time eating! Normally, when hunting, as soon as they have all they require for their supper, the king calls an end to the hunt.

Cook has been left with only his younger daughter to serve his guests. The tavern is full on a daily basis with every kind of passing traveler. Earlier that day, just before the big meeting, they had struggled to serve the many customers, and as a result, their supplies have become very low. The cook asks his daughter to take the wagon and visit the nearby town to stock up.

The hunters have also run out of supplies, literally and metaphorically. They have used their allotted number of bullets for the day but have failed to catch enough to feed and fill everyone. As darkness falls, they return, hungry and exhausted, to their camp. The governor orders the tracker to find the nearest tavern, and as he looks up at the sky and sees the heavy gray clouds, he instructs the tracker to find a nearby lodge instead. The tracker rides swiftly off into the thick fog, and the only sound is the neighing of his horse as he gallops away. To his good fortune, he meets the cook's daughter on the road, and after getting directions from her, he sets off back to the camp with the good news. The governor and the tracker choose to stay with the dogs and enjoy a well-earned rest. The king and the other four hunters follow the tracker's instructions and set off for the tavern. As they tie the horses in the tavern's stable, the king reminds his company once again that under no circumstances are they to reveal his true identity.

On entering the tavern, they are greeted somewhat hesitantly by the cook, as he knows he doesn't have much to offer them from his almost-empty storeroom. Reminded of the Arab saying, "You don't fill my eye," the king tries to charm the cook with a smile and a generous offer.

"Bring us the best meal you can, and prepare five rooms for tonight. We can pay you in advance!"

"I thank you for your generosity, my lord, but I will disappoint you. A swarm of hungry locusts passed by my tavern today, and they came close to eating me as well! I am afraid that I don't have all the necessary supplies left to fully satisfy you. In fact, I had decided not to open the tavern tonight, as the clock shows seven, and I have no provisions at my disposal."

"Well, we're out of supplies too, my kind cook. We've been hunting all day, but bad luck got the better of us. Make the best you can with what you have left, and come join us for supper. It seems you have the same need for rest as we do. At least, will you provide good beds for us to retire to afterwards?"

The cook is taken aback by the king's wide smile and his kindness, as he is not used to receiving such gracious responses from other travelers. "With the greatest respect, my kind sir, I have only ten rooms, and six are already booked. I can accommodate four of you upstairs, and one of you can rest in my older daughter's room, as she is away on a trip." As soon as he says this, he regrets it. He can't believe that he has just suggested that a total stranger spend the night in his house with his younger daughter and him. But at the same time, he looks into the king's eyes, and an overwhelming feeling of peace and security takes over his mind.

"My dear cook, we accept your offer. But you must allow us to return the favor. We want to eat and rest like peasants and pay you like kings. This is our only condition, and it is non-negotiable. If you do not agree, we will just drink the water you brought us, and then we will disappear into the mist!"

The cook, bewildered by the king's generosity, agrees with the terms and rushes to the kitchen to prepare the best possible meal he can for his surprising guests, who all radiate such wonderful kindness.

He takes the two portions of his special pasta that he had reserved for himself and his daughter, prepares an inviting salad of fresh vegetables gathered from his own garden, and makes a hearty fry-up using the eggs and sausages put aside for tomorrow's breakfast. He remembers that he has some cheese and dried meats at his house and doesn't hesitate to add those to the meal. Finally, he fills a bowl with fresh olive oil and a plate with green olives, and he takes a homemade loaf of bread from the firewood oven.

Taking a quick look at his offerings to make sure there is enough food and of good quality, he hurriedly changes into a clean shirt, washes his face and hands, and heads to the table to join his guests. Earlier, he had taken the precaution of putting a large pot of red wine on the table, and he now finds them cheerful and amused. The youngest of the group, the king's banker, has begun to sing, and his angelic voice spreads throughout the tavern. As soon as he sees the food prepared by the cook, he stops singing and looks at the delicacies in anticipation.

The cook places the dishes on the table and sits down. "I am not totally pleased with what I lay before you, but I am honored by your kindness and tolerance. I hope you will give me the opportunity of preparing your breakfast tomorrow morning, as my daughter will return from town later with fresh supplies."

"My dear cook, I was under the impression that your daughter was on a long journey, and I was about to accept your offer to rest in her room. Since she will return tonight already, then we will flip a coin, and one of us will sleep in the stable with the horses!"

"Oh, no, that's not necessary. It's my fault for not explaining it better. My elder daughter is married to a gold trader, and they are currently traveling to the Persian Gulf to meet a new trader. He will be hosting them for a few months as they work out their plan of partnership. Once that is accomplished, I would hope that they will find their way back home. This daughter's room is indeed at your disposal. My younger daughter is the one who has gone to town to get the supplies. It's a mission she's been carrying out for the past two years, and I have complete confidence in her. Indeed, while each time I give her more coins than she needs, in the hope of her buying something for herself, in all these years she has not spent a single one, not even for a simple dress or a piece of jewelry."

The king can only admire the cook's humility. He then becomes lost for a moment in his personal reverie, his happy mood changing as he recalls his own tragic story. The cook notices that his guest has not put a bite of food into his mouth, while the rest of the company licks their fingers and, every now and then, congratulate him on the meal he has provided.

Raising his glass high, he clears his throat and fixes his gaze on the king, exclaiming, "My dear lord, my dear guests! Here in the forests of Tuscany, we have a great custom! We frequently clink our glasses and make as much noise as possible. We do this especially when we are in *good company* and in *good mood* because pain is jealous and wants to join us. He wants a seat at our table. Since we don't desire his company, we try to drive him away by clinking our glasses and making a big fuss, with loud laughter and much clattering!"

The king, almost unconsciously, takes his glass and does as the landlord commands, taking a sip of wine before addressing the cook once again. "What else frightens and exorcises pain besides good company and good mood, my dear cook?"

"Pain's worst enemy is *good manners*, my lord. Pain takes hold of us and demands to be passed on to everyone else. He wants to see us all in pain and wants us to carry him through to others. This chain gives him immense satisfaction. The farther it reaches, the heavier it gets, and it makes him stronger and more powerful. Once he realizes that he is not getting his way—you are hurting yet manage to remain kind to everyone—then he mows down and afflicts you even more. If you manage to remain kind to everyone and everything, he eventually gives up and disappears, weakened!"

"So, pain is afraid of good company, good mood, and good manners, right?"

"Yes, but there are other elements that can help. The choice to be in good company, good mood, and have good manners comes from within. It's an attitude of mind, and no one should influence you otherwise. Even pain. Let pain come but not be welcome. And we have already stated how this is possible!"

"With good company, good mood, and good manners! Cheers to that!"

"Quite right, my lord, thank you! Therefore, let us not forget to clink our glasses as often and cheerily as we can. The next ingredient on my list that irritates pain immensely is when you have *good intentions*. Intention is a conscious will that motivates a person for action. The question is whether that action is for good or evil. As the sun has its moon, as the day has its night, as white has its black, so we, like nature itself, have the elements of good and evil within. Every human being has defined good and evil and makes decisions based on these two elements, thereby making distinctions. To someone, we owe goodness, and to someone else, we will return the evil. Good intention is the heart's ability to bypass the mind's discriminating process and offer only goodness to all. This causes incredible confusion to pain, as he cannot comprehend it. If you are always able to show *good intentions* toward everyone and not just at will, you discover a tremendous power that exists within you that is called *forgive, forget, and forward*. After that, how much damage can pain provide? Absolutely none or minimum! You will look pain in the eye and tell it that you have forgiven and forgotten far worse evils, and you choose to move forward!"

"So, pain will lose the battle with good company, good mood, good manners and good intentions!"

"Yes, he will lose a battle, but you'll still need to win the war. These four personal choices will help lighten your pain, but you are not a star in the sky. You are not a sun, a moon, a planet. You are not a mountain that sits still and silent through the ages. You are a person who lives with other people and who lives by other people. You are a human being living with other living creatures. Sometimes we give, and sometimes we take. The balance must always be fair!"

"When you say *fair*, you mean even? To receive what we give?"

"Yes, assuming you want to lead a normal life, my lord."

"What if I want more than that? An eminent life!"

"Then, you have to tip the balance. You have to give far more than you get and never check the balance on a daily basis. The final balance will come when it is due. Believe me, the one who chooses a life of giving more than he gets will live a happy life. To imprint this behavior on our minds and souls, I am afraid that good company, good mood, good manners, and good intentions are not enough. At least, not enough to win the war. It still takes a few special ingredients to make the best pasta in the world!"

The banker, who has been sitting quietly, chooses not to put another morsel into his mouth as he prepares to argue with the cook. "Look, we were talking about pain and how to scare it away! How did we get onto balances, final accounts, and total reckoning? That's my area of expertise, and I'm telling you that bills have to be paid on time—here and now—with no delays!"

"Please forgive me, my lord! I am old, and there are times when I lose my reasoning. The first choices—good company, good mood, good manners, and good intention—are entirely one's personal affair. The other elements, the ones we're about to discuss now, are for others to benefit from as well. They are the choices we make that impact the lives of others. Since we are talking about winning a war, no one goes into battle without armor and an army. Good company, good mood, good manners, and good intentions form your own armor. No matter how much shooting there is, it is not susceptible to serious damage, only a few superficial abrasions. Internally, you will remain safe and sound to continue your battle. And since you yourself are indestructible, you should help and guide your supporting troops. Unfortunately, they may not have learned or have been given this valuable knowledge, and not everyone wears the same armor as yours. If you don't help them, they will experience the pain of misery, sadness, melancholy, panic, fear, anguish, loneliness, anxiety, despair, and certain death, as they are indeed vulnerable. No one wins a war on his own. You will need to prepare and lead your troops if you want to ultimately win the war. Therefore, in order to win, the strategy is quite simple. We must first dress ourselves in our own armor, then immediately support everyone else by any means possible. This is where my other ingredients—or, if you like, choices—come in that will ultimately help us affect others in a good way."

"And what are those options, mighty general?" the banker asks disdainfully.

"Choose to generously share your knowledge with all, even if they want to take your title and your position. They will then advance, and you will be promoted! If your troops advance, the squad will progress and gain more ground. Therefore, *good progress* is the fifth ingredient—the fifth choice—and it is beneficial to all! Next, you must organize and plan your activities. Life is given to us as a gift, but a successful life needs effort and good planning. I call it a *choiceful journey to a successful life.* For this, you make wise choices, win your daily battles, and, at the same time, enjoy each day as if it were your last day on earth. The way you manage your daily time and activities will play a significant role in your success and happiness. Your steps must be completely synchronized, or the fire will burn the food. If it does, everyone will go hungry, including you. Therefore, *good timing*—the sixth choice—plays a very important role in having a successful life. If your good food pleases their sense of smell and thereafter fills their bellies, then everyone will want to eat at your tavern again and again! Does this make any sense now?"

"You've gone back to cooking advice again! Is the wine affecting your judgment?" the banker challenges.

"Where I come from, wine is always on the table to accompany the beautiful moments of our lives! A happy life includes beautiful moments with our loved ones. Therefore, we should spend as much time as possible with them. It is our choice to be happy, and that has not changed since humans first set foot in this world. Happiness is sewn, day by day, with beautiful memories and becomes a beautiful blanket. Someday, you will need it to cover your old feet and gain the strength to take another step, take another breath. Therefore, creating *good memories*—our seventh choice—will fuel your future journey and beyond. I'm rambling now, and I've tired you!"

The cook stops talking and waits for a response. The audience is totally mesmerized by the wisdom he imparts, and their souls are satiated. The only *sleeping student* who doesn't want to wake up is the banker. He chooses yet another intervention.

"Well said, my cook philosopher, but how about getting out from the comfort of your tavern and taking a walk through the poor streets and alleys of the cities of this world? All you will find are wounded souls and lost battles with pain. What are your comments on that?"

"I say it hurts my soul to think of them, and I take responsibility for my share of the blame. Since I'm so sure that my philosophy is like a suit of armor, then I need to shut my cookhouse down and go find everyone who is suffering on the streets. It is my duty to share this knowledge, but on the other hand, I have the responsibility of raising my daughters. Maybe one day, what we are talking about today will become scripture and be given to the whole world. Something similar already happened on Mount Sinai in 1470 BC. We are now heading to AD 1470, and I am afraid we have not been the best students since then. Even if we give all this knowledge to the world now, I am afraid that by the year 2000, we will encounter the same problems!"

"Then what's left for us? Absolutely nothing! We have no salvation!"

"We have three more ingredients, my young lord. I have already mentioned the previous seven to you, and who knows? Our pasta might save the world from soul hunger!"

The king is in no mood to let the nonbelieving banker continue to push the cook to the limit, so he takes the floor once again. "Remind us again of the seven choices you mentioned before, then continue with the other three, my great master!" The mighty king honored the cook by calling him master!

"Good company, good mood, good manners, good intentions, good progress, good timing, and good memories are the choices we have already discussed. What remains, my lord, is first of all to leave your candle always burning. Even the blind man will sense this special flame and come straight to you. For as long as the flame is lit and available, you will give support to all who need it. The flame of this candle is called *goodness*! With this value—or, if you prefer, the eighth choice—you can live a full life. Once you are replete and your storehouses are overflowing with goods, then you will open your doors and welcome everyone and everything. Your ninth choice, *good purpose*, will bring you to the ultimate destination: the *good life* you seek. These are the final three ingredients: *goodness, good purpose,* and *good life*! These three choices will bring faith and hope to even the most unbelieving of all. They will help even the most desperate human being, even if that person seemingly has lost everything. A hope in a higher one, a higher form, a higher being, can work magic. It is like a humble beggar who dares to ask the king for a coin to feed his children. Once the higher king gives him a shilling, then the king's blessing begins. If the beggar feeds his family with that shilling, then his own blessing begins as well. If he deceives the king and spends the shilling on alcohol, then his own sin begins. I say this to explain that our balances must be heterogeneous. We must constantly provide without caring what others do with our help. That is how we will become higher beings, as close as to the image of our higher God!"

The king is speechless. He feels that he has graduated overnight from the school of life. He has learned more valuable things from a cook than from the forty teachers he had for twenty years in the palace. He finds the strength to rise from the table, take his glass in his hand, and invite the company to toast the master's health. At that moment, the young daughter enters the tavern, greeting the guests politely. As the daughter unhesitatingly takes charge of clearing the table, the king asks his friends to retire to their rooms to rest, while he chooses to spend some time alone with the cook.

"Let's go and sit by the fire, my lord, until my daughter has finished with the cleaning."

"Tonight, I am honoring you with the title of the master! You've managed to teach me more in one night than my teachers did in years. We should definitely pass on the ten choices to all the kings of the world! To all the priests, the masters, the philosophers, the writers, the poets; to all those who have a strong voice and the courage to pass on this teaching; to anyone who can warm the soul of the suffering, as you have done tonight to my aching soul!"

"My lord, why do you say this?"

"My dear master, I came on this hunt with my friends with a real need to hunt and kill the pain I bear inside me. While I managed to kill enough game, I failed to kill the dark beast within me. I am not claiming that one hour with you is enough to win the war, but I want to bear witness that it was the brightest, most true, most important hour I have spent with another human being. And believe me, in my profession, I have met, conversed, and dined with quite a few—let's call them bright—people. But you are the most luminous of all!"

"I am speechless, my lord! Thank you for your kind words!"

"My kind master, I want to study your choices in depth, put them to the test, and become a good disciple, worthy of his master. For now, I will thank God for bringing me your way tonight. I also thank you for letting me rest in your house. I must say that you have treated us like kings, and I feel we will pay like peasants."

"What really counts is the time spent together."

"I have one last request. Tonight, I will leave my boots outside the room. Before I leave at dawn tomorrow, I want to find a manuscript of your *ten choices* inside. In return, I will leave outside your door the payment I consider fair, in view of all you have offered us. Outside your young daughter's door, I will leave a gift to reward her frugality over the years. Do you agree to that?"

"I agree, my lord. You have already honored me with the title of the master, and you honor me tonight with your presence. I promise you that tomorrow morning, you will find the manuscript you seek. But I feel the need to tell you something. You strike me as a very knowledgeable man, and I have not set foot in school one day in my life. Do not expect to receive a complicated, incisive document containing the secrets of the world, which needs wise men and clerics to explain. Expect simple and understandable content, as humble as were my words tonight. It will be no different from the list of ingredients I use to make the best pasta in Italy! Nevertheless, I have to warn you. If you omit even one ingredient, the pasta will be inedible, and everyone will be left hungry, first of all yourself."

"I totally understand. I am so eager to receive your manuscript!"

"When you read it for the first time, you will assume it's a simple and easy process. However, the application requires great effort and courage. It requires you to walk the long path of your transformation. This long path is called *La Grande Strada*—the Great Road—and contains four stations. The first three stations complete your *application* phase, and the last station brings you ever closer to *recognition*. The four stations are: *I choose, I dare, I become,* and *I am*. Perhaps your teachers know it by the name *tetragrammaton* and have already explained it to you."

"Could you give me an example?"

"If, for example, I choose to have good manners, then I have reached the first station of the Great Road. I am at the *beginning*, and the execution of my mission will be based on my order, so the choice must be clear. The thought inside your mind—*I choose to have good manners in my life, and I have the unwavering courage to overcome all obstacles that come my way*—should be kept alive until it becomes a deep desire. Create the thought, convert it into a desire, and make it a choice. *Think, desire, choice!* How does the first station sound to you?"

"Perfectly understandable and relatively easy. How do we get to the second station?"

"Take your time, and don't rush on this special journey. Each station needs time to settle in your heart and mind before you dare to go further. The previous station should give you momentum and energy for the next, rather than calling you to go back to complete it. The Great Road has only one direction: ahead and at full speed!"

"Got it! Thank you!"

"At the second station—I dare—you will go into action. You will need to prepare and write your *plan* in detail. You will then have a personalized handwritten action plan to carry with you at all times. Every time you look at it, it will remind you of your mission: *I choose to have good manners in my life and have the unwavering courage to overcome all obstacles that come my way!* And remember, this is action number one out of ten!"

"So, for each new choice, I will need a new strategy, right?"

"Exactly, my lord! As for the *plan*, you can go back and revise it whenever you feel it needs updating. However, the *choice*, assuming it is spiritually correct and beneficial to all, you will never change."

"Clear! Once the choice has been made and written down, it doesn't change in any way!"

"Provided it is spiritually correct and beneficial to all. Having said that, you will reach the second station with your spiritual compass and map. The earth is a huge magnet that keeps the compass needle always pointing to the north. You will set your personal direction and your spiritual compass to guide you wherever you wish; for example, *I dare to be respectful!* Do not let others get in your way, as they unwillingly and blindly head to their north. Your Great Road will take you to your chosen destination. The second station—I dare—is extremely important. It's a clear instruction to the mind, not just a wishful thought written down on a piece of paper. Arm your mind with specific instructions on how to reach the designated destination, and the mind will work, day and night, to help you get there as soon as possible. The mind is a wonderful machine, but very few people use it appropriately these days. Give it special attention, because it will offer the same levels of help if your choice is bad. This is why our world is getting worse. People choose dark thoughts, and their minds obey the dark master."

"So true! Will I need any help at this station?"

"Well, you could find a person you trust to observe or mentor you."

"This is the first time I've discussed the power of the mind, and I'm fascinated by our conversation. Walk me through the next stations please."

"I am glad you find value in our conversation, my lord. The third station—I become—is the toughest and will be filled with challenges. The good news is that most of the obstacles exist only in our minds; therefore, with the same ease that we put them there, I assure you that we can remove them. At this station, you need a powerful ingredient and a drastic action for your mind to get started. I will give you both of these. The powerful ingredient is *desire*, an unwavering dedication to completing your every task in this stage. It's the intensity you put in every action, the management of every reaction, until you reach satisfaction. So, *desire, action, reaction, satisfaction.* The drastic action is our *internal dialogue*, the voice you give to your heart to handle the difficult negotiation with your mind. It is no good making all your important decisions using the mind alone. It takes mediation and mental reflection. Negotiate your unfruitful principles, challenge your fixed beliefs, stop your useless habits, implement effective practices, dare to take new actions, and make adjustments utilizing your new attitude toward life, until you discover your true self, until you achieve your higher purpose—to become a higher being! These are the three stations of the application phase: *I choose, I dare, I become.* And the outcome is entirely up to you!"

"I have a mountain of work to do. Please help me!"

"I will, my lord. You'll find it all written down in my manuscript. However, you'll also have plenty to write and plan yourself. You should be able to create a miracle, to transform the intangible gold within your mind into real gold within your hands."

"I do not know from where I should begin."

"Your journey should begin with a heartfelt desire. Let's say, *I choose to be respectful.* You should thereafter write down on paper, in detail, your entire action plan. Next to each action you will nominate a mentor, and both of you will commit to completing the task in the most time-efficient manner—operating has added value when cooperating! You will study what you have written twice a day, and *declare* your action plan in hand to the sun and the stars. You have no excuse for not doing so! The sun and the stars will provide the light you'll need for reading and planning. The sun will help you plan your day, and the stars will help you evaluate your day. Once the *plan* is instilled in your spirit, then you will be able to describe it in just one word. This word—your life's purpose—will be so powerful that it will bring you back to the Great Road every time you get lost. So, you will welcome the sun and the stars with just one word! Some call this process *meditation,* others call it *prayer,* where I've simply chosen to call it *declaration.*"

"How will I know that I have succeeded with the ten choices? I guess it has to do with the last station."

"You'll know you've made it once you successfully pass the fourth and final station—I am. This is the station that has the potential to boost your spirit. It also has a secret ingredient: *respect.* Recognition depends solely on others, as they must *detect and tell* your achievement."

"What do you mean by detect and tell, my master?"

"Take a leaf from my book of life. I have never said that I make the best pasta in Italy. In fact, that achievement can be claimed by a fellow cook at the tavern a stone's throw from here. I will insist on my opinion, and my colleague will insist on his. Only fools try to change other people's opinions. They only waste their time and, in the end, lose their right to any opinion. The only ones entitled to evaluate and rate the outcome of your efforts are the ones who receive the results—the clients, or if you prefer, the recipients. If my reputation is verified by all and maintained over time, then I can claim to have obtained the coveted station: I am. *I am the best pasta cook in town!* Likewise, you will claim and acquire the glory of being respectful if your coworkers, your friends, your family, and everyone who gets to know you *detects and tells* that you are indeed respectful, every day and over long periods."

"Perfectly understandable! All this information tonight is indeed gold in my mind. Why are you so generous to me?"

"My lord, some teachers mistakenly talk about knowledge they have not really acquired. They rely on their rudimentary understanding, and their teachings only touch the hearts of their students in superficial ways. Some writers make the same mistake and produce books with insubstantial content. They often use content from old books, or even worse, they use incomprehensible language that makes others feel inferior. Some priests also make the mistake of creating fear in the hearts of believers. Teachers, writers, priests, and many others have convinced people that the Great Road is a very difficult road to travel, only feasible for the few. My story, on the other hand, is quite different. The ten choices flowing in my mind want to eventually come out and reconnect with the mountain river. The river will carry the knowledge to all who are brave enough to climb the mountain, find the river, and relish the crystal-clear water. This knowledge has been flowing freely forever; however, we must climb and search for it. All those who have been climbing and searching for years have become experienced enough to have applied some ground rules. If you want to climb to the highest mountain, then you need to have a reliable, strong, well-equipped base camp on the ground for your supplies and your protection. Within your shelter, you will rest, eat, and replenish your powers for tomorrow's adventure. The same goes with our own daily battles. We also need to follow some ground rules and have a solid base camp—our foundations—if we want to reach the top."

"Would it be too much to ask what those rules might be?"

"Not at all! My father called them the Gardener's Five Rules. He didn't have my gift; in fact, every time he tried to cook, we were all left with empty stomachs. He did, however, have his own blessed talent. He was a man who could 'speak' to the earth and conjure the tastiest vegetables and fruits from the stony ground of the mountain foothills. He could plant, grow, and crop wondrous harvests in the hostile, arid fields that other men would pass by. His produce was to be found in all the markets and bazaars in Florence."

"Will you be kind enough to give me these rules?"

"I have done so already, my lord, while explaining to you how to walk your Great Road! It's just that the information is too much for you at the moment. I will make sure to explain very carefully in the manuscript. But briefly, let me remind you that *beginning, planning, cooperating, desiring,* and *respecting* are, indeed, what my father called the Gardener's Five Rules. Therefore, let me set your mind at ease by telling you that you will find the Ten Choices, La Grande Strada, and the Gardener's Five Rules, along with other secret family recipes, in tomorrow's manuscript."

"Thank you, my master!"

"Just never give up your efforts. I can promise you that your life will be transformed. Can you promise me that you'll try your best?"

"I promise on my royal crown to try with all my heart and never give up! Your Ten Choices will become my Ten Lanterns, your La Grande Strada will become my Great Road, and finally, the Gardener's Five Rules will become the King's Five Rules."

The cook then bursts out laughing, as he had not yet realized that he was conversing that night with a real king; an exhausted king, who then drags himself away to rest in the room of the absent elder daughter—a luminous king, who, as soon as he lays his head on the pillow, feels it relieved of pain and filled with more understanding than ever before. The cook stays up as late as he needs to, in order to fulfill the king's final request. Upon opening his eyes the next morning and bringing to mind the events of the previous night, the cook leaps from his bed, wishing to invite the king for breakfast. But the king is already halfway back to his camp with the cook's manuscript in the leather bag hanging at his chest. That bag, the very night before, had held ten gold lira coins, as much as the king had counted on for the needs of the entire hunting group for the journey that could last for several more months. Feeling extremely thoughtful and fulfilled that morning, he had decided that the hunt was over; he now had the greatest prize of all. He had left the ten gold coins on the table and picked up the ten gold choices. He had also left a note, along with his royal ring, outside the bedroom door of the cook's young daughter. On the ring were the four golden lions, each with a diamond eye, which was the symbol of his monarchy and kingdom. On the note, the king had written,

To honor your kindness, generosity, and hospitality, I offer this, my royal golden ring, to you, my dear cook and master, with a profound wish. May my new choices benefit my people and my kingdom in the years to come. May my choiceful journey lead to a successful life—a full life for all. This letter certifies that the royal artifacts belong to your family by king's order.

With royal honor, King Christian

One year later, another wonderful surprise awaits the cook. The caravan of his elder daughter and the merchant arrives in the tavern courtyard. The cook tries to identify the two travelers with the baby in their arms in the darkness of the night. He cannot contain his joy when he realizes who they are, and he bursts into tears when he meets his grandchild for the first time. The trip to the Persian Gulf had been so successful that it had lasted longer than expected. This gives the cook cause for complaint for a while, but once he holds his first grandchild in his arms, he forgets all about it.

Two important events follow that night. First, fascinated by the story of the king's visit, as recounted by the cook, they decide to name their baby boy Chris, in honor of King Christian. Then later, because the caravan had returned home that night with the ten candles from the sanctuaries showing the way, his elder daughter urges the cook to name his lodge the Ten Candles.

And they all lived happily ever after, with the light of the ten candles. We also have lived happily for more than half a century!"

Grandpa takes a sip of his brandy. He sighs as he lets go of a burden he has carried for so long.

Replenishment:
Disclosure and Confession

Disclosure

We are all here for some special reason.
Stop being a prisoner of the past and
become the architect of your future.
—Robin Sharma

"And they lived happily ever after, with the light of the ten candles. We also have lived happily for more than half a century" are Grandpa's concluding words.

The coincidences and information are beyond intoxicating, and I have yet to put a drop of wine in my mouth. The only thing I really need at this point is to clear up all my concerns. Despite the fact that Grandpa has been thorough, and his eloquent storytelling calmed my mind, my heart is beating like crazy. For the first time in my life, it is my heart that is looking for answers, not my mind.

"Grandpa, I have many questions so please be honest with me!"

"I am still here."

"First of all, the way you related the story tonight seemed different. Is it the same story that you used to tell me when I was a little child? I remember it being much shorter and falling asleep right afterward. Tonight, it felt like an eternity, and I'm not going to sleep because I am so tense."

"It's exactly the same story, my boy. Back then, you heard it with your ears; tonight, you've heard it with your heart."

"Very well. Then, can I buy this fairy tale from any bookstore?"

"No, you won't find it in any bookstore in any country in the world."

"So it's a story you made up just for me. Because if my memory serves me correctly, you always told me that this tale is our secret and never to reveal it to anyone."

"I didn't make it up, and there is one more person who is aware."

"The custodian?"

"You see! You are not a fool after all!"

"Grandpa, this is no time for jokes and evasions. I want to understand what the story has to do with me and what part Mom has to play in it. I beg you to explain why it has all these similarities to the life we have now."

"I will never forget that Wednesday evening in 1977 when the phone rang at seven o'clock. For the first time, I ran faster than your grandmother to answer it. On the other line, a thin, trembling voice announced to me that my first grandchild had just been born in perfect health. He weighed 3,500 grams and had a little mark on his ear. 'This mark will set him apart from all the other newborns, Daddy,' said your mom, whose main worry in the previous few days had been that the nurses could get the babies mixed up, and she would end up at home with another couple's baby. I don't remember how I got to the clinic that night, but I'll never forget the wild beating of my heart while driving like crazy. This was mainly for two reasons. First, I wanted to see my grandchild as soon as possible, and second, I wanted to 'tell the rest' to my daughter. For your information, your mom and aunt also grew up eating, reading, and playing only. But the time had come for your mother to take on her new responsibilities and her new assignment. You, my first grandson, had come into my life, and my hands were finally free to take on the role and purpose of the custodian. That night, once everyone had left and I was finally alone with her in the clinic room, your mom heard the story of "The

King and the Cook" for the first time, and I told her all that needed
to be done. She had the same questions and concerns as you do right
now. Therefore, I am prepared for everything. What else do you want
to ask me?"

"OK. Let me try to summarize. There's a fairy tale—a story,
anyway—that has to do with your family?"

"Correct."

"This means that the story was passed down from generation to
generation and has managed to survive from 1500 to the present day.
Is that correct too?"

"Yes! That's right."

"If I relate the ten candles of the cook with the Ten Lanterns of Chef
Takis, I assume that we are descended from the cook, and I have no blood
relationship with the royal family. Is that correct too, Your Majesty?"

"That seems right, my chosen boy."

"Oh my God! I am Italian! That explains everything. My passion
for pasta and Italian sports cars. *Sono un Italiano!*"

"And what else are you?"

"Your chosen boy, but I still have a hundred questions to ask. But
before we get to that, only tell me that the custodian currently has the
king's ring and the note among our family possessions, and you will
completely blow me away!"

"In the fifteenth century, Italy was experiencing its Renaissance.
It was a particular period in history when the world was enjoying—
perhaps for the first time—total freedom. Inspired by it, a wave
of changes came about that later spread throughout Europe. This
wave washed away misery and oppression and brought about the
flourishing of literature, science, art, religion, and political science.
People finally had a thirst for studying and reading. The revival of
the study of classical authors, the creation of new classical works, the
passion for painting, and the widespread reform of education changed
the world forever."

"Grandpa, are you saying that King Christian is behind the
Renaissance with his new choices?"

"Unfortunately, I cannot confirm this. From what I know, those were very rough times. Evil and good were in constant struggle, and good didn't always win. That's why the king left the necessary documentation to certify the cook's royal possessions. In those days, if you were found with gold coins and royal artifacts among your belongings, you would be tried for theft and have your right hand cut off without even being allowed to speak for yourself."

"Please tell me that you have at least one piece of evidence that attests to this story; otherwise, you've got me fantasizing wildly!"

"Just be patient, my boy, and we'll get to that. I've told you about the Renaissance that began in Italy and eventually spread around the world. I've also informed you that battles between good and evil were on the daily agenda. On February 7, 1497, thousands of protesters, dressed in white and under the direction of the Dominican friar Girolamo Savonarola, gathered in Florence's main square after looting entire districts and properties and burning all works of art, books, musical instruments, mirrors, and generally everything they thought served human vanity. Paintings, sculptures, ancient books, and great manuscripts—all deemed unsuitable, according to their own conception, which was apparently influenced by the fanatical teachings of Savonarola—were destroyed in what is today called the Bonfire of the Vanities."

"Oh my God. Seriously?"

"It was indeed a cruel setback and a mighty blow to the flourishing Renaissance. Many were those who eventually left Italy, as they could no longer endure the ascetic life imposed by Friar Savonarola during the period of his leadership, from 1494 to 1498. Finally, on the instructions of Pope Alexander VI, the crazy monk was arrested in May 1498 and put to death. Unfortunately, irreparable damage had been done because objects and works of immeasurable spiritual value were lost. Along with them were lost many families who chose to immigrate to other European countries for a better way of life. Among these was the cook's family."

"Shocking! So our family left Italy, and nothing was saved?"

"You say the words *our family*, and I am deeply touched."

Grandfather's eyes fill with tears, and he cannot utter another word. It's the first time I have ever seen him so moved, and I spontaneously jump from the couch and find myself in his arms. After this emotional episode, I finally take a brave swig of the red wine that has been warming by the fire.

Visibly moved, Grandpa gathers his thoughts to continue. "Everything has been saved, my child! Some of the knowledge is in our minds, many feelings are in our hearts, and a few artifacts are in a safe deposit box. Together, they are as the seed that was planted in the fertile ground, after which came the magical effects of the water and fertilizer until the first delicate shoot emerged from the ground. The gardener then worked hard to support the tree, to prune it, and to protect it from winds, fires, and disasters. The tree grew to nourish souls with its spiritual fruits for half a century. They may have destroyed our house and our belongings, but they failed to destroy our history and heritage. Hence, this is not a fairy tale! It is the spiritual map and compass of your great-great-grandfather Amadeo Conali!"

"Amadeo Conali! My God, what a story!"

"A story, a history, your heritage and your roots, my chosen boy. The name Amadeo has Latin roots and means "the one who has the God within"; thus, the one who truly loves and embodies God. Grandpa Amadeo honored his name and honored his grace until his final breath. He was never afraid to carry the word of his Lord to all people."

"What took you so long to tell me all this, Grandpa? This is not the first time we have discussed serious and complicated matters. You always told me that you trusted me completely."

"All these years, you've been prepared in small doses until I was sure that you were ready to carry this spiritual load. Today, what matters is that you're ready to understand it and submit your will to carrying it forward. It is all yours. From the moment you used the words *our family* and *our history*, I have felt completely at peace."

"Exactly what is all mine, Grandpa? Be more specific, please. And finally, explain to me what part Mom and I play in this story."

"Oh, yes, forgive me! I am a bit old, and I am losing my reasoning. I've told you about the first time I recounted the story to your mom. After I had answered her hundred or so questions, she was finally ready to grasp all the facts. I also handed her a leather pouch with a key in it."

"The safe deposit box key, I assume."

"Nothing escapes your attention! Yes, the key opens a safe deposit box located at the headquarters of the bank where your godfather manages our accounts."

"Grandpa, before you go any further, I want to make sure of something. For everything we've discussed so far, nobody knows but you, Mom, and me, right? Neither my godfather, nor Dad, nor Grandma has any idea?"

"Yes."

"How is it ever possible? And above all, why all the secrecy?"

"This is the legacy that has been passed down from grandfather to first grandchild for half a century. And you are the tenth receiver—the last recipient! From now on, everything will be in your hands. You will choose how the tale is to end, or rather, how it will continue."

"But do you realize how many risks were involved in this mysterious family process? I wonder how it was kept alive for half a century. What if someone died prematurely? What if something had happened to you, Grandpa, and you took your secret to heaven? What would have happened then?"

"I lose my reasoning by getting old, and you lose your faith by being impatient. I will answer the previous questions, and everything will become clearer."

"Sorry!"

"First of all, don't worry about my health. I am strong like our oak! As far as the key to the safe box is concerned, your mother has never visited the bank, as the content is the property of only the sender and the recipient. This is ensured by registering the safe box to our joint account. If something were to happen to the sender, as you mentioned, then the custodian—the key holder—accompanied by the adult recipient, would have access to the safe deposit box. As you can see, in this story that is passed on from generation to generation, the protagonists are not only the respective grandfather and grandson but also our precious mothers. Obviously, you will find everything you seek in the box."

"I do feel more comfortable now. But some troubling doubts remain in my mind."

"Why have we kept it as a secret? Even from family members?"

"Exactly! If I recall correctly, the cook gained the honorary title of the master because he so generously shared all the secrets with the king and his company, except the recipe for Pasta a la Crème. If I also remember correctly, Grandpa Amadeo did not refuse to hand over a written manuscript with the secrets to success. So why all the secrecy from there on—for half a century already?"

"First of all, the cook did not deliver the secrets to success but only a simple and clear list of ten choices and various spiritual aids. He who will eventually succeed in crossing the four stations of the Great Road—*I choose, I dare, I become, I am*—will have a successful life. By using the word *success*, we do not refer to professional achievements that result in prosperity only. This could be one of the many carriages you have to manage in your life, if, of course, you choose it. The Ten Lanterns do not have riches and fame as an end result, but I assure you that their dedicated usage will lead you where your soul desires. Some of our family members have chosen spiritual realization as a final destination, some have chosen professional success, and some even decided to take up monasticism. You have a list with limitless options. You can have one or as many wagons as your soul desires, so choose wisely, my young captain."

"What did you choose, Grandfather?"

"I became a mountaineer. Look at our mountain mansion and count our blessings. One thing is for sure. This spiritual map and compass can turn a mountaineer into a teacher, a cook into a master, a king into a student, and a priest into a vessel of God! Apparently, they also will help any adventurer to find his treasure. Anything is possible with the Ten Lanterns in your possession. Now that we've got that out of the way, let me remind you that our family left Italy in a hurry, as Chef Amadeo's teachings contradicted the tyrant monk's wishes. This fear of persecution and the differences they encountered in the cultures of the other countries to which they traveled made our family take the decision to temporarily keep the beliefs secret and stop broadcasting them."

"Understandable! Therefore, in the safe deposit box I will find the manuscript that Cook Amadeo bequeathed to his grandson Chris Conali when he came of age. Then Grandfather Chris passed it to his own grandson. And then the same process over and again up to now?"

"This is the Conali family process, and all your ancestors had the same mission. You are the tenth recipient, and you are the most important of all! You are the only recipient with a different mission from the previous nine."

"What do you mean?"

"In one of the banker's many frivolous questions, the cook had commented, 'I am afraid that by the year 2000, we will encounter the same problems!' Do you remember that?"

"How could I not remember, Grandpa! I was extremely impressed that the cook referred to the year 2000, coming in seven years from now."

"Good. At some point, a very important decision was made. In the year 2000, according to the calculations, the tenth recipient will have received the family secrets. Provided that the world is still doomed to arrogance, jealousy, anger, laziness, greed, and envy—in short, a world that is still hurting and suffering from pain—then the process changes. The tenth recipient acquires the absolute right—not to use the word *obligation*—to bypass the secrecy process and reveal the ten choices with the hope that the new century will be better."

"Oh my God! Grandpa, what are you telling me? Will I need to do all that, seven years from now?"

"Take another deep breath, and don't panic. We have all the time in the world to organize our next moves. You, my chosen boy, have other more important choices to make first! What is really urgent is to choose the course of studies that will help you in your future endeavors. Your studies are of great importance, as they will help and support you in the future, not only professionally but also in terms of your mission. Next, you need to deeply study and learn the Ten Lanterns. This is not a difficult or complicated task; on the contrary, you will find all choices extremely familiar, as they are already in your mind, in your heart, and in your DNA. You will not find a single lantern that will cause you surprise or wonder; they are all familiar to you from the most important chapters of your life. Then you must complete the three stages of the *application* before you can pursue your *recognition* stage. Only when other people *detect and tell*—that is, to recognize, identify, and associate you with the Ten Lanterns—will you be able to represent them as a master."

"I see a marathon ahead, and I'm still at the starting line."

"I'm glad you can see ahead! My chosen boy, you have already come a long way without knowing it. Obviously, you will need a lot of deep breaths and strong lungs to finish, but the ultimate goal is not the finish line but the journey itself. Having a victorious finish means that people are waiting for you at the station to applaud and congratulate you on your achievement and hard efforts. You must strive to achieve your fourth stage of recognition, and that depends entirely on your outcome. Only when other people honor you with the title of master will you have reached the end of your mission."

"Like I said—an endless marathon!"

"You're closer than you think. Do you want me to remind you of all the kind words we hear every year from your teachers at school? Sociable, kind, courteous, gentle, enthusiastic, supportive—and the list goes on and on."

"It's not enough! How am I going to accomplish such a mission on my own?"

"The only sure thing is that in a few years, I will go to find the rest of the Conalis in heaven. What a feast we'll have up there! We'll keep a watchful eye on you, and we will be constantly clinking our glasses so that pain will never find you. You'll never be alone, my chosen boy!"

"I can't believe my ears. Let me at least enjoy the story, and then we can decide on the family legacy. Grandpa, I tell you again, I am not ready to take on such a serious task."

"The final decision will be made by you alone. It will not be made today or tomorrow. You will study, you will work, you will struggle, and once you are recognized by everyone, only then will you be able to make the big decision. All I ask of you, for now, is to love the story like a fairy tale and respect it like a legacy. Other than that, the only answer I seek from you tonight is just this one: to what extent are you willing to devote yourself and your life to properly infuse the Conali spiritual legacy in your heart and mind, and thereafter transmit it to the rest of the world? I promise you that your life will be transformed. Can you promise me that you will try with all you've got?"

"My legs are shaking, but I promise I'll never give up!"

"Is your fear greater than your desire?"

"Absolutely not! My desire to succeed is much stronger!"

"Then I urge you to walk the Great Road with the Ten Lanterns lighting your path. Use all your persistence, my child, and never give up for as long as it takes. The cinema of life offers soft drinks and popcorn to its entire audience, but those who ardently want to take control of the big picture and become protagonists in it must have, first and foremost, a *declaration* and the necessary *persistence* because a drink and a snack will not be enough. Apply the Ten Lanterns until they become embedded in your soul."

"Why do you make specific reference to persistence, and why do you say it will take me a long time?"

"Persistent people do not fail. They simply become the winners of the obstacle-course race until they honor their declaration. You, my chosen boy, will be the judge and henceforth either condemn the Ten Lanterns to prison or release them to the world. If your decision is the latter, which I wholeheartedly hope it is, you will have the choice of presenting them as a master, writing them as a tale for your younger students, or offering them in a book for your older ones. Why not all the options? The choice will still be yours."

"Got it! And why is the La Grande Strada a long, long road?"

"For all of this to happen and for you to make the right decisions, it will be years before you become the Ten Lanterns yourself—not to live by them but to be them. Not to present them but to represent them with your passionate experiences. Not to train them but to educate them properly. You should be able to honor them like a master and be able to write them in simple, humble, and understandable language. Be completely honest and humble like the chefs in your life, Grandpa Amadeo and Grandpa Takis."

"I promise on my royal honor, Grandpa."

"Well done, my chosen boy! And you are absolutely right on one thing. The Ten Lanterns are not sacred secrets that have mystically survived through the ages to benefit only the privileged few. You don't need to use the word *secrets* for promotional and advertising purposes. We have no such need, and we do not expect it. Just as we don't seek to be given a Michelin star for our food, we don't expect validation of our story from anyone. We respectfully expect the recognition to come from those recipients who will detect and tell the value of what we provide. Our only concern is to help as many people as we can with a simple family recipe. We are simple cooks with a complex mission!"

"Well noted! Any last advice to ease my fears?"

"I know that I have placed an enormous spiritual burden on your shoulders tonight—as heavy as the sign we have in our restaurant: 'Choose to have a good mood, or choose to leave right now!' It is my wish that you carry the burden properly and always in good mood."

"And if I tell you that I'm really afraid? How can I accomplish a mission that no other recipient has dared to undertake for half a century? I haven't even read the manuscript, and I don't even know how easily I will understand all this information. You have just admitted to me that I will need years to understand it."

"There is no shortcut on La Grande Strada. You will need

persistence for the implementation, patience for the recognition, and respect for all fellow travelers. When you finally become the master of the Ten Lanterns, you will also be able to handle all the Doubting Thomases you'll find in your path. Using the same courtesy that Grandpa Conali used with the banker, you must communicate a story so that they love it as they would a fairy tale. To do so, you must be the protagonist, not just another storyteller. You have to be the hero of the fairy tale in their eyes. How else will they accept you as their master? Are you still wondering why I say that you will need years to accomplish all these things?"

"All right, Grandpa. Maybe my fear has to do with the fact that it's all new to me. That's exactly how the king felt when he heard the story for the first time."

"Then let me remind you of two major factors. First, our dear master Napoleon Hill has taught us, 'Our only limitations are those we set up in our own minds.' Second, I remind you that it's all already programmed into your mind and soul, my chosen boy. You have grown up with the Ten Lanterns, metaphorically and literally. Let me explain why. Could you please remind me what our family does every Sunday?"

"We all gather around the table."

"What's the first thing your dad says every time, and we all burst out laughing?"

"That we're a crazy bunch!"

"Express it more elegantly, please."

"We are a good company!"

"Excellent! *We choose to have good company.* Let's move on. What's the first thing I say before we start eating?"

"Choose to have a good mood, or choose to leave my table right now!"

"Brilliant, my boy. *We choose to have good mood.* Remind me of the comment Grandma Vasia makes as your dad and your godfather disappear from the table to catch the football match on the TV?"

"She asks if they went looking for their good manners!"

"Extraordinary! You're my chosen boy after all! Look how effortlessly you found the third choice: *we choose to have good manners.* Being respectful is not a value necessary only when eating but for every event in our lives. Even while watching a football match, right?"

"Exactly! We should tell that to my father and godfather when they shout during the match!"

"That's right! Last question—because it's getting late, and Alanis will forget his good manners at five o'clock in the morning. How do we finish our meeting every Sunday?"

"You shout loudly, 'Where are you all going? Who's going to pay the chef's bill?'"

"What do my beloved grandchildren answer loudly?"

"We tell you with one voice, 'Grandpa Takis will! It was his good intention to invite us over!'"

"Exactly! *We choose to have good intentions.* Then what happens?"

"You say, 'Will someone please bring me the bill?'"

"And how much is the bill, usually, my chosen boy?"

"The greatest amount in the world, my dear grandpa. The bill is always for ten plates of love, nine plates of happiness, eight plates of kindness, seven plates of confidence, six plates of gratefulness, five plates of purposefulness, four plates of comfort, three plates of joy, two plates of anticipation for the next Sunday, and one plate for the coming day!"

"Excellent. *We choose to have good memories,* right?"

"Absolutely!"

"Tell me about the next day's dish."

"We begin our Monday in full—a full belly, a full spirit, and a heart full of goodness for the rest of the world. If we help others, they will advance, and we will be promoted, just as Grandpa Amadeo said."

"Are you sure you haven't read the manuscript? That's why I'm telling you that you've grown up with the Ten Lanterns within you. Take strength from our legacy, and do not be afraid. You now have a *good purpose* and the choice for a *good life.*"

"When are you going to tell me the rest?"

"For now, eat, read, and play, my young master, and soon you will finally discover the rest. I have nothing more to tell. Tonight, God blessed me by allowing me to tell you almost everything."

The fire is almost out, and we don't have another log at our disposal. Grandfather, exhausted from the whole process of the delivery, has dropped his brown bone spectacles onto the table, clearly indicating, *I neither want to hear nor see anything more now.* After all, everything has been said.

After a few moments of silence and contemplation, he rises from his throne, stretches his long arms upward and then backward, and takes a few steps in my direction. His face is suffused with light, even though the flames have died. I jump from the couch and enfold him in my arms.

"Good night, my chosen boy. Never forget this—you will be the judge. Henceforth, you will either condemn the Ten Lanterns to prison or release them to the world."

"Good night, Chef Christakis."

I blow out all the candles and go to my room. Finding Mom's letter on my pillow, a smile forms effortlessly on my face. Under normal circumstances, I would read it over and over again, but the information in my head is already too much for one night. I rest my head on the pillow, and it's the first time it's ever felt so full. It's as if all the information and emotions are trying to escape the prison of secrecy. I think to myself that I won't be able to endure so many years, carrying this heavy legacy, until I finally pass it on to my own grandson. What happens if I don't have a family or don't have any children or a grandchild? The question passes through my head like a flash of lightning, and I hide under my sheet. I'm ready to make the decision to spread the word before I've thoroughly read, studied, and applied it myself. I silently acknowledge the fear in the depths of my heart and finally close my eyes.

Grandfather has forgotten to close the shutters on the kitchen window, and the wind forces them back into place with a loud bang that takes my breath away.

A sharp pain, low in my operated lung, literally takes my breath away, and before I even realize where I am, I instinctively struggle to find the red panic button to call for help, desperately pressing it as my breathing becomes heavier and heavier. Two nurses come into the room. Using frantic gesticulations, I try to show them that I can't breathe. Fortunately, they quickly understand the problem, once they inspect the twenty-centimeter rubber tube that goes through my chest and into my right lung. The other end is connected to a ventilating machine that helps the lung to fully expand. The tube has crimped during my sleep and filled with blood and fluid, preventing the lung from functioning normally. Once the tube is released and cleared, the lung works again, and with the first relieving breath, I begin crying and moaning. The nurses think I'm crying from the pain, but this isn't the case.

My return from the mountain mansion to the hospital room was so violent and abrupt that I lost the battle with pain. After a few minutes, one of the nurses returns to the room, holding a large syringe. This is inserted into the IV at my wrist and not my shoulder. The relief is delayed much longer than I expect, and I am left staring hard at the ceiling, trying to ignore the pain.

One thing is for sure. My flight to Patience Island was probably the best journey of my life. I found what I was looking for, talked to those I needed the most, and took another breath as strong as my very first one back in 1977. For a second time, I take the first breath of the rest of my life. A different life!

I replay my grandfather's ending words over and over again in my mind: *You will be the judge. Henceforth, you will either condemn the Ten Lanterns to prison or release them to the world!*

These words spin in my head like a whirlwind.

"Thou shalt judge and thenceforth condemn the Ten Lanterns ..."

Just before the painkiller kicks in and my eyes close, I put on my black judge's robes to deliver my final verdict—a life-or-death decision!

Confession

Everything can be taken from a man but one thing: the last of the human freedoms. To choose one's attitude in any given set of circumstances, to choose one's own way.
—Viktor Frankl

November. What a blessing!

"Good morning, Judge! Your coffee is on your desk."

Every morning, I hear this greeting from Aria's lips, together with the presentation of my cup of fresh, aromatic coffee. And that's not all—next to the coffee I find my daily newspapers, my window is opened for ventilation, my legal briefs are on my desk in priority order, and there's a pile of little notes with my missed calls on my keyboard. Missed calls from my family are noted on a yellow Post-it on my screen, with a smiley face next to the phone number just in case I've forgotten it, which is likely to happen, considering the pace I work at and the long hours I put in at the office.

Aria is a charismatic woman. When she first started as a trainee lawyer at the Attorney General's Office, everyone declared that a star had been born. A brilliant, hardworking, diligent, tireless, and unstoppable young lady who was a pleasure to work with. It wasn't long before we nicknamed her the Whirlwind, despite the fact that she was the last to learn about it. At a Christmas party when we were exchanging gifts, she was left staring at us in wonderment and persistently asking us what she had to do with the spinning top she held in her hands, a present from her Secret Santa. When the joke was explained, she was so fond of her nickname that in some internal emails she signed, "With honor, Miss Swirl."

Aria and I parted ways when I became a judge and moved to the district courts next to the Municipal Garden. The last time we saw each other was at her wedding celebration, held at her new two-story home on a wooded hill just outside of town. She married a stockbroker, Leo, and they were very happy that night. It was, admittedly, a glamorous wedding with all the extravagance she deserved. The most glamorous of the evening, by far, was Aria, especially the moment when she stood under the fireworks that turned the night into day for ten nonstop minutes. Their crackle and sparkle were the starting point for the frantic dancing that lasted until the early hours.

As I said goodbye to her just before sunrise, she was so happy that the first thing that came to my mind to say to her was, "My dear Aria, please stay away from judges if you want to stay happy forever! Don't call me for work, only for fun!"

She shook her head awkwardly and threw herself into my arms. That was the last time I saw her.

However, news of Aria and Leo keep coming to my attention, one way or another. Various mutual friends, knowing of my close relationship with her, keep me up-to-date with everything. Sadly, they neglected or avoided telling me the most tragic news of all.

She had to ignore the advice I gave her five years ago, and a call is her only choice. "Your Honor, do you have time for an old friend?"

Time for a little prank. "Who's there? You're speaking to the top judge in the district, and I am quite busy. Please do not waste my time!"

"Oh, how much I have missed you! I can definitely testify that you are the top drinker! But I am not confident about the top-judge hypothesis."

"My dear Aria, I am so happy to hear from you. If my memory

serves me right, the day we succeeded in passing the bar examination, I did indeed win the tequila-shot contest at the party!"

"The good old days, my dear friend! There are rumors of your return to the Attorney General's Office. I am proud of you doing so well."

"As you say, rumors! I'm not moving. The view from my current window will take your breath away, so I'm not coming back to the dungeons. How are you doing? How old is your little boy?"

And as I expected the small talk to continue, Aria burst into tears.

"What's wrong, dear? Did I say something to upset you? Is your little boy all right?"

"My Leo ..."

"What's happened to Leo? Please try to calm yourself because I can't understand what you're saying when you're in tears."

"Haven't you heard?"

"God is my witness! If I knew something bad had happened to you, we wouldn't be on the phone right now. I would have you in my arms."

"Oh! You are so sweet! Did I tell you how much I miss you!"

"Yes, but you did not tell me what's wrong?"

"We lost Leo."

"Where are you now?"

"At my house, talking over the phone to my best friend."

"Tell him he's a villain, and then hang up the phone! If he was your best friend, he would be there for you. I'll be at your house in thirty minutes!"

"But it's very late! Aren't you tired? Don't you want to go home?"

"I'll get a coffee from the coffee shop downstairs and be on my way. Black with brown sugar for you, right?"

"Yes, but it will be cold by the time you get here. Just get yourself a cup, and I'll have some fresh when you get here—or shall I have your favorite Valpolicella Blend chilled and ready?"

"I really admire your good mood right now!"

"Did I tell you how much I miss you?"

"Hang up the phone, please. I'm in a hurry to go visit my best friend!"

It is particularly hard to grasp the tragedy that had befallen my friend's family. I am overwhelmed with everything she told me. As I left her house at midnight, she made me swear to respect her decision and to consider her proposal seriously.

Driving back home, I am compelled to call her once more.

"Hello?"

"Sleeping already? I still have fifteen miles to go!"

"That's what comes from spending time with you."

"Boredom and sleepiness?"

"No, are you crazy? Total serenity and security. What have you forgotten this time? Did you leave your glasses on the table?"

"I didn't forget anything. I just wanted to make sure that you haven't forgotten what a talented lawyer you are. It's inconceivable that you want to give it all up and work as paralegal!"

"So, you are rejecting my proposal already?"

"The only thing I reject is your decision to quit practicing law. I beg you to reconsider."

"Then, I'm really sorry. It looks like you haven't heard a word I've said to you tonight."

"I did not miss a word, my dear!"

"Then let me ask you one question, Mr. Judge!"

"Please proceed, ex-Counsel."

"How did my Leo lose his life?"

"He missed a red light and crashed his car violently."

"My Leo, Your Honor, lost his life because he didn't manage his time correctly. I'm not going to make the same mistake. I have a responsibility to my son to find the time to raise him right. And to provide him with the time he deserves, I have to change my habits. Do you understand that, or should I send my résumé somewhere else?"

"Aria, take as much time as you need. Spend as much time as you want with your son, and I will expect you in my office whenever you are ready."

"Thank you very much. Good night."

"Aria? I've missed you too. Good night."

● ● ●

Less than a month later, Aria is responsible for all the administration and paralegal work. Not a day goes by that she does not perform her tasks with professionalism and efficiency. What she has forgotten—or rather buried, along with her husband—is her motivation for a better way of life. She is like a seven-hundred-horsepower Ferrari that produces half the power on route. Who would say no to such power and luxury? Nevertheless, what a waste, taking into consideration her full potential.

Before I take a sip of coffee, Aria opens the door hurriedly.

"The attorney general is asking for you!"

"Then why are you staring at me from the door? Put him through on line three, and close the door behind you, my dear."

Line three is a secure line that I rarely use. It's the only nonrecorded line for use when there is a need for absolute confidentiality.

"If he was asking for you over the phone, I wouldn't be here. He is waiting outside. He is talking with Judge Edward, but he told me that he is in a hurry."

"Don't tell me we have a scheduled meeting, and I forgot it?"

"No, this is an unexpected visit."

"How come? Ask him if he wants a coffee, and tell him to come in!"

I pace nervously until the door opens abruptly, and he walks in.

"Your Honor. Do you welcome all your guests at the door, or am I a special case?"

"Mr. Attorney General, welcome to my office. Obviously, you are a special case. This is your first visit to our district. To what do we owe the honor of your presence?"

I extend my hand for the customary handshake, and he grabs it like a clamp, pulling me closer to him and fixing me with an intense glare.

"I hear that you are trying to take my place, and I came to have a word with you," he says sweetly, winking his left eye.

"Even if this is the case, sir, your reputation precedes you. There is no chance that the president will ever choose a four-door sedan like me over a Ferrari."

"I am flattered. Thank you for your kind words and for likening me to a Ferrari. Your craziness for Italian cars is well known."

"Some habits never change."

"Are we to remain standing?"

"Please, do have a seat. Would you like a coffee?"

"No, thank you. Your secretary has already asked. I am in a bit of a hurry, so allow me to get to the point without delay. Mr. Pain had requested a personal hearing and came to inform me of his serious objections to your final decision on his case. He is considering an appeal to the Supreme Court, and he wanted to get my advice first. To his credit, he acknowledges that the young man is exhausted from his health issue and does not want to prolong any suffering unnecessarily. Well, I need to understand your decision. You have condemned his choice to remain depressed, scared, and angry, ignoring testimonials that prove beyond any doubt that this choice could be justified!"

"First of all, I would like to thank you for giving me the opportunity to explain the reason for my decision. I will agree that this is a young man who has suffered a great deal over these past years. To give you an idea, after the fourth operation, while the normal postoperative period in hospital should not have exceeded one week, the young man was finally discharged twenty-seven days later, due to serious complications and other postoperative difficulties that arose."

"Your Honor, I am well aware of all this. I made sure to get an update by reading the trial notes. Since I am in a hurry, I would appreciate a more explanatory reply."

"Understood. So you also know that the young man willingly confessed his actions while taking the stand."

"Yes, I am aware."

"Does it come as a surprise that Mr. Pain didn't address any questions to him after this confession? Has Mr. Pain explained to you why? He had the chance to cross-examine and did absolutely nothing!"

"No, he didn't explain himself to me, and he doesn't have to apologize for his actions."

"I think it's a good idea for us to read the confession together. It was short, concise, and effective, as drastic as a shot, if I may say so. It will be archived as soon as its conversion from shorthand is completed."

"Fine. Let's do as you suggest."

"Mr. Attorney General, may I call Aria in to do the reading?"

"What for, Your Honor? Are you not good at reading?"

"For goodness sake! That's not the reason! The young man's confession was redemptive for him, wasn't it?"

"Obviously. According to your wisdom."

"If I told you that this confession could be liberating for Aria as well, would you accept my suggestion? By the way, I can't read stenography."

"Are you talking about your secretary's liberation? I have told you already that I am in a great hurry! What is this nonsense?"

"I apologize. My intentions are good. Aria is not my secretary; she is the most brilliant lawyer I have ever met in my life."

"Then what's she doing outside your office? Don't you have a private office to give her, as the regulations stipulate for all lawyers?"

"She has chosen a more spiritual path, Mr. Attorney General."

"Look, I'm losing patience with you. I don't care about her role or path. Just call her and get it over with!"

I walk briskly to my desk, call Aria on the phone, and take the case file from the third drawer. Aria knocks discreetly and then enters, standing there awkwardly, waiting for us to explain what we want from her.

"Aria, come and sit with us. Please open this file and find the final confession."

"Here it is, Your Honor."

"Good. Could you please read it out loud?"

"I'd be happy to. Are we ready, Mr. Attorney General?"

"Let's go."

Final Confession

Your Honor. First of all, thank you for your patience. When my health adventure began, I found myself in uncharted territory. I looked anxiously out of my window, yet nothing within sight reminded me of my own life. It was all unknown. I was scared and in terrible pain. My mental state was shattered!

Most of the time, I choose to look up at the stars, but sometimes I catch myself looking down at the mud. I look up when my thoughts are bright and clear, and I look down when I am defeated by the pain. At the same time, the train never stops. It continues until it reaches the next station.

We all wish to find happiness in the next station or get to it as soon as possible. Some head in that direction on foot, some ride their bicycles, and some fly like the wind. Of course, there are also those who go in the opposite direction and seem to be completely lost. I choose the train because it travels at the ideal speed for gazing out of the window at the green landscape and having time to evaluate my options and make my choices.

Being young and impatient and with the further excuse of being bedridden, I sometimes try to take a shortcut and find an instant dose of happiness in the books I study. I am in good company with Stephen Covey, Dale Carnegie, Scott Peck, Napoleon Hill, Viktor Frankl, Robin Sharma, Wayne Dyer, Og Mandino, Leo Buscaglia, and Louise Hay. Don't be surprised when I mention my conversations with these great masters. I must admit that they have all been extremely supportive and helpful to me; perhaps they are influenced by my horrible image!

To see a young athlete end up in bed, skin and bones, cannot be a pretty sight. The tubes coming out of my chest were not the most pleasant sight either. All this has played its part, and they have all given generously to me, leaving no secret, choice, rule, practice, habit, concept, or principle undiscussed and always in good mood.

To be able to see the stars and ignore the mud you need to have good company and good mood. Despite the fact that I was in severe pain, my good company and good mood acted as an analgesic against the pain. One could argue that I had found a simple way to lighten my pain. At least for a while.

In one of the many conversations, I came to see that there is no such thing as bad luck! What really exists is our bad judgment and bad handling. And for as long as I blamed bad luck, other people, or—even worse—God Himself for my problems, I thereafter expected some good luck to arrive, and I demanded an apology from those responsible or pleaded for God's mercy. When none of this happened, I decided to punish everyone with my bad behavior. My misbehavior continued until I finally discovered that no one owed me anything whatsoever, and no one was to blame for my life. If I wanted to achieve anything good in my life, then I had to ask for it and work for it, using my good manners. Only by doing this will the support I need magically appear. With this new understanding of things, I was able to change course. I now understand that happiness has its own place and time. Happiness is located within me, and the time is now.

I have found happiness within! I have stopped blaming other people for my life's problems, and

I have stopped waiting for it to come from other people. I choose to create my happiness!

I have found happiness today! I have stopped expecting it to come in the future and have stopped looking for it in the past. I choose to live in the present!

Happiness is not the final destination but the journey itself. Happiness does not have a starting point and an end point to measure how fast or how slow we have traveled the necessary distance. Happiness is not near or far to quantify the distance left. We don't lose or find happiness. Happiness is within us, and it is happening right now. It is the most precious commodity and, at the same time, the hardest thing in the world to acquire. Why?

Unfortunately, it's not wine to store in a bottle; we cannot fill an entire warehouse and stock up on happiness for every future occasion. If it were that simple, then Grandpa would not have remarked, "The best wine in the world is the one you share with your company!"

Happiness is my own affair—something internal and personal—but in order for it to manifest, to take shape, to be tangible, to have taste and smell, I have to share it with other people and create a good company with good mood and good manners.

After this awareness given by my luminous masters, I have finally taken responsibility for my life and have stopped blaming others or expecting help from others. I have finally stopped my miserable behavior and have started to live again, with good intentions. I have stopped expecting and started giving. One could say that my good company, my good mood, my good manners, and my good intentions are enough to lighten my pain again—for a little while longer.

The issue of my health is one of the many milestones in my long journey through life. After being at a standstill and having plenty of time at my disposal, I want to find out what was behind this unpleasant event. I do not want to remain stagnant; I want to take slow, steady steps and make some good progress on my own, even if everything seems to indicate that I am not making any improvement at all. Once free from the negative thoughts clouding my mind, I have discovered that behind every obstacle, a wonderful opportunity is hiding. You can only find it if you have the desire for good progress and the microscopic view of good intention. One of my wise masters said, "Do not let your emotions control you with a sudden event!"

What was happening to me was indeed a momentary event, and only by taking a positive approach could I overcome it. Otherwise, the daily uneven battles with pain, both physical and mental, would exhaust my body and my mind. As a result, I would lose the war as well. One could say that my good company, my good mood, my good manners, my good intentions, and my good progress have become enough to lighten my pain more frequently. Therefore, today I process my thoughts differently.

I choose not to complain that my life doesn't change.

I choose not to complain that my life has stagnated.

I choose to get on the train and continue my journey.

I choose to get behind the wheel and steer my life again.

Today, I will learn how to lighten my pain indefinitely—again and again! The slightest mistake on my part is capable of leaving me stranded at the same station. A fatal mistake on my part is capable of making me miss the train altogether. I am prepared to pay for the most expensive ticket to avoid being thrown off as a stowaway. I must excel at everything before I can be trusted with the steering wheel again. I'm ready to find the courage and make the right choices—to take effective actions that will take me to the next station; to design my action plan based on carefully chosen steps that will bring value to my life. Today, I process my thoughts differently, and my good timing will not let a single minute go unused, even if I have to toil while everyone else rests. Only in this way will I make up for my lost ground!

When I was preparing my confession, I realized in an instant that I would never have been in this dilemma if my choices had been better from the beginning. Whenever I use the word *choice*, a howling wind pushes my boat down memory lane. And then, sixty horses pull a wagon, taking me to the mountain mansion. My good memories are alive, the fire is warming my heart, and a sweet voice echoes through my soul: 'Good luck on your choiceful journey to a successful life!' A balm for my wounded heart. Goodness is finally back in my life, and, like a strong lantern, it points my way down the Great Road. Half a century may have passed by, but a promise still stands. I found my good purpose in the mansion, and I revisit my vows for a good life. I will not allow myself to lose another minute. The time has come to honor my name and my family. No one can argue that my good company, my good mood, my good manners, my good intentions, my good progress, my good timing, my good memories, my goodness, my good purpose, and my good life are good enough to lighten any pain indefinitely. The Ten Lanterns are enough to win the war over pain!

Your Honor, please look closely into my eyes, and try to discern my achievement—from painful to painless with the right choices! Then, look at my smile to locate all the happiness I have discovered on my journey. This is what happens to people who have managed to completely lighten their pain. It happened to me when I found the blessing hidden in my misfortune. Thank you for your time.

Date: Friday, December 3, 2004

End of the final confession

Aria closes the file, puts it on the coffee table, and takes a tissue to discreetly wipe away her tears.

At seven o'clock the next morning, along with my coffee and newspapers, I find an email and a letter. The email is from the attorney general, congratulating me on my final decision. The letter is from Aria. The best secretary in the world has resigned, and I am so happy about it! She has decided that her choice is to become the best judge in the district and ultimately honor her name. The name *Aria* means noble but strong as a lion, so I have no doubt that her new choice will not affect the time she wants to spend with her son.

I pick up the phone and dial 1.

"Yes, Your Honor?"

"Aria, are you packing your stuff?"

"Yes, I am. How can I help you?"

"Call the young man's lawyer and put him through on line three."

"Gladly! I'll be going now. Do you need anything else?"

"No, thank you. I wish you a choiceful journey to a successful life!"

I open the window, in need of fresh air, and glance at the surrounding greenery. The content of Aria's letter has set me on the creative-thinking path. I stare at the little boy wearing a baseball hat and jersey. He bows to the "thousands of fans" who applaud him for his performance in the grand finale. By desire and visualization alone, he has, in a self-submission way, made his dream come true!

Line three interrupts my very important realization.

"Greetings, Your Honor! How can I be of use to you?"

"Today I have received congratulations from the attorney general on my ruling of your case. I feel I must share the praise with both you and the young man. My congratulations!"

"Thank you very much for the update and the congratulations you share with us. Your Honor, may I ask you a question before we hang up?"

"Please do."

"How do you feel?"

And before I can think about it or wonder why he has asked me that, only one phrase escapes out loud: "*I feel free!*"

"Then, Your Honor, at this particular moment, all three of us are feeling exactly the same way. We have become one! We are one! One soul in three dimensions of time and place. We have succeeded in meeting in the Asynchronous Zone of Today and made the right choices. Goodbye, and good luck!"

I put down the phone, and within moments, I am responding to the attorney general's email. I thank him for his kind words and provide him with my resignation. On the last line, just before I bid him farewell, I quote a line from the wisest man of the twentieth century. Mahatma Gandhi once said, "Be the change you wish to see in the world!" Finally, I have decided to get back behind the steering wheel.

The time has come to honor my name and complete my mission. I leave a final message on a yellow Post-it note, for the next hungry tenant who will replace me and enjoy this office:

> Desire backed by faith knows no such word as impossible!
> —Napoleon Hill

I pack all my personal belongings and leave the office spotlessly clean, ready to welcome its next guest. I leave the stereo on, selecting one of my favorite songs by which to say farewell to this journey in time and space—"Send Me an Angel"[2] by Scorpions fills the empty space as I return to my time.

> Wise man said just walk this way
> To the dawn of the light
> Wind will blow into your face
> As the years pass you by
> Here I am
> Will you send me an angel?

Just before the song ends, I open my eyes and realize that I am still confined to the hospital bed. Turns out, the legal drama wasn't as boring as I thought it would be. And the judge, the stern voice inside, chose life rather than death.

---

[2] If you want to find me in the Asynchronous Zone of Today, search for the song on the internet, and enjoy it with me right now!

Station 6

The Exit

The truth is, our finest moments are likely to occur
when we are feeling deeply uncomfortable, unhappy,
or unfulfilled, for it is only such moments, propelled by
our discomfort, that we are likely to step out of our ruts
and start searching for different ways of truer answers.
—Scott Peck

June. What a blessing!

I have the VIP invitations in an envelope and wait anxiously for the moment when Coach will find our tickets for the launch event of his favorite book. I want to give him a gift as a token of my appreciation for all his support—for his help at the hospital, his defense at the court, his guidance through my darkest moments, his understanding of all my fears, his support of my efforts to lighten my pain, and for all the endless conversations regarding our past and our future.

In his book, Coach makes a special tribute to the author's adventures and quest for the most precious thing in the world. He speaks with great admiration of the author's life while describing the dreadful event that left him stranded for years. Taking a leap of faith, the author had begun a journey to recover his lost treasure.

He had embarked on a trek, without a compass or a map, that eventually led him to find valuable rewards after a years-long adventure. He may not have been able to recover what he initially lost, but along the way, he was blessed to acquire much more; he discovered the most precious thing in the world!

The author finally has found his lost self, his purpose, and a spiritual map and compass. Having possession of a new treasure, consisting of artifacts and valuables, he knows that he cannot keep all this wealth for himself alone. The journey itself taught him that the more you give, the greater the treasures will be at the next station.

His book has quickly become a best-seller around the world. From there, he continues his mission of giving meaning and purpose, compass and map, to other lost travelers. He has reached his final destination, has tasted the fruits of happiness and success, and wants to take as many fellow travelers as he can to this wonderful station. His book is now presented in every corner of the globe and has gained countless fellow passengers. Wherever he goes, his lectures are always sold out. He is blessed to have become a universal writer.

I was anticipating the moment when his train would make a stop in our small country and made sure to get two tickets through a good friend of mine, who works for the company sponsoring the event. I received the tickets last week with a funny note!

> You have assigned me quite a difficult task, but I know how much you really need it. I am enclosing two VIP tickets and hope you have a great time. Who's the lucky girl?

Time passed by in a flash—a cool summer breeze caresses my face as we enjoy our cocktails in the reception area of the Politelia Resort. Coach is already on his second glass, and his eagerness for the presentation to begin is quite obvious. Most of the time, he gazes at the billboard that shows the book cover and the author's photo. After a generous sip, he whispers to me, "What a journey! *From painful to painless with the right choices!* Can't wait for it!"

He is now nervously looking for the waiter so he can order another cocktail. He seems to be overwhelmed with anxiety, more nervous than the protagonist himself. This is the first time I have seen him so mentally distracted.

The announcer has switched on his microphone, and a hum inelegantly interrupts the classical music we were enjoying. "Ladies and gentlemen, welcome to Politelia Resort! We would like to kindly ask you to make your way to the Sky Theater and find your seats, as indicated on your tickets. The event will begin in ten minutes. Thank you, and we wish you a wonderful evening!"

Coach had put down his glass before the announcer was even finished and is on his way to the Sky at a brisk pace, clumsily passing other people who had preceded him. As soon as he realizes I have been left well behind, he turns and nods, like a little kid running to get into the theater to get a good seat.

"Don't worry! No one will take your place," I call to him almost mockingly. He ignores me and continues on his way, unabated.

Within minutes, we find ourselves in a huge hall that is packed with people! I am now sitting comfortably in seat 7A, and I am trying to estimate how many people have a seat tonight. It's impossible to do that, as the hall is vast and packed with people. Luckily for all, our excellent hosts have placed giant screens in every corner so that everyone will be able to enjoy the protagonist of the evening. Thanks to my good friend, who is under the impression that I'm trying to impress a girl, Coach and I have the good fortune of being seated right across from the author's seat on the stage.

Coach understood what I was trying to do and notified me directly. "More than two thousand people are in the Sky tonight!"

"It's impressive! Coach, could you ever do something like that? Go on stage and speak to such a huge audience?"

"You must have a special adventure to tell—a story that the audience needs to hear. It's a real blessing to have an opportunity to positively influence other people and make them better or wiser or, at the very least, stimulate them with your story."

"You've already done all that! That's why my mom has named you my bodyguard! You can unfold our true story to the rest of the world!"

I keep my eyes fixed on his face, as I want to hear a positive response to my challenge. At that particular moment, the lights dim, and two thousand people simultaneously close their mouths.

The room is in complete silence. We are all ready to welcome the wanderer of the world, who tonight has chosen to make a stop in our city, at our station. I have a quick look at my watch; it is exactly seven o'clock.

The giant screens light up the room as they show us an olive-colored train traveling through an evergreen forest. The imagery and sounds are so vivid that as we sit in our seats, we feel every bend, enjoy the movement of the air through the open windows of the carriages, and hear the whistle of the iron wheels that hug the rails as the train takes steep uphill turns.

In the distance, I spot some lights in the thick forest and realize that the train is rapidly approaching a station. Almost unconsciously, I count the lanterns, and I can't believe my eyes when I see ten in total!

"Oh, my dear grandpa, you're here with me once again," I murmur, tears now filling my eyes.

The music that comes with the vivid image is now more rhythmic, and we spontaneously begin clapping to the beat. Soon, the train arrives at the station, and a small boy debarks from the first wagon, carrying his suitcase. Wanting to make sure he got off at the right station, he raises his head to read the sign bearing the name of the station. Along with the boy, two thousand people are at the same station on this beautiful night in the Sky.

"I am finally home," he turns and says sweetly; then he sits down on the station bench with his little legs dangling clear of the floor. Bringing his suitcase onto his knees, he opens it slowly and gazes curiously at the contents.

"I found it!" he shouts loudly and shows us the book. "I want to read it to you, but I'm too young for that. I only have permission to eat, read, and play, but my reading is done by my father. Do you want me to call him?"

We all shout a loud and coordinated *yes*.

The theater is now completely dark, and a bright spotlight directs our eyes to the stage. Our author, like a star in the Sky, is sitting on the station bench. Next to him is the same suitcase the little boy was carrying in the video we have just witnessed. He holds the book in his hands and glances around the hall as we stand and clap furiously. No one intends to stop; the applause is getting more and more enthusiastic.

Finally, we sit down, and as if there was a sound switch, the whole room falls silent in a flash. All eyes are fixed on him, and we are eager to hear his voice for the first time.

Taking a quick look at seat 7B, I catch Coach wiping away his tears. I discreetly turn my head back toward the stage as the author is about to begin.

"Good evening and welcome! Thank you for the invitation to this wonderful station. Do you by any chance know where the station foreman is?"

He pauses, waiting for someone in the audience to reply. Some awkward laughter and mumbled comments follow, and then, once again, our lively applause begins. He stops us with a gentle wave of his hand.

"It's a very comfortable bench, but the screws need a little tightening."

That's when we all burst out laughing and resume our vigorous applause. He acknowledges our applause, then continues.

"With all the smiles I see on your faces and the noise you make with your applause, you have managed to scare my worst passenger and drive him away—God bless you! Mr. Stress has been traveling with me for years now, and what is more, he does not buy the appropriate ticket. He's the only stowaway on my train. You may wonder why I am nervous when I've done this over and over again for so many years now. Well, I have a confession to make. Every time, Mr. Stress is not just traveling with me; he also wants to take the stage! But when I have such good company, good mood, good manners, and, above all, your good intentions, Mr. Stress disappears into the crowd. Then, all we need is some good progress, good timing, and a desire to create a good memory! Our goodness and good purpose will lead all of us to our final and most desirable destination: a good life!"

Our applause rises up once again and won't stop for anything, since he just mentioned the ten choices in one sentence. For the first time, we are hearing all choices from the creator's mouth!

"Enough, enough! I don't understand why you are so excited! I am nothing but a simple storyteller. I have my own fairy tale that, although it is supposed to help little children go to sleep, ends up keeping the big kids awake all night. But don't worry; it's not a horror story. I truly believe that it is more of a love story, able to wake up even those who pretend to be asleep. These are the most difficult students in the class because no matter how much you poke them, they won't wake up, simply because they are just pretending to be asleep!"

Several in the room laugh out loud, revealing their guilt.

"The best students have eyes for learning, ears for improving, and an insatiable desire for developing themselves, for becoming better and better. They choose to learn something new even if it comes from another story. Good students always choose to have good progress!

Choose to have good progress.

"I am stressed because I want my story to awaken every good feeling that is hidden in your hearts and, at the same time, to prompt you to immediate action, as immediate and effective as a shot! When my *shot of goodness* intoxicates you, know that the effect lasts for a very short time, and then off we go again.

"Sadly, it is in our nature to easily forget and return to our original states. Nevertheless, our hearts are like a rubber band that keeps changing size as you stretch it. It needs daily expansion, and the more you stretch your heart, the more your heart will grow. To be able to open your heart wide will take small and daily acts of love.

Daily heart expansion will create its new dimension—a new state. This is your heart's evolution. You choose to progress through daily acts of goodness. If you don't, some other—better students than you—will keep overtaking you. They will progress, and you will get a punishment from Father.

"Now, I want to warn you about something. The shot I am preparing for you will be very strong! It will be almost impossible to find the time to do everything your heart desires tonight, so I'm going to let you take some notes so you don't forget. We'll do that at the end of the presentation. For now, stay glued to your seats, and don't let outside factors interrupt our journey. That's the only way to fully enjoy our train trip. Agreed?"

Our applause testifies to our consent.

"Speaking of shots, I hope the cocktails at the reception were just as effective, as I have no desire to be decorated with lettuce and tomatoes by any who don't like my story!"

The laughter and the noise return to the theater. He has this amazing ability to psychologically lift us up and bring us down like a roller coaster. As soon as he feels the audience sinking into a maze of contemplation, he throws a joke at us and fixes us back into our seats. Once we're again in need of a spiritual dose, he buys us another shot, and we fly off into the Sky again.

"I hold my book—my own fairy tale, as I prefer to call it—but at the same time, I recognize that you all have your own stories to tell. The storyteller always has a great responsibility—not the one who wants to put the small children to sleep but the one who wants to awaken the big ones.

"I accept my responsibility, and I am ready to unfold my experience in my quest for the most precious thing in the world, provided that you are ready to listen to it with your heart. Whether or not it becomes precious to you too, your heart will reveal this to us at the end, when you hear the familiar words beloved by everyone—*and they lived happily ever after!*

"Especially today, more crucially than at any previous time—whether you are reading your story to adults or to children—it should abound with meaningful messages and have a happy ending. No more horror, and no more pain! We've had enough! Tonight, we will tell a different kind of tale! A magic one!"

The lights are lowered; the stage is now in total darkness, and the music prepares us for what is to come. The introduction, for what it's worth, is magnificent! I take the opportunity to look again at Coach, giving him the chance to speak to me.

"I am living in my own fairy tale tonight, and I thank you from the bottom of my heart for the invitation. This man lightens my soul. I close my eyes as he speaks and I know the next words that are to pop out! How is this ever possible? Oh my God!"

While I am trying to understand his optics, a small group of people appear on stage and quickly change the scenery.

The song "Pelago Vathi"[3] by Ermogenis Skitinis starts up and throws us into the deep!

> On your shores I have also walked, seeking your precious secret. With tears He made you and formed you, I presume. I stand beside you and I look at the sky through your eyes.

---

[3] If you want to find us in the Asynchronous Zone of Today, search for the song on the internet, and enjoy it with us right now!

Station 5

Time Zero

Any fool can criticize, condemn and complain,
and most fools do. But it takes character and self-
control to be understanding and forgiving.
—Dale Carnegie

May. What a blessing!

The new setting is the interior of the train's locomotive. The author
sits in the driver's seat and wears the captain's hat. He takes a quick
look to make sure we are all in our seats before starting his engine. He
lowers his eyes to the book, takes a deep breath, and begins.

"Once upon a time, there was a traveler who traveled around the
world on his train. My life is a train that carries wagons full of people,
and my sole mission is to find luminous people in every corner of the
planet to ask them a simple question: *what is the most precious thing
in the world?*

"I am the captain, as my colleagues like to call me, and I am
responsible for the speed, safety, comfort, and joy of everyone on
board my train. My first concern is the speed and the travel time from
one station to another. Obviously, I can push my engine to the limit
and reach the next station at breakneck speed. But I do wonder: How

pleasant will it be for me and my fellow passengers? What marvels will I miss if my eyes are just fixed on the next destination? How much comfort will my nervousness allow? How secure will my fellow passengers feel with my impatience? How much fuel will I consume because of my greed? How much damage will my pressure cause to the engine? How long will the captain, the passengers, and the train endure?

"Besides, I must not forget the tough competition. There are many other means of transport, and I have no intention of losing a single passenger. So sit back and relax, and I will take care of everything.

"Although I have chosen the lowest speed possible to enjoy your good company, look how time flies! We've already arrived at our first station—the Time Station!"

The giant screens make our collective imagination run wild. Here we are at the Time Station! Built of red bricks, with large arched gates and green wooden shutters and doors, it's impressive how clean and tidy it is; almost spotless. An imposing iron sign hangs from two heavy black chains, welcoming passengers in calligraphic lettering: "Welcome to Time Station—Since 1955."

A huge antique clock shows seven o' clock, and everyone is in a rush. We meet all kinds of passengers going back and forth frantically, some looking for a train, others looking for a destination. They are pushing each other; a mother is pulling her two young children by the hand; a well-dressed gentleman with a hat on is shouting and waving his hands vigorously at the conductor. Boarding announcements and last calls are made, one after the other, alerting the lazy-comers and scaring the life out of the latecomers.

A little girl is standing by the station cafeteria door, playing angelic music on her violin. A violin case is open at her feet. She keeps her eyes tightly shut, but her little heart is wide open as she moves back and forth to the rhythm of the music. There are just a few coppers in her violin case, but she doesn't lose hope. On the contrary, she keeps trying, hoping to freeze time for the hurrying passersby, offering them a tune, a melody, a break, a breath. Unfortunately, the case remains empty, just like the passengers who have passed her by.

Before our eyes, the giant screens show the image of the girl and amplify the sound of her violin. So mesmerized are we by the image and the music that when the author resumes his narration, we almost scowl at him.

"Wagon doors are wide open! I put on my official jacket and take a quick look in the mirror to fix my messy eyebrows. I like to make an appearance during boarding time to personally welcome each one of the first-class passengers. My colleagues very often drop the prefix 'pr'—dubbing them 'ominent' rather than prominent—when reporting their various eccentric requests over the intercom: 'Captain, the ominent in suite 1A wants you to go faster because he has an urgent and important business meeting to attend!' I always respond to such requests by immediately lowering speed. I want Mr. 1A to get a good look at the forest spreading out to his left. I hope he'll forget for a moment the soulless concrete jungle of the city that draws him like a magnet.

"I was once blessed to meet a truly prominent man at Time Station. I will never forget our initial conversation as he boarded the first-class carriage."

● ● ●

"Welcome to our train, my dear sir."

"A glass of water please, and make it quick," he said. A shadow of loneliness fell on his face as he returned to his VIP suite, tilted his head back, and closed his troubled eyes.

"Right away," I replied, leaving him alone and making sure that I brought his glass of water as promptly as possible.

"My apologies for being abrupt earlier, Captain," he whispered as he took his first few sips. "I've had a long day. But at least I caught the train, unlike my friend Alan." He cast a sad look out of the window.

"Do you want me to make arrangements so that Alan will also make it?"

"No, thank you. He has chosen a different journey."

I discreetly avoided asking more questions, but I felt the need to offer him more than a glass of water. "Sir, there are two seats in the locomotive. Obviously, one is for the captain, but as for the other one, I can invite anyone I choose. My guest will enjoy two things: the panoramic views, and hopefully a pleasant conversation with me. You are more than welcome to join me if you wish." He nodded affirmatively, and I continued to welcome the other passengers to the first carriage.

The last-call siren is forcing the last few passengers to get aboard just as I am preparing to fire up my engine. Within seconds, no one is left on the platform. There is absolute silence in the station, apart from the little girl's violin. She is now playing Vivaldi's *The Four Seasons*, a reminder, despite the challenges we all face, that no matter how difficult our day, spring, summer, autumn, and winter always circle around to reappear in our lives. A new season, four times a year. What a blessing!

At times, the girl opens her eyes to see how foolish we all are to be chasing time. She sometimes wants to open her lips too, to explain that we all carry our own season. Regardless of the weather with which God has chosen to gift us today, it is our choice whether we take an umbrella, sunglasses, both, or neither. Nature lovers need no gear and will gladly dance in the rain. Simply put, we can carry our own season. Those carrying the summer heat in their hearts will warm up their fellow passengers too, even if it's pouring outside.

All passengers are now seated, watching the girl behind their closed windows, trying to catch their breaths after their last-minute rush to get aboard. Unfortunately, the double glazing does not allow the sound to sneak in to soothe their hearts. They are watching a silent movie from a distance, regretting that they missed the chance to catch a single note. Of course, there are always those who stubbornly choose to stare down at the mud.

My train's engine is now warm. I've got the go-ahead from the station master, and I am setting the speed and course of travel on the autopilot. Along the way, I allow my eyes to enjoy the greenery flooding the horizon as the sun's rays warm my face. I keep my eyes open to enjoy all the different shades of green. Despite the fact that I've been on this route hundreds of times, I still have an inexhaustible need to observe, to search for that single thing that I hadn't previously spotted.

As I gaze out of the window, my undying curiosity resurfaces, and my innocent childlike inquisitiveness returns. Last time, I was left staring dumbfounded when I spotted an old wooden sign with an arrow pointing to a road leading to a motel. When I looked it up on the internet, I discovered that the motel had closed twenty years ago. Apparently, no one had bothered to remove the sign, unless it was destined to stay there forever to show us an alternative road. The arrow on the sign had almost completely faded, but the message remained clearly visible from many yards away: *Make a Stop! Let the lush greenery give you a deep breath!*

Since I first saw it, I had started a ritual. Two hundred yards from this spot, I slow the train down for two reasons. First, I hope that all the passengers who left their souls at Time Station will notice it. And second, so that I can open my window, stick my head out, and draw a deep breath. The oxygen from the lungs of the earth mixed with the cool breeze and the aroma of the towering cedars, godly sequoias, red alders, and proud oaks is almost intoxicating. How beautiful May is, with mild rains and warm sunshine. It is one of God's gifts to nature. What a blessing!

My nature healing was cut short; the conductor interrupts me on the intercom: "Captain, have you invited 3A to your cab?" I close the window and immediately give instructions to escort him to me.

"Thank you very much for the invitation, Captain. My name is 3A!" He extends his hand with a wide smile, and I hope he forgives and forgets the radio communication he had obviously heard. "The view is indeed impressive from here. Are you sure I'm not keeping you from your work?"

This gives me a chance to tell him a few things about my work, but my intention is to listen rather than to talk. I got a sense that this man is in need of letting off some steam.

"Time is cruel sometimes! If we could have waited for a little while, or if your friend Alan was luckier, we'd certainly have him with us, wouldn't we?"

"Well, we should be really careful using the word *certainly*, my dear captain. As for your comment about time, let me share my nickname with you. My colleagues and patients call me Dr. Time. I am a surgeon, an oncologist. One may assume that my job is to give time to patients who are in their final stages of their lives—some quality, pain-free time, if possible. I try my best to help them live for another minute, another hour, another day. For many of them, this extra time is crucial, as they have left the most important unfinished business for last. An apology, a hug, a thank-you, or even a simple goodbye. Anything that needs to be said before the long journey!"

"What exactly happened with your friend?"

"Since you ask, Alan was one of my bravest fighters. He never allowed pain to win him over. He never missed an opportunity to cheer up anyone who passed by his room. He had chosen his own season, and it was always sunny in his room. He was like a ray of sunshine, strong enough to warm our stormy hearts. Every day, he had a fresh joke to share or a compliment for my tie or shirt. Alan was in such physical pain that he could not get out of bed. Mentally, though, it was a different story. Alan had found a way to fool the pain! He didn't let a single moment go to waste for the sake of pain!"

"How did he do that, Doctor?"

"Alan and I spent a lot of time discussing and theorizing on this. In fact, we even joked about it. We used to hold a small plastic cup that we called *the shot*! His shot contained strong painkillers, and mine contained vitamin booster, but the real boost was what this luminous man taught me regarding pain management. Practices that I had not come across before, not even at university. I occasionally called him Professor Alan and he always came back with the same sarcastic line: 'If I'm the professor in the room, then we're screwed!'"

"And all this while he was in unbearable pain?"

"Exactly! Alan chose to live his final days in good company, good mood, and good manners. That's how he managed to lighten his pain. He also had good intentions to endure one more minute, one more hour, one more day, so that he had time to say goodbye to his son, who was traveling from New York to see him. The big-time lawyer with a reputation in many states had missed many appointments with his father in the past due to urgent and important cases that he always had to attend. Birthdays and special occasions were celebrated online. However, this appointment was different from any other. This time around, no case was urgent enough, no business meeting was important enough to stop the big-shot lawyer from getting to his father. He is traveling first class to meet him as we speak!"

Dr. Time opens the window to get some fresh air. I choose not to ask him any questions, allowing him to compose himself. I let the lungs of the earth take care of him and recharge him. A couple of minutes later, he closes the window and continues, visibly moved.

"Life doesn't always give you what you want. Alan boarded the train to his final destination this morning at seven o'clock, while his son arrives late tonight. You see, I was not able to keep Alan alive long enough to see his son one last time. Cases like these make my job both a blessing and a burden!"

"I am so sorry for your loss, my dear doctor. For what it's worth, my job is also a blessing and a burden. My blessing is the opportunity to get passengers safely to their destinations without any undue delay or danger. No one wants to waste their time unnecessarily on a train, especially when their family is waiting for them at the station. Nor do they want to be put at risk by a careless driver."

"And what is your burden?"

"It's an intense fear. We are not getting any younger, Doc! I go for blood tests more often than visiting the cafeteria nowadays. My prime concern is my health because passengers depend on me every day. I'm really scared! I shudder at the thought of having a sudden event with no time to alert the conductor or the deputy captain. Can you imagine a driverless train full of people?"

"Indeed! Very alarming!"

"This is why I have become a prevention advocate. I get regular blood tests, and I watch my diet. I get up at half past five every morning and walk seven miles; then I eat a healthy and energizing breakfast to help me cope with the demands of the day. My grandfather taught me that breakfast is the most important meal of the day. In addition, I have instructed the conductor to check on me every twenty minutes. By the way, he also brings my detox tea so he doesn't come empty-handed!"

"Excellent strategy, Captain! A big thumbs-up for your prevention plan!"

"The most important measure I have implemented is what we are doing right now. I often invite a guest in the passenger seat. I tend to choose someone who looks like they need a break, but in reality, I am the one in need. In your case, I just nailed it; you are a doctor!"

"Why did you choose me, Captain? What did you see in me?"

"I saw a true gentleman who had forgotten to wear his most important adornment—the number-one ingredient in making a good first impression."

"What was missing? Though I've got something in mind."

"You were missing your smile, my dear doctor. My grandfather, God bless his soul, had one of the best restaurants in the country, and his favorite quote was, 'For catering, you first have to cater a smile!' If you wanted to enjoy his famous dishes you had to make a reservation a month in advance. Another of his oft-told lines was, 'The best elixir is your smile; you just need two drops—one for you and one for me!' Grandpa was a wise man; he gained his wisdom by interacting with thousands of customers who passed by his restaurant."

The author pauses the narrative to look at the audience. As I am in the front row, I have the impression that he is staring right at me, waiting to see my reaction. My breathing is heavy. I reach for the water bottle under my seat. I feel dizzy, and my vision is blurred. Coach, sensing that something is wrong, leans toward me, his left hand on my back, and asks if I need any help.

I respond anxiously, "You told me that you can foresee the author's next sentence, right? If I tell you that I have similar symptoms tonight, will you believe me? How is it possible that there are so many events in his life that coincide with mine? He talks about his grandfather, the restaurateur, and it's like I'm transcending on stage and telling my story under the ten lanterns! This is extraordinary! My heart is about to burst!"

Coach doesn't have time to comfort me as the narration continues.

• • •

"My dear doctor, please forgive my frankness. I don't want to insult or judge you. It's just that as I get to know you better, I've noticed your smile as you recount Alan's sunny season. You become a different person from the one who entered my carriage. I also acknowledge that instead of showing the appropriate courtesy, I have taken off my captain's hat and put on my coach's hat to give you a mentoring lesson. You see, I wasn't always a train driver. I used to guide souls; now I guide wagons. But it looks like I have never been able to let go of my former job. I should be more patient!"

"Don't apologize for being truthful, my dear captain. I too acknowledge my attitude in response to your warm welcome. To be perfectly honest, if I were in your shoes, I'd have poured cold water over my head to wash away my rudeness! But it's all water under the bridge, as my colleagues in London used to say. Could you please keep your coach's hat on for a little longer and tell me more about your former role?"

"On my train, the only thing that changes is the passengers; therefore, I sometimes change my hat, depending on my codriver. Everything else remains the same. The route is the same, and the stations are always in the same place. Sometimes, though, there are surprises or new signs along the route, if you keep your eyes open for them. For example, did you happen to see a wooden sign that we passed fifteen miles back?"

"I don't think so, probably because I was looking down."

"And what did you see, looking down?"

"The mud, Captain. What else could I see?"

"Anyway, I started telling you that while everything seems to be the same, in every journey a wonderful opportunity presents itself, provided that you keep your eyes open and search relentlessly. If you spend meaningful time with a passenger, you will find something of value, as long as you have eyes eager to learn, ears willing to understand, and an insatiable appetite for progress. Every minute I spend with you today is like joining another life class. In order to learn, it is necessary to change hats, roles, and practices. A student becomes a teacher, a patient becomes a doctor, a defendant becomes a judge, a captain becomes a coach, and vice versa! Stepping into the other person's shoes and assuming that you retain your childlike innocent curiosity, you get to look out of another person's window and see what he sees. It's as if someone is handing over their role so that you can get a better sense of them, lending you their glasses so that you can see their landscape. And if you don't use those glasses, you will continue to limit yourself in your own myopic version of the world only."

"How do you achieve this?"

"It's simple, Doc! You only need a desire to learn and a will to understand!"

"I experienced something similar with my friend Alan. I offered him my doctor's hat when I chose to learn how he managed to lighten the pain. Our roles were reversed, and I became his student."

"Exactly! You had a desire to learn and a will to understand. Therefore, I would like to put my student's hat on to ask you a very important question."

"Sure. Go ahead!"

"My dear professor, what is the most precious thing in the world?"

"Captain, two years ago on my birthday, I received the most precious gift in the world. My young daughter gave me a magic stick. She thought that pink was my favorite color so she bought me a pink pencil! It has a fuzzy ball on one end and the tip of a regular pencil on the other. In her card, she began with a complaint about not spending as much time as possible with her. At the same time, she provided the solution: 'Daddy, I give you this pink magic stick to help you make the whole world well, especially the little children. This way, you will be faster and more efficient and come home on time. With LOVE, your magic girl.' She chose to write the word *love* in capital letters. Since then, the pink magic stick has always been with me."

"Did the miracle happen, spending more time with her?"

"I'm not entirely sure if I eventually managed to leave work on time regularly, but the magic stick has gained great reputation in our hospital and beyond. When I am with my patient at Time Zero, just the two of us, alone in the Intensive Care Unit, I present the magic stick, explaining that my young daughter chose the color. It's never too late for a joke, right? This is the moment when science and medication have exhausted all possibilities of help, and the pain is at its peak. All that remains is one's own determination—how much drive the patient has left to live. It could be Time Zero for the desperate, or one more hour, one more day, one more month for those who want to deal with the pain and complete their missions."

"How is ever possible to have no more drive to live?"

"That's a very good question! Unbearable pain is capable of exhausting even the most ferocious lion. At this stage, when patients have given up and science is useless, my last trick is my pink magic stick. I take it out of my bag and say the same thing every time: 'What I hold is a magic stick, capable of granting you one last wish, as long as you let me touch the fuzzy ball to your forehead. What do you need right now?' I eagerly await their response."

The doctor pauses, waiting for my reaction. I shake my head awkwardly, as I have no idea what will follow.

"The answers I've received over the years are overwhelming, Captain! I now have the hard evidence, like every good statistician, to document that seven out of ten patients always ask for the same thing."

He is now waiting for me to guess what that last wish usually is. First thing that comes to mind is the obvious—"I want my health back"— but for some reason, I suspect that the answer would be quite different.

"Most answers have nothing to do with their health. I bet that was the first thing that came to your mind. It's not about money either, as that's completely useless at this stage. Nor is it fame, posterity, or any of the things we run like zombies, from station to station, every day to acquire. Take, for example, the giddy bunch we met at Time Station earlier. Next time, we'll do a poll—you'll ask ten of your passengers what they really need today, and I'll ask ten of my patients the same question. Put on your coach's hat for a moment, and tell me what answers you think you'll collect at the station."

"Probably similar to the ones I've been listening to in my office for twenty years:

1. I want a promotion.
2. I want to have many friends.
3. I want my childhood dreams to come true.
4. I want to find my lost self-esteem.
5. I want them to stop gossiping behind my back.
6. I want to stop hating the one in the mirror.
7. I want everyone's respect and dignity.
8. I want to lose twenty kilos and have a beach-fit body.
9. I want a sports car and a house by the sea.
10. I want to be successful and famous.

"I want, I want, and I want! As soon as I urge them to pick up their life's remote control to switch from *I want* to *I am*, they do pick up the control to push the red power-off button!"

"My dear captain, I can sadly confirm that all the above are correct. We run after our vanity on a rusty bicycle, while it speeds off in a sporty convertible. The answers I will get at Time Zero will be completely different from yours:

> Doctor, I need just an hour!
> Doctor, I need one more day!
> Doctor, I need one more week!
> Doctor, I need one month!

"I need, not want! And it is surprising how specific most of them are. They have a specific task or tasks in mind, and they have already worked out the time they need to complete them. They will then add the following:

> One more hour to say *I love you* to my wife!
> One more day to say *I am proud of you* to my children!
> One more week to say *I am sorry* to those I have hurt!
> One more month to say *welcome home*, my son!"

"That is indeed remarkable, Doc."

"It is, but we continue to do absolutely nothing about it! Even us, right now—of all the daily worries we have, the last thing we worry about is time ticking away. Our real worries should be quite different, such as:

> How much time do I have left with my loved ones?
> How much time do I waste on my mobile phone?
> How much time do I spend with my friends?
> How much time do I need to visit my parents?
> How long do I stay angry until my partner says *amen*?
> How many summers have I left to enjoy the sea?

"Speaking of summer, Captain, August will be knocking on our doors in three months, but I'm sure you've already made plans, organized, and prepaid for your vacation by now, correct?"

"You're absolutely right."

"You see what's going on here? We wrongly assume that we have time in the future, and as a result, we don't live in the present. We run from station to station with our clock hands broken! Is there a guarantee that three months from now, we will all have reached August? Why have we packed our luggage already? What about the luggage we carry every day? Is the most valuable luggage you have in your life packed away safely, Captain?"

"What exactly do you mean by *luggage*?"

"Simply put, each relationship is like a piece of luggage. If you forget or neglect to pack the essentials, then you will face shortages during your trip. Harsh words and long absence make the luggage increasingly heavy, sometimes impossible to carry. It's no surprise that we end up avoiding carrying the heaviest ones! We get new ones, ignoring the important ones we already have in our storerooms. Just ask the station porter to tell you what happens when he carries heavy luggage—he gets breathless, becomes exhausted, and has no energy left for the rest of the day!"

"Oh my God! You are so right!"

"We wrongly assume that we have unlimited time ahead of us, and as a result, we hold some heavy, often painful luggage! Very painful luggage from our work relationships, our family relationships, from the relationship we have with ourselves. When was the last time you came to a brave and selfless settlement with a special piece of luggage? We put off our apologies to our partners, we postpone expressing our love toward our children, expressing gratitude to our parents, voicing our need for help. We put off the care of the most important luggage; after all, we have unlimited future time for it. And so the luggage is left in the storeroom, gathering dust, lacking care and love. After all, we'll definitely take care of it sometime in the future!"

"Unbelievable! I am stunned! You should let your enlightening words warm your own heart too, my luminous doctor! Never again speak of the burden of your profession. You are a blessed man. With your unbreakable will, you give time to those who truly need it."

"You're going to be punished for not being a good student, Captain! Do you really think I have the power to do such a thing? That I have the choice to give or deny time to anyone? That I have the option to give someone an hour and someone else a whole month? This is the prerogative of my *Director*! I am only a *vessel of God*!"

● ● ●

The giant screens interrupt the narration; we are looking at an empty calendar page that shows the twenty-four hours gifted to us each day, as a loud ticking noise disturbs us all. The heading above the calendar reads, "Choose to have good timing."

Choose to have good timing.

● ● ●

Dr. Time went on. "And I still wonder why we never learn to manage time, since it is clearly a personal choice how and where we invest our most precious commodity. Why do we have to reach Time Zero, only to ask third parties to give us more time? Why is it only when we arrive at Station Zero that we realize time is all we have left?"

"Please, dear doctor, tell me what I should do about it. I urgently need your help to manage time properly!"

"It is your choice to make time. We all have twenty-four hours a day at our disposal. Some choose to build a pyramid, and some choose to dig a pit. All who came before us and those who will succeed us, no matter whether they are famous or ordinary folks, rich or poor, lucky or unlucky—they all wake up each morning with the same gift from God: twenty-four fresh hours every day! I am not a photovoltaic cell, doomed to have life only when it is sunny. I am not a wind turbine, doomed to have life only when there is wind. I am a human, all-weather living organism, blessed to produce work and energy around the clock, if I so desire, even in the dark of the night when everyone else is asleep. Name one person who loves you and who would be annoyed if you woke them up in the middle of the night to say, 'I need your help,' or 'I just called to tell you how much I love you.' Not one! When will we finally wake up, and when will we finally wake up the others?"

"You've just woken me up! Thank you for passing on all this knowledge!"

"Captain, in the arena we call life, no one will hand you the weapon you need to save yourself from the lion! Likewise, you will not be given free time by anyone. You must make time for yourself. I say this often so that I also can hear it myself. I must honor my magic stick and my nickname. I need to better manage my time and spend more of it with my family. This was indeed a long answer to your question, but I hope I've proved to you that the most precious thing in the world is time!"

"My dear doctor, my heart is now filled with your wisdom, but please allow me to share a last concern before we part. My mission is to offer a safe and pleasant journey to all traveling on my train; my purpose is to seek the most precious thing in the world. This is why I asked you earlier. Once I complete my mission, I would like to share my treasure with the rest of the world. Therefore, I want to be absolutely certain that this spiritual fortune will be appreciated by everyone. Forgive me for saying this, but how can I pass on your wisdom without fear? How can I speak about the luminous doctor who insists that the most precious thing in the world is not health but time? In my opinion, there will be objections, and I will end up getting embroiled in a bras de fer with Doubting Thomases!"

"I was under the impression that I had been talking to an experienced coach all this time. Correct me if I am wrong, but coaches never argue with other people's perceptions, do they? In fact, they never express their personal opinions but simply guide the coachees with questions that are as powerful as fertilizer, for as long there is fertile ground for a base. Coach will thereafter plant the seed and water and fertilize the soil, as necessary. You put in the seed and let the others decide whether to grow roses or nettles. It's their choice. However, I will not leave you without the necessary garden spray that is ideal for all the *weeds* you will encounter along the way. With the seed, the fertilizer, and the weed-killing spray in your arsenal, you will become the best gardener in the world and fill the globe with roses!"

● ● ●

The giant screens are now filled with all sorts of roses: small and dainty; big and full-blossomed; red, white, and yellow.

● ● ●

"Captain, to those who don't like roses and want to cultivate nettles, you will tell Ms. Aria's story—a story as effective as a shot. This story is capable of killing all weeds and germs, so I compare it to garden weed-killer."

"I'm all ears, Doctor!"

"For this story, you will need a strong heart rather than ears: 'I shouted after him with all my strength—*Leo, come back! Leo, don't speed!* But he just slammed the door as he left in haste. It was the last time I saw him, Doctor!'

"This is how Aria began to unfold her story to me outside the hospital. Leo, her husband, had been having breakfast with his family and was visibly nervous about the morning meeting coming up at work. It had been an extremely difficult week, as stock markets around the world had crashed. He was facing the risk of losing almost all of his clients and the portfolio he had built up with hard work and sacrifice over the years. He had to take his son to school, as he had done every morning for the past three years, so he looked again at his watch, which now read seven o'clock, and he kept pushing his son to finish up quickly. After all, he had an *urgent and important* meeting! He had transferred so much negativity to his son that, in an awkward move, the poor kid spilled coffee over his father's pants and crisply ironed white shirt. Pandemonium ensued, shouting and blaming, before Leo shut himself in the bedroom to change his clothes. Even with the door closed, his angry voice reverberated throughout the entire house and panicked his family. From his point of view, he had lost precious time. He made his way out, leaving his mortified son behind. His last words before he slammed the door angrily was the commanding instruction to Aria: 'Your son is all yours; you take him to school!'

"He left, ignoring his wife's pleas for him not to speed. Leo never arrived at work, and—for the sake of history—the stock markets bounced back just a week later. Leo's *final bounce*, unfortunately, was taken that day. Thank goodness he was alone in the car, I hesitate to say. A police officer informed Aria that her husband had run a red light at a road junction, crashed violently into a pole on the opposite side of the road, and had died instantly."

This was the last lesson delivered by my luminous doctor. Before he left the locomotive, he opened his briefcase and took out his pink magic stick. He touched me on the forehead with it, giving me a soul whisper. "May your quest be short and the story that will be written immortal. May your words encourage the desperate and your voice waken the asleep. Invest your time wisely. Bon voyage, my dear captain!"

He took out a notepad and his luxurious pen, wrote a message, folded the paper, put it in an envelope, and set it on the passenger seat. He gave me a warm hug and a heartfelt farewell as we arrived at the station. My first thought is how quickly time flies when you are in good company. I put my jacket on, take a quick look in the mirror, and I am ready to bid farewell to my passengers, with the note he left me constantly in mind. There is no time to read it yet. I didn't even have time to say a proper goodbye as he already disembarked. At least he left with a smile on his face. He left his sorrow on 3A.

The doors of the carriages are now wide open. People are getting on and off quickly, as they do at every station, and I once again welcome my first-class passengers with a wide smile on my face.

I return swiftly to my cab to open the envelope. The letter is written on paper carrying the doctor's and the hospital's contact details. Underneath, his handwritten message reads:

My dear captain,
  Lao Tzu wrote, "Kindness in words creates trust. Kindness in thinking creates wisdom. Kindness in giving creates love." In our brief meeting, we got full marks in trust and wisdom! Love is all there is left; love, I will give to my patients every day, and love, you will give with your book when you finish your quest and adventures.

When you finally give up all your hats and put your writer's hat on, I hope you'll remember that the most precious thing in the world is time! If you ever find yourself in trouble with the weeds, even after you fertilize and spray, then I have one more drastic shot for you to use! Tell them that Dr. Time has confirmed and scientifically validated that hundreds of healthy people are dying every day because they have failed to manage their time properly! Invest your time wisely!

With love, Dr. Time.

Station 4

The Other Road

I will act now. If I delay, success will become
wed to another and lost to me forever.
This is the time. This is the place!
—Og Mandino

As I leave work and am driving home, I can't get the doctor and his words out of my mind. I frequently check the passenger seat beside me, where I placed the envelope containing his message. I want to be sure that my time with him was not a creation of my imagination but was something real. At the first red light, my mind recalls Ms. Aria's story, and I feel the need to call home immediately, despite the fact that I am almost there.

"Hello?"

"I'm twenty minutes away, darling."

"Your food is ready! Shall I heat water for your shower? I suppose your delayed afternoon nap will follow right after?"

Nothing of the sort, my May girl! Just put on your best dress and get ready for a night out at your favorite restaurant!"

"Did you just call me girl of May? Is everything all right? You are worrying me! It's been years since you surprised me like this!"

"Well, then, we won't waste any more time. In a few minutes, I will be at the door. Tonight, I'll give you all the time you want and deserve."

I hung up the phone quickly to hide my fragile emotions. This is my most important luggage of all, which urgently needs to be lightened. This is clearly a side effect of my beloved doctor's story. After his drastic shot, I know that I must act immediately before myriad meaningless excuses come up and distract me. Neither my exhaustion, nor hunger, nor bathing, nor the eight o'clock TV news are capable of disrupting my new action plan. It's seven o'clock in the evening now, and I am ready to have the best time of my life. Tonight, I choose to be different. Tonight, I choose a different path. Tonight, I have taken my life's remote control and changed from the usual channel. I choose to create another good memory!

● ● ●

The author's eyes sparkle with joy and happiness as he pauses and turns his attention to the giant screens. They are projecting a slideshow featuring dozens of personal photos of him in moments of absolute pleasure. Simple, everyday moments. Beautiful, happy memories—enjoying a nice meal, swimming in blue waters, dancing with friends, sitting at a big table enjoying his good company. I cannot take my eyes from the photo of him holding a guitar and singing with a large group, as I usually do!

Choose to have good memories.

Before I can intertwine his memories with my own and the resemblances become the protagonists of my night, a caption appears on the slide—"Choose to have good memories"—interrupting my anxious thoughts.

The author's eyes glow from the light of the screen as he also gazes at his good memories. I allow a ray of light to suffuse my soul, and I recall my own good memories from my personal album of life. They are identical, but this time, I will not allow my mind to fly me away from the Sky Hall. I look at him, and I just smile. I now look at him and see a quite familiar person. I am sure he is also looking at me as he prepares to continue with his love story.

● ● ●

As I approach my house, just two blocks away, I feel very strange. It is like the romantic nervousness that usually precedes a first date. And how fitting—as I open the passenger door for her to enter the car, I notice that she is also terribly nervous, somehow anxious. As we drive away, it is probably the only time we've been together in the car without her talking nonstop. There is an awkward silence because we don't want to spoil the moment with mundane daily matters.

I take a quick glance at her and notice that she is wearing her favorite dress. She has done her hair the way I like it, and she smiles like a sunny afternoon. Literally, her smile radiates light, like the face of an angel. I feel warm, and I open the window to let in some cool air. The evening air is wonderful, one of the few evenings without unbearable humidity. A cool breeze refreshes the mind.

I now look at her fingers. Slim and clean, with neatly trimmed nails, they rest gently on her knees. No sign whatsoever of the exhaustion, the discomfort, the hard work she puts them through every day. No sign of all the times she has held me tight, each of us trying to give the other the strength to go on. No sign whatsoever of the suffering we've been through together—afflictions that few people go through and eventually overcome without losing their sanity. Capable hands, hands full of memories, but no sign of mistreatment.

I switch on the radio to bury my negative thoughts, going through several radio stations until I find the most romantic option. The night continues to do me many favors!

I turn up the volume and let her favorite band, Melisses, serenade her with "Mpalanta ton Asterion."[4]

One night on a blank piece of paper, I hid what I had in my heart but I didn't tell you. I took a deep breath and blew the words far away. And the syllables became bright stars and the paper became the sky when the light fades. Every time you look up and the verse grows stronger a syllable wants to be heard.

"Today I met a doctor who, while he deserves to see only the stars, lowers his eyes and sees the mud! Do you want me to give you the message he wrote to me?"

"Let me enjoy the song, and I'll let you tell me all about it in the restaurant."

The syllables became bright stars and the paper became the sky when the light fades.

"I told my mom that we are going to dinner for no special reason, and she was touched by it. Are you sure you're all right? Did you get a promotion and want to celebrate it with me?"

"I don't need a special reason to celebrate with you. Every day should be like a celebration! It just took me a little longer to get the engines started. You always say that I am as slow as a train!"

"Yes, but I'm not changing you for anything. You're my own train. What should I do? Sell you and get a Ferrari instead?"

The mood is great, and we continue our jokes and small talk until I park outside the restaurant. As they open the door for us to enter, she clings to my arm as if escorting the president of the country. We sit down, and I immediately instruct the waiter to bring only one menu.

"That reminds me of something—our first date when you

---

[4] If you want to find us in the Asynchronous Zone of Today, search for the song on the internet, and enjoy it with us right now!

decided to order the whole menu to impress me! Thank God you had connections with that restaurant; you had a family discount, didn't you?"

"Worked like a charm back then, so why not tonight? Sit back, and I'll take good care of you. You do it every day, and you don't even bring me the bill at the end. Well, tonight, I'm paying!" I exclaim, and we both burst out laughing.

A delicious dinner follows, and we manage to drink two bottles of Italian red wine, which enhances the pleasant atmosphere even more. We are encouraged to leave by the waiter discreetly bringing the bill. We are the last table, and it is getting late, very late. She takes the keys from my hand, as I have not been fair in sharing the wine. She has had only one glass; therefore, she is the only one capable of driving us back home.

"What a fantastic night, my darling! Thank you for the wonderful surprise and for the extravagant dinner. Next time will be my treat. How about next Tuesday?"

I agree, kiss her good night, and turn off the light—more than ready for bed. Before surrendering to sleep, I acknowledge again how important the time is that we spend with our loved ones. Time flies, but good memories last forever!

● ● ●

The author closes the book, as we open our eyes, breathless from the effects. For the first time, we see a glimmer of light, like a blind man seeing a ray of sunshine for the first time, like a short-sighted child putting on glasses for the first time. We see and understand for the first time because we see and understand with our hearts. And slowly, our hearts are making little expansions and changing size. Growing bigger and beating harder.

He returns backstage, leaving us with another piece of evidence. The giant screens display a photo. He is posing outside their favorite restaurant, holding his wife in his arms. There are captions as well: "We take a break twice a week! How about you?"

The Sky Hall will also take a break with us. With halting, almost numb steps, we find our way out to the poolside, where an array of delicacies awaits us. I notice that the night air is much warmer than the sunny afternoon before the event. Yet again, maybe it is my overheating heart or the season I choose to have for this evening. I have chosen my own personal temperature, and I am radiating warmth and love. My eyes are wide open, and I see everything as vividly colorful as the roses on the screen had been. I am kind, romantic, positive, and smiley. I am in love with life!

Coach returns from the bar, bearing our cocktails. He brings the same exotic drink we were drinking before the event began. He even explains to me how to properly order an *old fashioned*—"But go for Jack Daniel's instead of bourbon and a cinnamon stick next to the orange peel," he advises. Apparently, he has changed it to a *new fashioned* drink with his alterations.

He has recognized that I need a spiritual lifeboat, as I am drowning in a million thoughts.

"Young man, in order not to lose our minds tonight, I suggest that we start trying to understand with our hearts, rather than with our minds. All I can tell you is that we all, at certain times, increase the frequency of coincidences when we mentally elevate a person who appears in our lives. We are able to do this without losing our inner connection, while at the same time tuning in perfectly to that person's frequency. Therefore, let us try to stay tuned in to the author without losing our own inner rhythm. If we can do this, we may eventually feel, instead of just understand, what we really need to experience."

We clink our glasses and stand in silence for several minutes. At other times, we don't have enough time to say all that we want to say, and here, we are unable to say a word. We are in this idyllic beachfront hotel, with cocktails in hand, and are unwilling to interact because we don't want to spoil this magical evening with trivialities.

What keeps bothering us for sure are all these similarities

that we interpret as mere coincidences to avoid completely losing our minds. It's extremely difficult to comprehend and accept the coexistence of the three of us in the same time dimension, within an infinite asynchronous dimension, where time and space lose their boundaries—within the Asynchronous Zone of Today, where the soul can travel whenever it wants but never the mind.

During the break, something else happens that I have never experienced. After only ten minutes and without any warning or announcement, we all begin returning to Sky Hall. Under no circumstances do we want to miss the train as it leaves the station. When the announcer calls for us to return to our seats, we are already there, physically and mentally. We have left the cool May breeze out at the poolside and have found a wintry December chill inside the hall.

The scene is now of a large station in a big city, and we can see snow that has piled up from the previous night when it snowed nonstop. The low temperature in the room enhances the setting; the air conditioners having performed their job well while we were outside.

The giant screens artistically bring Christmas into the room. Christmas lights dance to the rhythm of the song "Last Christmas," and a large Christmas tree stands proudly in the station square. Many of us sing along, mentally transported to the festive period. Once again, my mind discovers an opportunity to ponder. *What gift shall I get for Grace? What plans shall we make for spending the holidays with family? Where can we go with our friends to welcome the New Year?* Many other fleeting thoughts fall like snowflakes into the Sky.

I am mumbling, "This year, to save me from tears, I'll give it to someone special," when the lights are lowered again and our own personal Santa Claus comes onto the stage.

Station 3

The Old Friend

The best way to find yourself is to lose
yourself in the service of others.
—Mahatma Gandhi

December. What a blessing!

He opens his book and turns his eyes toward the pages. He clears his
voice until complete silence reigns in the hall. Our journey in the Sky
is about to resume.

• • •

Several months have passed since the day I met Dr. Time at Time
Station, but not a day has passed where I have not thought of him. On
many occasions over that period, I was tempted to give him a call to
catch up, but each time I thought that someone else needed his time
more than I did. I have framed his handwritten note so that it is forever
protected. It now hangs next to my travel log, under the electronic clock
that shows the time as well as the temperature of the train's interior.

My carriage doors are wide open and the temperature is minus
three degrees Celsius. I need to start greeting people and wishing
them *Merry Christmas,* but it is so cold that I do not dare step out

of the locomotive. Besides, I do not see anyone coming towards our train. *Well, everyone should be enjoying their Christmas holidays with their loved ones,* I tell myself.

Four station workers are furiously throwing salt on the train tracks, a reminder for me to check the weather forecast once more, until I am absolutely certain that the journey will be completed without any unforeseen trouble. One of them comes toward my side window, waving at me to open it.

"Good evening, my good friend! What do you reckon? Will you give us the green light to start?"

"Good evening, Captain! Haven't you received the update from the control room?"

"Not yet. What is wrong?"

"All routes have been canceled! A huge avalanche has covered the tracks completely, three miles from here. We have made all the relevant announcements at the main station building, and as you can see, it is now completely empty."

"Now it all makes sense! I cannot understand why the station master did not radio me. Tell him that as soon as I lock up here, I want to have a word with him!"

I pick up the radio and ask my team to join me in the driver's cabin.

"Well, guys, I've just been informed that an avalanche will be sending us off for Christmas Eve earlier than expected."

They all burst into cheers and applause.

"Since we are all here, I want to wish you a merry Christmas! I hope your wagon is full of your loved ones enjoying your good company. Make sure you all make good memories to add to your personal albums."

We exchange Christmas wishes. We hug and kiss, and within minutes, there is not a living soul on the train or in the station. I lock up my train, and I get myself ready for a fight with the station master, who neglected to give us notice earlier.

I am now in the main building, climbing up the stairs towards the station master's office. I end up in a long, dark corridor on the third floor. I walk past one closed door after another until I reach the end of the corridor and the last door. I can clearly hear rock music blaring from the office and spreading throughout the hallway.

The louder the music gets, the angrier I get, as I am now certain that the control room has been turned into an entertainment venue. I am convinced that behind the closed door, the entire station staff are standing around the stereo, drinking and partying. I am absolutely certain that this is taking place with the station master's blessings, and I stand outside the closed door, preparing myself for a big fight. The music is so loud that I decide it is utterly useless to knock, which would be the polite thing to do. With a determined push, I open the door. To my utter surprise, there is not a single soul in the room. I cast my anxious eyes over the desk—a half-empty bottle of superior whiskey, a coffee mug, scattered potato chips. The rest of the room is clean and tidy. The rock music is not my cup of tea at all, and I quickly turn it off. At last, there is absolute silence in the room.

"Who's there?" a thunderous voice booms behind a closed door next to a huge bookshelf overflowing with books.

"The captain of C77, who you obviously forgot to invite to your party," I exclaim abruptly, if not rudely.

For a couple of minutes, no one speaks. I hear some strange noises from behind the closed door. It sounds like a child is riding his bicycle and clumsily banging back and forth across the room. Finally, the door opens with difficulty, and the station master appears in a wheelchair. The first thing I notice are his still, slender legs. I try to find the courage to raise my eyes to his face, and when I do, I freeze! I am so tense that I can feel my heart pounding in my throat.

Time is also frozen; it carries me back in time at supersonic speed. It seems that not a day has passed since the last time we met. Truth be told, it's been decades since we served together in the military police. And I now recall the summer of our discharge, when we rode across the country on our Harley-Davidsons. Memories of us partying until morning with empty beer bottles in our hands—we lost count of the empty bottles—so drunk we couldn't move. This time around, it seems it is not the alcohol that's rendering this amazing man unable to move. What happened? I am determined to find out tonight.

"Back in our army days, you used to drive me crazy with your rock music, and from what I hear, you have not changed a bit." I regret this unfortunate comment as soon as I let it slip.

"You think so? As you can see, I put new wheels on my bike."

"Even your twisted sense of humor remains the same. You must admit, though, that I still am the most handsome of the bunch," I respond tactlessly, in an attempt to patch up the earlier gaffe and hide my embarrassment.

"Apparently, you did not get over that night when the Lebanese girl chose me to take her for a bike ride. It's about time you admitted that someone else was the charmer of the group." He keeps his eyes fixed on me, desperately seeking confirmation of his statement.

I quickly cover the steps separating us and give him a heartfelt, long hug, as well as the reassurance he seeks. "You were by far the coolest of us all!"

I hold him in my arms, and I feel two beasts struggling within my soul. The *black wolf of sorrow* and the *white wolf of joy* are devouring each other until one of them prevails. I choose to side with the white wolf, as the opportunity to catch up with my old friend trumps the sadness of seeing him confined to a wheelchair. As for the anger that brought me here, the black wolf grabbed it and disappeared down the snowy mountain slope.

"I have to admit that some things have indeed changed Mr. Station Master! For God's sake, whiskey in a coffee mug? And you, alone on such a lovely white night?"

He gives me a sly smile. He opens the second drawer of his desk and takes out another cup. He pours whiskey like it's coffee, passing it to me with glee.

"First of all, I'm not alone tonight, unless the years that have gone by, since the last time I saw you, have gifted you not just this hideous belly but myopia as well. Can't you see there are two of us in the room? Come to think of it, you're either blind or incurably discreet. Either way, I totally agree with you that some things have changed. Good things and ..."

"Bad things." The words escape my mouth while he pauses for thought.

"Good things and great things, my dear brother," he corrects me without a moment's hesitation, and his smile lights up the room like a spotlight. He takes a sip of disguised whiskey and leans his body toward me; it was obvious he was about to tell me something important. "My only mistake in this life is that I didn't get to marry that Lebanese girl, my brother. I remember, as if it was yesterday, when I took the microphone at your wedding, fixed my eyes on your wife, and told her that every summer, you and I would ride around the world on our motorcycles. Then, she got up from the wedding table, grabbed the microphone, and made a counter statement. Do you remember what she said to me that night?"

"Yes, I do remember! She said, 'I promise you that my husband's motorcycle will be sold next week! Tonight, I'm marrying an able-bodied man, and that's the way I want him until the end!' Oh, my brother," I exclaim with a heavy sigh, wiping away a tear.

"That's right. If my luck was similar to yours, tonight could have been completely different. We could be enjoying Christmas Eve dinner with our wives at your place!"

"Why did you disappear? The last time we spoke you were packing your bags to go to Arizona to study. After that, we only exchanged two or three messages, and then you fell off the face of the earth."

"I lost my way before I found myself, my brother."

"What does this mean? Do you want to tell me exactly what happened? I need to ask why you're in a wheelchair."

"Remember what I always told you guys? That all I wanted was to spend the rest of my life on two wheels? Well, be careful what you wish for, buddy! On one of my many road trips, down historic Route 66 to be exact, my wish finally came true."

"What happened?"

"I worked on my bike for a whole week. I was about to embark on the most demanding journey of my life. The goal was to get from

Arizona to Chicago riding 1,700 miles! Obviously, there would be stops along the way for rest and refueling. However, every morning, upon waking, the rush was always the same. You know what I mean— riding with a thousand horses between your legs and with the wind blowing through your long hair! Rider's 101: thirsty horses, eager rider, rock music in your ears, a leather jacket, and a bony finger on the brake."

"So far, so good. And then?"

"I made it all the way to Missouri; my exhausted body and my tired horses were looking for a quiet place to rest. Now, what I am about to tell you may sound like a lie. Even I couldn't believe my eyes when I saw it. The first suitable venue I came across had the most unexpected name! Oh, my dear brother, of all the names in the world, the neighborhood I'd arrived in and in which I used my legs for the last time in America was called … Lebanon!"

"Jesus Christ! Are you kidding me?"

"Nope, I wish I was! Some coincidences can surely drive you crazy! No need to say more about this sad story. You remember how many trips I made to Lebanon, trying to persuade stubborn Mr. Bilal to give his blessing for me to marry his daughter Roro. What were the odds?"

"So many huge what-ifs, my friend."

"Exactly! What if Roro had decided to spend her summer vacation of '97 in a different country? What if she had decided to visit a different bar instead of ours that night? Or what if she had decided to go for a ride with another man that night? And what if she had decided to disobey her strict dad and follow me back here? All these thoughts still haunt me every night. I imagine a different life, trying to understand the true meaning and purpose of the life I live now."

"I remember how tough it was for you back then."

"Then you can also understand that when I finally chose to spend the night in Lebanon, Missouri, rather than resting and sleeping, I got to watch my entire life flash before my eyes like a horror movie. I literally didn't sleep a wink that night; I relived the cruelest chapter of my life. As you can imagine, the only company I had was the minibar in the room—"our treat," the note read.

"Slowly and painfully, the sun came up at around seven that morning. The new day found me sitting on the balcony of the room, a broken man, holding an ashtray full of cigarette butts. I couldn't take my eyes off my motorcycle, parked right in front of the motel reception, under the dirty entrance canopy. That's when it started. Without realizing it, I began talking to my bike: 'How many roads and miles together, my dear? You alone have been faithful to me on every journey, my precious girl! Thank you, my love! Thank you for being with me to this day!'"

"Strange things, indeed!"

"Well, they were perfectly normal to my aching soul, my brother! An overwhelming dark feeling soon interrupted my conversation with her. I tried to bring myself around: 'What are you doing? You are not being serious now. Saying goodbye to a motorcycle?' I was talking to myself, uncontrollably shaking my head left and right, as if I would drive the negative thoughts out of my mind. This was the first time I'd ever had this strange feeling. It was like an omen!"

"How did this end?"

"I had a hot bath. All the negative thoughts, all the painful feelings found their way to the trash can, along with a dozen or so empty bottles of booze that I'd had for dinner the night before. I put my leather on, some rock music in my earphones, and woke up my horses."

"You decided to continue this challenging journey without a right wing? Completely unprotected and unaccompanied? Incomprehensible!"

"Maybe! But before you label me as reckless, I am telling you without hesitation that deep down, I knew that this was my last journey. It was like my last tragic trip to Lebanon, when Bilal had the police arrest me as I was showing him the diamond ring I had bought for Roro. Since I survived that, then I could endure the longest road trip alone. What was I supposed to do? Pick a moonless night to come and steal you from your sweetheart, or ring your doorbell and tell her that I needed my right wing? She'd have cut my legs off before I lost them myself."

"Can't deny that, buddy."

"So here I am, at dawn, riding down historic Route 66, with heavy eyelids from the night before. The last thing I remember was the sound of a loud truck horn. From there on, others took care of my ride."

"Oh my God! What are you talking about?"

"I'm about to tell you something that might be quite difficult to comprehend. As I was lying, there waiting for the ambulance to arrive, I felt a divine peace that I never felt before in my life. It is impossible to find the words to describe the experience in simple earthly terms."

"Please go on. I will do my best to follow."

"Think of it as lying naked on warm golden sand at a beach. The sun is about to set, and the light is playing tricks on you, with the sunbeams hiding behind little clouds. It's a very strange feeling, but you don't care about being naked because you soon realize that all the people passing by on this extraordinary beach are also naked like you. The weirdest thing of all is that even I—and you've known me well over the years—didn't sneakily stare at the naked women."

"As if that was ever possible!"

"And yet, how else can I explain it to you? It was as if we had no bodies at all! We looked at each other only to appreciate one another, without exchanging a single word, as if we didn't even have lips. One glance was enough to know who the other people were, what they did in their lives, and, most importantly, what had brought them to this celestial beach. Lying on the road, the pain was unimaginable, but now, on this sandy beach, I was in absolute peace. I spotted a boat in the distance, and I soon realized that it was my body. I was watching it as a bystander, looking at all the damage from the collision, but I was not *in it!* Do you understand what I'm trying to describe? The boat was cold, wet, and dirty. I didn't want anything to do with it. I just wanted to stay lying on the warm sand on the beach, enjoying the chime sounds coming from the sky."

"In other words, you were lying on the road, injured from the collision with the truck, but you were no longer in any pain?"

"The pain disappeared when I experienced an inner connection with the divine energy that existed on that beach. It was a feeling of lightness, as if I was a seagull flying over the boat—*over my body*. As I looked at it, right next to my shattered motorcycle, I didn't want to connect with it again; there was only pain left in that carcass. What bird would give up its wings to connect to a heavy burden?"

"So, what happened then?"

"I continued to enjoy the flow! It was an invisible flow of love! Like being madly in love with everyone and everything. Everything I cast my eyes on was a source of love. Everywhere I looked was a stream of love. Everything I touched energized me with a high-frequency sweet sound. Even when my invisible hands touched the pebbles in the sea, I received vibrations of love! What fool would sacrifice this paradise to return to a broken boat that is taking in water?"

"How do you explain all this?"

"I experienced something unreal, my brother. Once I experienced that dimension, I was already ready to fly like a bird and leave my last breath on Route 66. But as soon as I thought of this, a determined voice responded, *'You will leave your last breath in your book!'* I turned around to see who was talking to me. The scenery changed in a heartbeat; I was in a helicopter! I was seeing the panorama out of the window, and everything was crystal clear, as if I was looking into a camera lens. Then again, a clear voice: *"You will leave your last breath in your book."* I realized that the person who was talking to me was the helicopter pilot. He had not yet turned his head toward me so I could only see his helmet and hear him through my headset. For a moment, I thought that I was being airlifted to the nearest hospital. However, I could not know for sure because I was completely alone in the passenger compartment and was dressed in a suit and tie. Who, me? In a suit and tie on a private flight? Funny thing!"

"And then?"

"After two weeks of cutting and stitching my body in three consecutive surgeries, I finally decided to open my eyes. I soon realized what had happened and where I was, as the nurse at Missouri Hospital was quite descriptive. She made a mistake in her description, however, and I urged her to correct it. I told her that I was not brought in by an ambulance and that I actually had been airlifted. In fact, I asked her to put me in touch with the pilot, as we had discussed many things that morning that I couldn't remember at the time. Now, what can I tell you? You'll think that the whiskey has kicked in! But I can assure you it's not that."

"Come on, then."

"My brother, I never went to any warm beaches, nor did I find naked people. Most importantly, I never was on a helicopter! It had all happened in the realm of my wild imagination, the nurse explained. Some physiotherapy followed, and as soon as I found the strength, I took the first plane back home. And this is why I disappeared from your life."

"Did you finally write a book, or did you lose your appetite for life?"

"I accept the summer sunshine just as I accept the winter storm, my dear brother! You know why? Because now I am capable of choosing my own season on a daily basis. Putting all my past and current suffering aside, I never lost my sense of humor and my good mood. On the very first page of my book, I have noted, *Life has many stories. Not all of them are pleasant, so I chose the most beautiful one to tell you!* That's all my news, my brother."

"I'm so proud of your courage. You're amazing!"

"Just amazing? Not amazing and handsome?"

"Yes, my old friend. I must admit that you're even more handsome now. This experience, regardless of the disability, has given you the ability to lighten your pain. I guess that's how you finally managed to write your book. First thing tomorrow morning, I'm going to visit my neighborhood bookstore and buy your book. Next time I visit Bliss Station, make sure you're sober enough to write me a dedication."

"Did you really think you would leave tonight without a Christmas present? Here it is! Wrapped and personally inscribed to my best friend from the old days. I won't let you open it in front of me and burst into tears. We're big men, still riding our wheels, right? Go to your family; if you have some time, open it then."

"But, I don't get it. How did you manage to write the dedication and wrap it up? Since I invaded your office like a barbarian, I haven't let you out of my sight for a minute."

"My brother, the answer you seek has two parts. Your heart should try to grasp the first part. As for the second part, which is much easier, your mind will understand it."

"You're giving me a hard time again. Tell me what you mean!"

"That morning, as my body lay on the cold asphalt next to the metal scraps that used to be my motorcycle, my soul was picking up the remaining pieces of my life, making an exquisite quilt of square blocks. Each block of this one-by-two-meter quilt corresponded to the most important and meaningful chapters of my life, from the day I was *created* to that particular moment. In the first square, I saw myself standing over a stone-built well. In it, instead of water, there were pairs of crystals connected by a golden thread. As I tried to select a pair for myself, I realized that the choice was very difficult, as there were millions of options. They all sparkled brightly in my eyes, almost blinding me, as if they were trying to attract me. I closed my eyes and chose my own pair of crystals. As soon as I picked them up, the golden thread that bound them together grew longer and longer until it wrapped itself around both my wrists, like handcuffs. Then, the golden thread merged the two crystals into a large one. Its blinding light dimmed, and I got a glimpse of two smiling faces inside the crystal; they were my parents' faces! Not as I know them but as I remember them from photos taken when they were in their early twenties, when they had just met. What this meant, I guess, was that I had my parents before my parents had me."

"Unbelievable! I'm in shock!"

"Wait, there's more coming! In the next square block, I saw the day I was born into this world. It seemed like a movie playing before my eyes. I was never told that my father had fainted or that they rushed to revive him. There were others in the room that day, but I didn't know who they were. I was very happy to see them again and felt an incredible attraction and warmth, despite the fact that I had no idea who they were. To give you an idea of how confusing it all was, the one who really stood out was wearing a red cloak. As soon as my mom gave birth to me, this person put a strange ring on Mom's finger. Anyway, in another square block, I saw my school years; in the next one, my first time making love, and so on. I was able to see and enjoy each square, even the ones that reminded me of some difficult circumstances. Suddenly, my mother appeared, took this blanket in her hands, and covered my injured body. It was after that when I found myself on the beach I told you about, and then I found myself talking to the pilot."

"I really don't know what to tell you. I can't find the words to comment on what you're saying. I'm waiting to understand what this has to do with me."

"I'll tell you! But I repeat, try to understand it with your heart because the mind has not yet acquired this ability. Remember I told you that as I was looking out of the helicopter window, I saw everything with camera-lens sharpness? I could see an ant carrying crumbs to its nest, a mother cat feeding her kittens, two pigeons dancing on a branch. But most importantly, I could see, hear, and understand what was happening inside people's homes—not in each home individually but simultaneously and collectively. I was taking the pulse of entire neighborhoods. Once I thought to myself, *This can't be happening to me,* the signal started getting weaker and weaker. When I changed the frequency and contemplated, *It's my choice, and I can deal with it,* the signal became transatlantic, and I could hear and sense whole districts, states, countries, and then, the whole planet."

"Oh dear! And how did that feel?"

"Brother, there is only one word to describe it—pain! Unbearable pain! Pain everywhere! Pain in our bodies, in our hearts, in our minds, in our relationships, in our jobs, in our churches, in the parks, in the streets, and in our homes. Pain so intense that it turned my heart to stone. Then my heart slowly stopped beating and cut off the blood supply to my arteries, and my mind decided it was time for me to take my last breath. I closed my eyes, and I was ready to let the pain get me. It was beyond any human capacity to endure all that pain."

"I am shocked!"

"The most shocking thing is that in every corner of every home, there was help—a break, a solution, an answer, a blessing available to help ease their pain. Sadly, people bypassed all those aids like zombies! No one could see, no one could hear, no one could feel happy. They all carried an unbearable burden of heavy luggage. And it wasn't just these numerous aids they had before their eyes; there were also endless sources of inspiration at every corner of their neighborhoods. In every bookstore, in every school, in every church, in every wise man's home, there were signs that read, 'We buy weight at a great price!' Still, no one could walk in while everyone was hunched over from the weight."

"It is unthinkable!"

"Zombies, I tell you, looking for bargain prices and cheap solutions! They sold their values and their valuables to arm themselves with useless weapons to win the vanity battle. As you can imagine, I could see no more, hear no more, had no more strength to deal with the pain any longer. It was beyond my will and power. A second before I closed my eyes forever, you, my dear brother, interrupted me! Your voice still echoes in my ears: 'You will leave your last breath in your book!' I was amazed to see you! 'How did you get here, and more importantly, since when are you a helicopter pilot?' Those were my first words to you before we continued our illuminating conversation!"

"It's not much different to riding a motorcycle. You might as well be in the cockpit. In fact, I can take you anywhere by just reading your mind, your thoughts. A thought is a destination in itself, so you have to be precise. Your reflection is the coordinates, so be certain before you make your final decision. Your life depends on your next choice. Plan accurately, and you will reach your chosen destination;

plan inaccurately, and you will reach a destination you dislike. Fail to plan, and the captain will take you wherever he likes."

"I am exhausted, brother! It's all the unbearable pain I have experienced on this journey that has shattered my soul into a thousand pieces and my body into a thousand bits. Just fly me to my mother."

"Your mother flew to the angels when you were ten years old. I'm not entirely sure that she wants you to join her today. For that to happen, you must want no more, take no more, seek no more, endure no more."

"What more is there to do?"

"Light your way and lighten your pain! By doing so, you will enter your final coordinates into the helicopter's navigational system. I will simply follow your instructions to the letter. However, because of our brotherly relationship, I'm going to give you another option to consider. You may leave your last breath in your book."

"How?"

"Since you have been blessed to see, hear, and understand other people's pain, then I am sure you can do something about it. There's no value whatsoever in just looking down on them and feeling sorry for their pain. Get into their homes, in every house of every state, in every country, and generously share your experience with them in a book as a gift of life. Like the gift that God has given you today."

"What gift?"

"To see, hear, and understand the pain of other people and never give up. Choose to survive another hour, another day, another month, another year, until you complete your mission. If you choose this, then they will also have a choice."

"Complete what mission?"

"Learn how to lighten your pain, and then educate other people how to do so."

"And why would I want to do that?"

"Despite the pain that will accompany you on this journey, you will ultimately accomplish the purpose for which you are destined."

"And what would that purpose be?"

"To conceptualize and illustrate what happens just before someone decides to take their last breath! To describe the options available in that particular moment in Time Zero. To explain why you, personally, chose to give us your book, rather than give up your life."

"And why is this task so important?"

"Your words will encourage the desperate, awaken the asleep, welcome the lost, and above all, comfort those in pain. Your story will arm them with the inexhaustible power for self-improvement and the will to move forward. To live! To live a good life! You will leave your last breath in your book so that you get to educate the whole world on how to lighten their pain and live the happy lives they deserve! Do you hear me? You will leave your last breath in your book."

Our cups are now empty, and our hearts are full. With his eyes radiating love and optimism, he reaches out and hands me his book, wrapped in Christmas paper, while my eyes tear up.

"I warned you that the first part of my answer would require an open heart, rather than open ears. As for the second part, you're smart enough by now to understand why the station master never radioed you about the cancellation. When I saw your name on the list, it was like seeing the holy star pointing the way of your return to me. I was absolutely sure you would demand an explanation for being ignored, and I made sure to fuel your anger further with my rock music. My only wish for tonight is that the holy star will illuminate the way and pick up our friendship where we left off."

"That goes without saying. Your right wing is back!"

"I hope you like the book. I look forward to hearing your comments. I am also giving you my favorite rock music CD to listen to and to think of me whenever you miss me."

On my way out, I shut the door quietly and carefully—the same door I wanted to knock down a few hours ago. The corridor now seems to be a 1,700 miles long.

I don't remember how or when I got home, but I find myself parked outside my garage.

I don't remember us saying goodbye.

I don't even remember the drive from the station.

It was like a helicopter picked me up from Bliss Station and, within minutes, dropped me off at my house.

I have now been sitting in my car with the engine running for about ten minutes. Suddenly, my cell phone rings and interrupts my mental snooze. My watch reads seven o'clock in the evening, right on time for supper.

"Do you want me to serve your dinner in the car?" my wife says, chuckling.

I make up an excuse that I am checking out a noise in the engine. I turn to the passenger seat and pick up my friend's wrapped book. It is neither the right place nor the right time to give in to my curiosity and read it all in one go. Whatever he wrote, however long or short, I want to break it down into pieces like his magic quilt and absorb it bit by bit, square by square, breath by breath.

What I definitely swallow in one bite is the stuffed turkey my wife has prepared. She looks at me curiously, as I am still flying my helicopter. I haven't been able to land back to reality, even though several hours have passed. I limit myself to describing some highlights of my afternoon, but it is still impossible to share with her all the light I am carrying within. It is too much—almost unreal, I would say. I need time to digest and process it. Fortunately, I have all the time in the world over the Christmas holidays.

I pour some whiskey into a coffee mug and sit by the Christmas tree with my gift in my hands. I carefully unwrap it and hold my friend's life in my hands for a second time.

I check the book cover as well as the back of the book and stare at his picture, with my eyes brimming with tears.

I fix my gaze on his and think of his achievement: *From painful to painless with the right choices.*

I lose myself in his smile and mentally thank him for the best Christmas gift of my life.

Then, I bring the book close to my face. I smell it, browse the contents, read the publisher's contact information, all in an attempt to delay the climax of the evening as much as possible—reading my friend's dedication. This process is called *delaying gratification,* as taught by my beloved Dr. Scott Peck.

I flip through to the end. I do the math to figure out whether there is a possibility of reading 273 pages in one night.

The clock on the fireplace gets on my nerves with its heavy ticking. Of my classical music collection, I choose my favorite, Beethoven's "Moonlight Sonata," to isolate two major distractions—the annoying ticking of the clock and the noise coming from the kitchen.

I look again at the clock; it's time!

I kiss my wife good night and I warn her, "I'll be a little late; I want to read his book."

"Don't stay up too late, please! You promised to go Christmas shopping with me tomorrow morning, remember? If you don't wake up early, I'll go alone, and I will probably forget your present. You'll find an empty stocking by the fireplace," she warns, knitting her brows.

I take a generous sip of fine whiskey, put my glasses on, and finally open the book at page seven, where my personal dedication begins ...

(7)

My captain!

Thank you for the trip and for helping me get the coordinates right. I have not yet reached my final destination, and I have not yet taken my last breath. Thankfully, the quest continues until its purpose is achieved.

Dalai Lama said, "The purpose of life is to be happy." Who can argue with that? But what is happiness?

In my journey while writing my book, I learned that happiness is something personal and special, as special as my breathing. And no one can breathe for me, no matter how much they love me, no matter how much they want to help me.

Happiness has four ingredients. First of all, it requires a dose of *freedom* and a dose of *health*, just enough to allow participation in the experiences one wants to go through. Just a dose! There are many who wait for the perfect day when everything will be as they imagine, but happiness begins today, through our gratitude for the gift of life. Research done in 1978 by Brickman, Contes, and Janoff Bulman showed that paraplegics who lost their legs alongside lottery winners were just as happy a year after the event. And I tell you that I am no less happy today than I was when we were riding together every night. Remember?

(8)

What are the other two ingredients of happiness? It requires a strong dose of *purpose* to inspire your active participation and many doses of *quality relationships* to facilitate the release of positive emotions.

So, freedom, health, purpose, quality relationships! All four ingredients are multidimensional. That is why when one thinks about happiness, one gets lost and concludes that it is an abstract concept. Something we cannot perceive with our senses but only with our cognition. But we know very well that we feel happiness. We feel it when something good happens to us, and we feel it when we do something good. Happiness comes out of good; it sounds absurd to me to expect something good to happen to me in order to feel happy, while I, myself, do nothing good. There is nothing simpler than doing something good—not necessarily extraordinary, just something good!

Everyday when I wake up, I say, "Thank you, God. Thank you for giving me the opportunity to be, to feel, to have, to hope, and to keep dreaming!" And then I ask God to fill me with love in order for me to sow love. To make me able to give good so that I am allowed to receive good. Goodness for me, for those I care about most, for those who need it most.

(9)

Choose to have goodness.

Everyone needs it, and everyone can give it! Choose to have goodness! This is what I wish for me, for you, and for the whole world.

Another breath, another good deed, and never give up no matter how much it hurts! The most precious thing in the world is our *perseverance* until we complete our life's purpose, with a little help from God.

With love,
Your old friend

His dedication is great—huge, incredible! His words fill pages seven, eight, and nine, but the meaning fills my heart with goodness.

My good old friend, who lost his way before he found himself, like another Odysseus! Our brotherly friendship was forgotten for a while, but its flame was rekindled and revived our reunion. I am left staring at it, unable to turn the page and continue to the first chapter. I read the dedication one more time, then close the book for a few minutes. I am looking at the bright star on the top of our Christmas tree and recall his last words: *My only wish for tonight is that the holy star will illuminate the way and pick up our friendship where we left off.*

Then I glance at my wedding photo on the dining room table, the glass frame reflecting the lively dancing of the Christmas tree lights. How many parties and gatherings that dining room could have witnessed if my friend had finally convinced Bilal to allow him to marry his daughter, the love of his life. I feel so sad about it that I unconsciously stand up and turn the tree lights off. The living room is now more peaceful than ever. I can see the purple flame in the fireplace and have the unquenchable fire inside me to read the book in one go. I turn on the lamp on my side table, turn the music down, and finally turn to page ten.

I am immersed in a vast ocean of emotions, memories, desires, images, and hallucinations. Just before dawn, and as I reach the final chapter of the book, I stop feeling human. I see myself as a boat, made of oak wood, battered and knocked around. I feel like I should have been in the shipyard for repairs or sunk to the bottom of the ocean; nevertheless, I am still in the harbor next to the other well-built boats. I see people passing by and stopping to stare at all the fishing and sailing boats moored and roped alongside each other, but no one stops to look at me. Most of the boats have their nets neatly tucked away and tidied up in waterproof bags. Their ropes are carefully coiled in a corner, and their life jackets are hung prominently, standing by to aid. The sailboat hulls are strong, with keels of thick wooden plank; their footing is curved and high at the bow and low at the stern for calm and safe sailing. Their polished aluminum fitting, poles topped with different flags and names emblazoned on their sides, each tell of their travels and adventures, crafting their stories, inspired by their individual journeys across the seas.

I, on the other hand, am a boat without a name. I never have been able to tell anyone my own stories. I kept them all inside me under heavy anchor. I did not dare to go out and fight the furious waves of the sea because I was afraid! I was terrified at the thought of telling my own story and being devoured by the first bloodthirsty shark. I had chosen to stay tied to the safety of the harbor, letting time and the salty water adorn me as I deserved. While the heavy legacy bestowed on me was strong and sturdy, made from the trunk of a century-old oak tree, I had left that, too, to the mercy of time.

No one looks at me; I have no worth and no name. I remain nameless and useless, with nothing to offer. The other boats inspire interesting stories; I am a rusty, battered boat, attracting no interest from anyone.

As I reach the last paragraph, I am ready to name this book *A Tide of Emotions*. When the tide came in, all the boats, large and small, the luxury sailboats and the cheap, tattered fishing boats and cruising boats, were all lifted up toward the sky. They all came closer to the sun, and its rays would light up and warm them. When the tide went out again, all the boats returned back down to the calm of the sea. Up and down with the tide. The only boats that couldn't make the constant, repetitive journey of the *Tide of Emotions* were the ones that were covered in holes and were taking in water everywhere. There was no way they could tackle the positive emotions of the tide without eventually sinking.

The only reason I survived was thanks to the two boats tied on either side of me.

A noise from the bedroom wakes me abruptly! Before I cast my eyes to the clock on the fireplace, I manage to read the names of the two boats. The boat on my right is called *God Is My Captain*, and the boat on my left is called *Family and Friends*.

The clock ticks loudly; it's seven o'clock in the morning. A red blanket covers me, and the fire has been out for hours. I hold his book on my chest, on the left side, where my heart, my family and friends are. I let the tears flow until my soul is cleansed. I hurriedly open the drawer of my side table and reach for a pen. I turn to the last blank page of the book. I start writing as my soul dictates:

> Today, as another wonderful day dawns, before I put my feet on the floor and take my first step, I will count my blessings, one by one. Once I have filled ten books of blessings, I will thank God, who is always by my side, for His goodness in granting me another twenty-four hours. Merry Christmas. December 2017.

"Good morning darling. Merry Christmas! Were you comfortable on the couch?"

"Merry Christmas, my love. Well, not really!"

"Don't tell me that you are tired."

"No, I don't think so. What time is it?" The fool's role play is a disaster, getting the proper answer.

"The clock is right across from you, and I am quite sure you have been watching it all night. I'm going shopping, and you make sure you make up for the sleep you missed. We are having a barbecue party for twelve people tonight, in case you forgot."

"Thank you, darling. I'm going straight to bed. Will you forgive me?" I plead, trying to convince her with my best baby-face expression.

"Just tell me what gift you want Santa Claus to bring, you naughty boy!"

"I want Santa to help me write the book I've always talked about. I want to be a writer!"

"I'm sorry, but I don't perform miracles." That was her final shot before slamming the door on her way out.

● ● ●

The giant screens are alive, landing us violently from 2017 into today. We see a photo of three boats, side by side, while Natassa Bofiliou supplies the coup de grace with her angelic voice singing "S' Eho Vrei Kai Se Hano."[5]

> I've found you and I'm losing you, borrowed presence.
> I have so much to do, and there's no substance to it.
> Some days I hear your voice in the silence.

Every soul in the Sky is now deeply moved by the story, the song's video clip, and the lyrics of the song, as if Roro is dedicating it to her lost soul mate. As if the author is dedicating it to his friend from old days.

A bunch of people rush onstage to change the setting. The only one able to get up and rush backstage is the captain of our hearts,

---

[5] If you want to find us in the Asynchronous Zone of Today, search for the song on the internet, and enjoy it with us right now.

while the rest of us are still sitting, enjoying the song, having no strength to get up, even for a brief stretch. We all feel paralyzed from the waist down as we stare at the photo still on the screens. I cannot take my eyes off the middle boat as I whisper with joy, "From painful to painless with the right choices!"

Station 2

The Teacher

Too often we underestimate the power of a touch,
a smile, a kind word, a listening ear, an honest
compliment, or the smallest act of caring, all of
which have the potential to turn a life around.
—Leo Buscaglia

January. What a blessing!

We are back in the train's cabin with our beloved captain in the driver's seat. He opens his book and continues his narration in a hoarse voice. Fatigue has begun to leave its mark on his voice but his passion remains the same. I take a quick glance at my watch; entering the third hour, it still feels like the story has just begun.

● ● ●

It was by far the best Christmas ever! Despite the fact that I was a naughty boy, Santa Claus forgave me and didn't put coal in my stocking. He gave me a fine pen, with a note asking me to forgive my wife for not believing in miracles and telling me that he would help me to change her mind, since my pen has magic powers. With the magic ink, I will write my first word, then my first paragraph, and then complete my first chapter! I will write nonstop until I complete my mission and achieve my purpose. That way, the dream will come true, and my wife will finally believe.

We look forward to tonight's New Year's Eve party with our close friends at our place. The wedding photo has been removed from the dining table to make room for all the delicacies we have prepared. The clock reads seven in the evening, and we are surrounded by good company! Everyone is joyful and in the holiday spirit. The girls are sitting in the living room by the fire, enjoying their cherry liqueur and chats. They don't look particularly hungry, so we send Danny inside on a secret mission—to bring another dish out to us in the backyard. So far, so good, as the girls are excitedly discussing a matter of concern to Lena.

We, on the other hand, wearing scarves, hats, and gloves are trying to get some warmth from the barbecue fire and our whiskey. Lucas asks me to put on some music to warm up our minus-five-degrees-Celsius party. All at once, I remember his CD and warn everyone that we're going to rock. Where I expect reactions and disagreements, they all say in unison, "Thank God, a year without Beethoven!"

I press PLAY, and the first song is the famous Scorpions' ballad, "Send Me an Angel." The lyrics—*here I am; will you send me an angel?*—fly me at supersonic speed at Bliss Station. It's just a short flight, as my good company lands me back home by clinking glasses and shouting loudly, "Happy New Year boys!" Happily, I have just managed to also clink a cup with my old friend before leaving his station.

The only girl who interrupts our minus-five-degrees nirvana every now and then is my dear sister, with the order, "Don't burn the chicken wings again, Chef! I like them medium-well, like Grandma used to order them, you hear me?"

The third time I hear this request, I make sure to respond accordingly. "The apple never falls far from the tree! Same name, same grace." Of course, I'm referring mockingly to the quirky character of our grandmother. My sister leaves with a dismissive smile, while the rest of the group clink glasses to toast my brother-in-law's undying patience.

The chicken wings are indeed saved from burning, whereas the party is on fire all night! The coordinates set at the beginning were just right—good company, good mood, good manners, good intentions, good progress, and good timing. All the necessary ingredients for creating another good memory!

The next day, my wife finds a house bombarded by the partying, and I find a head bombarded from drinking! She is kind enough to suggest I go for a walk while she tries to clean the battlefield. It sounds like a directive rather than a suggestion, as she will not want me lazing around, so I have only one choice—take two painkillers for my headache, put on my trainers, and disappear from the house.

I walk out the front gate, take the first right, and walk at a slow pace down Liberty Street, just across the main avenue. Parallel to this road is a divine thirty-mile nature trail, consisting of rivers, trees, bushes, flowers, and whatever else has survived the city's concrete. It's astonishing that this arterial paradise is located in the center of the city to infuse oxygen and positive energy into all those who discover it.

I cross the avenue at a brisk pace, and in just a few steps, my right foot is touching nature as my left remains momentarily on the concrete. One ear listens to the birds, and the other one, the frantic vehicles. Carbon dioxide from the cars on my right, and God's oxygen from the assemblage of trees on my left. I need just one more step to slip in and be lost in a seductive green world.

Very few people choose the same itinerary. It's the first day of the New Year, and most of them have better things to do than walk alone on a nature trail. However, I am not discouraged by this, and I start taking pictures with my cell phone and forwarding them to our group. I notice that the name of the group has changed from "Men Only" to "Minus Five," but I can't remember which one of us did it. I might have some memory lapses from excessive drinking. I am not getting any comments, or thumbs-up, or likes for my early-morning nature photos; clearly, the other four members are still enjoying their sleep.

As my headache fades away, I pick up speed, and my pace is now more intense. The open-air exercise is warming my body, and nature is warming my soul. Time passes pleasantly, and more and more nature lovers make their presence on the trail. Some daredevils in short sleeves warm up before their run, while others, smothered in scarves and windbreakers, walk at low speeds.

My mind is full of good memories crafted from last night, and the thought of finally starting the book that I have neglected for so many years is constantly on my mind. I get even warmer and envision that my book has already been published. I am blessed to have become a best-selling author, and I am already famous in my city. This fleeting vision brings a smile to my face, and since I am now recognizable, I feel I should politely greet every fellow citizen on my path.

"Good morning and happy New Year, my dear! How are you feeling this wonderful day?" It's my first unsuccessful attempt to communicate with the lady coming from across the trail, just before the Swiss shepherd accompanying her comes within breathing distance of my chattering teeth. Next to receive my joyful arrows is a couple in their sixties who, when I greet them, both bow their heads, mumble some incomprehensible words, and go on their way.

"Strange things," I declare loudly and look to make sure I am properly dressed. Perhaps my smile was not big enough. By the time I have thought about this, I have encountered three girls and a boy. The Joker smiles, and his tongue dissolves again. "Happy New Year, guys!" This definitely spooks them. The girls gather behind the boy's back while he puffs out his chest like Superman.

I feel lost, as I can't tell the difference between welcoming people to the first carriage and greeting people while walking down the trail. I am utterly disappointed when my social experiment is confirmed as a failure by almost all other passersby. It makes no difference whether it's a man or a woman, young or old, in a hurry or relaxed. Only a few respond to my good wishes and smiling signals. The only one who cheerfully greets me is a three-year-old girl, pushed by her mother in a stroller. While her mother wears huge black sunglasses that cover half of her face, like a tombstone of emotions, the little girl, unlike her, stares into my eyes and sends me a flying kiss with her palm. I take her kiss and try to find my way back home, troubled by my thoughts. I open the main entrance door, expecting to find the house still a mess and my wife in despair. How she has managed to make the house like new and treat herself to a warm shower in only ninety minutes is like *Mission Impossible.*

I sit glumly on the couch and wait patiently for my turn in the shower. I still suffer from the spiritual assault I felt along the nature trail—and on the very first day of the New Year!

"The trail should be called Trail of Pain," I mutter as I head to the kitchen for a glass of water. On the refrigerator door, along with the dozens of magnets and notes my wife sticks there, I gaze at a Post-it note in unfamiliar handwriting that reads "Hope Wanted."

My wife walks into the kitchen wearing her white bathrobe, with water dripping from her hair. "Hi, my love. Has your headache gone?"

"Yes, thank you."

"Did you enjoy your nature walk?"

"Hope wanted ..." I reply, holding up the piece of paper.

"Yes, it's a book title. Olivia wrote it down for me last night."

Without realizing the pain my morning walk has caused me, she returns to the bathroom to dry her hair. My headache has been driven away with two painkillers, but my mental pain needs something much stronger than that.

The afternoon is much more enjoyable, as it's my sister's turn to host a celebration gathering. They've organized a party full of games, banter, and laughter. I anxiously await the time for the exchanging of gifts, as I am very proud of my choices this year. For my brother-in-law, I got a board game called Patience Maze. Basically, you try to guide your ball to the finish line, located in the center of the maze, and every time you awkwardly touch it against the walls, a light electric shock hits your hand through the stick you are using to guide the ball. In the greeting card, I didn't fail to express my praise for all the shocks he absorbs from my sister on a daily basis.

Once the loud laughter and teasing has stopped, my sister doesn't fail to remind me, once again, how big and curved my nose is, and, therefore, the only explanation for us growing up together as siblings is that I'm most probably an adopted child.

"A gorgeous woman like me could never be gene-related to someone like you" forms another of her apt arguments. I hold my fire and wait patiently for her to open her own gift to find the response she needs inside. It's a huge plastic chicken wing that I bought from the pet store. The label reads, "Intended for large-sized dogs that are obsessed with chewing and destroying everything." My card reads, "It's cooked well-done! Enjoy your meal, my Doberman! I love you very much!"

Our jokes, teasing, and laughter over the silly gifts we gave each other continue until midnight. The best gift is from Alexis, who had conspired with my wife a week before. It's a book of blank pages, with the title I want to give to my book on the cover. Alexis asked for an inscription on the first blank page, and they all started mocking me for my overconfident attitude as I wrote my autograph with a flourish. They commented that once I become rich and famous, my "Italian nose" will become a snooty nose, and I won't be hanging out with them anymore. Alexis makes me promise to deliver my real book in a year's time. They also make me swear to them that we will always be a crazy bunch, no matter how curved or snobbish my nose is.

My sister takes the opportunity to declare to everyone, "As soon as my big brother becomes a famous writer, he will pay off all my loans!" She doesn't seem to mind my nose's shape anymore, as she envisions her "adopted" brother paying off her debts.

The Christmas holidays passed by like a morning breeze, and I am already at the train station, getting ready for my seven o'clock morning route. All routes are confirmed, despite the sky being gray and full of heavy clouds. My predictions are also confirmed, and traffic is very low at the station. For one such shift, I summon the second captain and two cabin attendants only. Under normal circumstances, the team consists of ten people: the captain, who has overall command,

and the engineer, the second captain, the wagon master, and six cabin attendants.

The second captain brings me the final report from the ticket office: seventy-three passengers on board and 177 empty seats on our eleven-carriage train. The report shows about seven travelers in each twenty-five-seat carriage. The ticket issuer, in such rare cases, has the responsibility to place the passengers as scattered as possible for safety purposes. You will never find all passengers seated on one side or crammed into one wagon leaving the rest of the train completely empty. This is probably the first time I have no passengers in the first carriage—2A—that accommodates our distinguished travelers.

Our train offers three options. A regular train ticket will take you to the economy seats, located in the last seven carriages. Two carriages ahead and with the price rising significantly, you will be escorted to your business-class seat, where you can read your daily newspaper and enjoy some complimentary treats. Those who can afford it and wish to travel in carriage 2A, which is right behind the captain's carriage, C1, will be comfortably attended to their personal cabins in the first-class carriage.

Traveling first class means that passengers have their own private cabin that has walls that are luxuriously clad in walnut. On the left are two bunk beds; in the middle, a small lounge with three comfortable seats; and on the right, a small study desk. Passengers have the option of locking their cabin doors by leaving the red plastic tag bearing the message "Rest time," should they wish not to be disturbed. Inside the cabin, there is a small fridge containing refreshments and snacks, and there is also an attendant call button, if they wish to order anything else their hearts desire.

Last year, my request to upgrade C77 train was accepted, and now we offer multiuse sockets with USB ports in every seat and internet access via Wi-Fi. After this much-needed upgrade, my train was renamed C77i. Last but not least, pets are also allowed on the train, once prior permission is obtained and the appropriate ticket is issued.

All is set! It's exactly seven o'clock in the morning, and I have the green light to start my route. My right hand is raising the gear knob to position DRIVE, and with my left hand, I slowly accelerate the speed dial until it shows one hundred miles per hour. I then select the orange button marked with a capital alpha. Captain—A—will make sure we maintain a constant speed on uphill and downhill gradients and will constantly monitor the electromechanics of the whole train. He'll keep the interior temperature as comfortable as possible and will stream music to all wagons. If he has anything to report, he will flash one of the fifty buttons on the control panel and claim my attention.

I've put on the CD of Christmas songs to supply ninety minutes of nonstop joyful music that will fit my mood like a glove for the duration of my first journey of the year. It's impossible to predict the unexpected meeting to come; I am totally convinced that it will be a boring ride, as I am entirely alone in the first two wagons. Having this thought in my mind, I am again overwhelmed by the fear that something might happen to my health that will leave me no time to radio for help. And this is all my fault, as on holiday I ate and drank as if it were the end of the world. I think of the classic New Year's resolution—this year I will enroll at the gym—as I take a fleeting glance at my tummy that now competes with Santa Claus's belly.

My old friend was absolutely right about my belly, I muse, sinking even deeper into guilt. I am saved by the radio as it interrupts my thoughts about my weight.

"Joanna for Captain. Over."

"Go ahead Joanna. Over."

"Permission to approach. Over."

"Only if you are carrying a hot coffee with brown sugar. Over."

"Confirmed. Over."

"Roger that. Over and out."

I'm waiting for Joanna and my coffee while "Jingle Bell Rock" plays over the speakers. I open my desk drawer and take out one of the ten wrapped books I brought for my team. On the first blank page, I've written a small dedication, leaving room for the author to write his own. I have already warned him on the phone, as I was leaving the bookstore, holding the books, that he will need to sign them all the next time we visit Bliss Station.

On the CCTV screen, I see Joanna standing outside my cabin door. She's wearing a green elf cap and is making funny faces at me. She holds the coffee cup close to the camera until the lens is completely fogged by hot steam. I can see nothing now, as the naughty elf is drawing a happy face on the camera glass! I punch in the security code and open the door for her.

"Welcome to the captain's lair, naughty elf!"

"Your coffee, hot and steaming, my fat Santa Claus!"

Was it truly necessary to call me that? My mind briskly returns to my bloated belly, and I get lost in negative thoughts once again.

"Do you want your coffee, or shall I take it back?"

"Thank you, my dear! Don't tell me you're all wearing elf caps."

"Affirmative, Captain!"

"And you've convinced Jason to wear one too?"

"Of course. We left him no choice!"

"I feel sorry for my second captain! Well, I will not accept any disunity on my train. Be sure to find an extra-large one to fit my big head, OK?"

"Roger that, Captain!"

"Joanna, as a token of my appreciation, please accept this small gift, accompanied by my gratitude for working with me today and putting up with me for a whole year."

"Thank you very much, my dear captain. May I open it?"

"Of course!"

I explain who the author is, where he works, and that we will get his dedication and autograph.

"Captain, I have some great news to report. We have a VIP on our train!"

"Are you sure? Last time I checked, 2A was completely empty."

"Indeed, but she is humble enough to travel like ordinary people do. Other passengers spotted her in carriage 7, and they are taking photos and chatting with her."

"Don't tell me that we have Jennifer on board because my wife will kill me if I don't get an autograph!"

"Who is Jennifer? Anyway, her name is Jane, and she is the best teacher in the world!"

"Who?"

"The one who won first prize for being the best teacher in the world, among thousands of other nominees? The one who managed to come on top out of hundreds of competing countries? The one who gave interviews to many magazines? The one who was on all TV morning programs and on the eight o'clock news? Really? You have no idea who I'm talking about?"

"I really have no idea, but seeing you so excited, I suppose it is a great event indeed. Here's what I propose. As soon as she finishes with the rest of the passengers, you'll tell her that we are all so delighted to have her on board, and we want to offer a seat in carriage 2A for the rest of the journey. Make sure she accepts the upgrade and help her move to the first carriage. Understood?"

"Excellent idea, my captain! Thank you very much. As soon as I get her up front, I'll let you know. Thanks for your friend's book. I'll read it and let you know."

Joanna hurries off to perform her duty while I do a web search for our special passenger. I'm left speechless by her accomplishments, ethics, and philanthropy. And truly delighted! I am now hoping that she will accept the upgrade so I get the chance to reach out and meet her in person. I turn my gaze to my board to look at Dr. Time's referral.

"Will this be another special meeting?" I ask myself out loud.

Donning my captain's jacket and hat, I take a quick look in the mirror, straighten my crooked tie, and hopelessly try to button the jacket in a desperate attempt to hide my belly. It will not close at all, to the point that I am annoyed all over again. Grabbing my cell phone, I send a text to the perpetrator: "From today, I want you to please stop treating me with your delicacies. Starting from tonight, I want a plain pumpkin soup ONLY!" The word *only* was in capital letters because my wife will make the soup but will not fail to accompany it with many tasteful sins.

Joanna rings at my door, making the OK sign with her fingers to the camera. I pick up the radio and call Jason to the cockpit. He will have to take off his green elf hat and assume his captain duties for as long as I will be wearing my student's hat.

Ms. Jane has already made herself comfortable in private cabin E4, located on the right-hand side of the carriage. It was Joanna's good idea to pick this side, as all that is visible to the left for the last twenty minutes of the journey is an industrial area, while the evergreen forest continues to the right.

I enter carriage 2A and discreetly knock on the half-open door of the private cabin. Jane jumps up from her seat and opens the door wide.

"Please don't get up. I am here to make sure that you are comfortable enough in your new seat." I extend my hand for the customary handshake.

"Good morning. I'm Jane, and it's nice to meet you, dear captain. You shouldn't go to all this trouble. I was perfectly fine in my previous seat. Then again, this place is amazing! I didn't expect such luxury on a train. And so much kindness from everyone. I'm really impressed! A big thumbs-up!"

"Thank you very much for your kind words. The train has been recently refurbished to provide all the latest amenities and, obviously, a few more facilities for our distinguished passengers."

"Excellent! Excuse me for asking, but who's navigating the train as we speak?"

This brings a smile to my face, and I answer her directly. "Very good point. For every journey there are two captains. This gives me a chance to socialize now and then. But I won't bore you any further with my chatter. I'll leave you to enjoy your private cabin and get back to my wheel."

"No one can really enjoy something if left alone. Unless, of course, the real need is for silence and isolation. Since you know that I am an ordinary teacher, quiet and solitude are not in my repertoire."

"Not just an ordinary teacher? The best teacher in the world, from what I know! My congratulations, Ms. Jane! You have made us all very proud."

"Thank you very much! I would never have accepted such an honorary title if this recognition had not come from my students themselves, their parents, and my school. Simply put, I did not pass the exam on paper but on the field, if you know what I mean."

"Indeed! I have read your accomplishments, and you do deserve this distinction."

"Why have you remained standing, my dear captain? Perhaps you would like me to accommodate you in my private cabin," she returns with a smile.

"You are very kind. I'll accept your invitation if you'll allow me to buy you a drink and ask you a couple of questions that are troubling my mind."

We continue our small talk until Joanna arrives with a ginger and cinnamon tea for Jane and a fresh coffee for me.

"Joanna is a lovely girl. Congratulations on your crew! I imagine this is the result of your leadership."

"It's the result of our combined actions. Operations acquires substance with cooperation, hence the prefix *co* from the word *combine*. Cooperation produces added value to operation."

"Oh, my dear, how lovely! Are you a former colleague and you are hiding it from me?"

Bitterly regretting the time wasted in small talk with Dr. Time, I don't let a minute go to waste and go straight into the investigation phase. "Unfortunately, not. But I did grow up with the greatest teacher in the world. Really, may I ask you a question?"

"Of course, but don't leave me wondering who this great benefactor in your life was."

"My grandfather. I was blessed to be raised by two amazing parents, but I got my spiritual nourishment mostly from him. He inspired me to work for almost two decades in the training and development sector. I coached executives and employees with some success, I have to admit."

"You see! We are indeed colleagues. Oh, how nice! I never expected to find myself in a VIP seat, along with a distinguished fellow traveler on this trip."

"I am enslaved by your kindness."

"You've had your hand raised for some time now, and I've been ignoring you. What is your question?"

"I experienced an event yesterday that has shaken me. Do you believe in hope?"

"Although your question is vague—meaning that it can be interpreted as 'Believe in our inner hope,' or 'Believe in a higher form's hope,' or even 'Believe in the human species' hope to survive,' I will answer with a brave and forthright yes to all. Because quite simply, hope is the only value that has been with us indelibly for centuries. Hope is the last thing we lose before we give up our last breath. Do you want to tell me what triggered this concern so I can be more specific?"

"That is a genuine coaching question! Are you sure we're not colleagues, Coach Jane?"

"Get rid of all the titles and roles to discover who we really are! Under our Father Heaven and on our Mother Earth, we are all brothers and sisters. If this is ever truly understood, think of how our lives will ultimately change. We will march to help and comfort. We will shoot bullets of love. We will kill the pain and frighten the fear. We will deplete hunger and eliminate poverty. But don't let me get ahead of myself because, as a teacher, I like to ramble. So tell me, what happened that made you lose or look for hope?"

I stare into her eyes like a puppy, wanting her to continue to embrace me with her words. I want her to keep throwing me the ball of knowledge and keep me running like crazy to catch it. I manage to gather my thoughts and describe to her my experience on the nature trail. She listens carefully without interrupting. I get it all out of my system and calm down. I now have my ears open, and I am ready for her response.

"When you ask me about hope, I feel sure that some outer event, something outside of you—a third force, if you want to call it that— is affecting you in a negative way. Hope, my dear captain, is a flame that lives and dies with us. Thankfully, God, even with the most wannabe killers of hope, leaves a small flame smoldering within. No one has been able to extinguish it completely over the centuries. The dying still hope for grace, the hungry still hope for a loaf of bread, the unfortunate still hope for a chance, the sad still hope for a laugh, the unhappy still hope for a dram of happiness, and those in pain still hope for a moment without suffering."

"But I tried to ease their pain, my teacher. I am referring to all those people I met on the path, and not one of them accepted my pain-care kindness! Why?"

"They either don't need it, or they don't deserve it. The American writer Richard Bach interpreted it for us very simply: 'Allow the world to live as it chooses and allow yourself to live as you choose!' But why are we talking about other people? Are they sitting here with us, and I don't see them? Do you want to talk about hope or not?"

"Yes! Please tell me the magic solution."

"Listen carefully, then. I have infinite hope inside me; hence, I offer help and support to all my students. I do not seek hope from the world, but I give hope to the world. And I know how to disguise hope and offer it even to those who misuse the word *proud*. There is no pride in those who reject help and support, only insanity. Every student, every person, all living things have different needs. Even your classmate, your best friend, your twin brother, who shares so much in common with you, will have a different need than you. In conclusion, there is no magic solution that fits all. You will have to dig very deep until you discover the real need that each soul has."

"Do you have an example to share and help me understand this better?"

"One day I was substituting for a sick colleague who teaches at the primary school. I walked into the classroom and found ten little angels looking at me strangely. After introducing ourselves, I then asked them to each take a piece of cardboard and write on it—in big letters and in a single word—what they want to do when they grow up. Do you want me to tell you the answers I got that day?"

"I'm listening with the greatest of interest! You've piqued my curiosity. I suppose they all want to be doctors and save us from pandemics."

"You see the mistake you made? The same as I did, so I don't blame or judge you. Even I was intending to get them to think about how they imagine themselves when they're grown up. What profession they want to pursue, right?"

"Exactly! Where is the mistake in that?"

"The mistake was clear! I was just not the right teacher for those ten little philosophers. They didn't tell me what they want to do but what they want to be! Do you understand that? What a huge difference it makes! How much wisdom is behind it."

"I find it hard to understand the difference."

"Give me a minute to find the picture I took of them that day, and you'll know exactly what I mean. I still have it in my photo album on my phone."

As Jane searches for the ten philosophers, I philosophize about the deep meaning of our conversations. All I know for sure is that I am speaking with yet another luminous passenger on my train.

"There!" she shouts happily, turning her phone screen to me.

Sure enough, I see a picture of ten little people shedding some true light on all of us.

"I'll zoom in so that you can read what they wrote, and pay careful attention. Their answers were as follows to the question, 'What do you want to be when you grow up?': useful, cheerful, respectful, faithful, resourceful, mindful, grateful, thoughtful, purposeful, and insightful."

Jane remains emotional, and I am left speechless. If it weren't for the photo as evidence, I would never have believed such a story, even if it was told by the best teacher in the world.

She wipes her eyes and clears her voice to continue stoically. "Obviously, this is the result of good coaching by their teacher and their parents. So, how come a former coach and well-respected captain, with so many experience-miles on his clock, asks me if we have or need hope? With trees like these flourishing in our elementary schools, hope will never be lost. Rather, it will create a cluster of *illuminating trees* that will choke out even the toughest concrete. Hope is the foundation—our roots—and we all know what an earthquake can leave behind if the foundation is not strong enough. Whoever plants a tree plants hope. But just as trees need water, light, and care, hope needs sustenance. Hope is the roots, and if hope is strong, then let the earthquake and the rushing river come our way. Oh, my dear hope, I occasionally find you and lose you; nevertheless, I may well find you everywhere—in me, in others, and by looking down to the foundations. When in despair, I look up into the sky!"

Jane pauses to give me a chance to process all this valuable knowledge that spills from her mouth like poetry. I could ask a lot of questions, but I'm not a stowaway. I'm a former coach and an active captain, sitting in a VIP cabin with the best teacher in the world. I watch and listen to remember—not to learn—what I've always held in my heart. I just had to travel at supersonic speed back to my preschool desk and open my notebook once more. It's all written there, dated September 1983!

"I see that your mind is still traveling far from here, my captain. It looks like that walk of yours in nature probably sucked out all the oxygen from your soul. Let me remind you of something else. Don't wait for hope to fly in through the keyhole of your door. Make sure you open all the windows and all the doors for the sky to pour a rainstorm of hope onto your doorstep! Just open your heart."

"Awesome! Thank you very much, my dear teacher."

"Tell me what else is bothering you."

"Jane, when I was still wearing my coach hat, I had an endless thirst for offering and helping. A higher power was guiding me. I was favored with the ability to understand exactly what each of my clients needed. I became quite successful, and as a result, I worked fourteen hours a day to see as many clients as I could. Even so, finding an appointment for one of them back then would be possible only in a few months' time. After a health issue, I felt abandoned by my higher power and eventually lost my appetite for work. I lost my zeal for life in general. Today, hearing you speak to me with your uplifting words, I finally opened my eyes and realize that no one has abandoned me! It was I who had quit my job, I who had quit my clients, and I who had quit my higher power. However, you are absolutely right! That little flame still burns inside."

"And what does this flame offer?"

"When I began this new journey, I promised myself not to let any route go to waste. I made it my mission to search and solve the greatest riddle that has plagued us for centuries—what is the most precious thing in the world? If I succeed, then all that remains is for me to pass it on to the rest of the world."

"This is excellent! How's your mission going so far?"

"My new mission has been underway for a long time, but I still carry my old inner fears as heavy luggage. What is more, I have to face new challenges, rough paths, and insurmountable obstacles at times. To be honest, the most difficult obstacles come from the passengers I host in my wagons, especially from the distinguished ones. Nevertheless, even in the darkest parts of my journey, where the train's powerful headlights burn like a weak candle, when I still can't see light at the end of the tunnel, some luminous passengers magically appear to light my way again and get me back on track to fulfill my mission. I'm enjoying such a bright moment with a luminous person right now, my dear teacher! Thank you from the bottom of my heart."

"Let's get rid of the titles and the roles once again so I can thank you properly. My dear brother, remember that in total darkness, you can more easily spot the luminous people. Thank you for making this challenging trip for the sake of all of us. My wish is for you to reach your desired destination soon enough. If it helps you at all, the world chess champion for twenty-seven years, Emanuel Lasker, very aptly said, 'When you see a good move, look for a better one!' Consequently, keep collecting all the precious things along the way, and don't stop looking for even better ones! And most important of all, never despair, as the flame inside you is all the power you need."

Any further discussion after this would be inconsequential chatter, so I get up from my seat. As I reach out for a proper farewell handshake, Jane pulls me into her arms.

"A handshake is too little to convey my true feelings right now, my dear captain. Know that darkness and difficult passengers have artistically crafted the man you are today—a true captain! Challenges and obstacles will either become an avalanche to stop you or just a station to pass by. Obstacles will evolve you and make you even wiser. Good luck with your quest."

"Thank you so much! You have really cleared my mind, and you leave me with a revived soul."

"I have something in mind for the puzzle that's been troubling you. Do you want my opinion?"

"My dear, as it is only twenty minutes until the next station, I would like to let you enjoy some peace and quiet in your cabin or to enjoy the green landscapes on your right. You can share your thought by leaving me a letter with your answer to the question, 'What is the most precious thing in the world?' Is that possible?"

She nods affirmatively, and we part ways.

I nervously watch in my left outside mirror as the few passengers slowly disembark. I count them, one by one, until I am sure the train is completely empty. The next departure is in twenty minutes, enough time to clean the carriages and welcome the next passengers for the next station. Enough time for me to return to the "crime scene" and make sure there is no incriminating evidence of any kind left.

I have the teacher's letter in my hands, and I'm holding it tight, like treasure. I put on my glasses and hungrily read her message.

Dear Captain, Coach, Colleague, Brother,

Let's get rid of the titles and the roles for one last time so I can leave you with my final message.

My dear soul mate, when you asked me what the most precious thing in the world is, I didn't have to think about it much. Through my work and experiences, I have learned that the most valuable thing is *giving*.

By giving, we extend our hope to everyone else, as long as we make sure that we give what they truly need. A great teacher is one who has a true passion for education and training, whereas a great master is the one who builds close relationships with all students, learns what really makes them happy, and then does everything possible to provide it for them. There is no magic vaccine that can cure the pandemic of pain, but we all have within us the undying flame—that magical power—that can give hope to others by extending ours.

I honestly believe that people who dedicate themselves and work hard and passionately to develop another human being are very, very special. They offer the world tree saplings growing up in a luminous nursery garden. For me, educators, trainers, and coaches—like you are, my dear—are my true source of inspiration.

Choose to have good purpose.

Together, we can make a difference. Together, we can create a better tomorrow for our children. Teach them how to choose to have good purpose in life!

Education is not about filling a mind with knowledge but about filling a heart with beautiful feelings. As Marshall McLuhan rightly said, "Anyone who tries to make a distinction between education and entertainment doesn't know the first thing about either." Therefore, don't forget in your quest to choose to have good company and always good mood! May you have good progress and never lose your hope! It's inside!

Love, Jane

The letter from the best teacher in the world has been given the distinguished place it deserves—laminated and protected from time and hardship, next to Dr. Time's referral letter, along with the other evidence of the luminous people I have found along the way.

Station 1

The Last Route

There is no end. There is no beginning.
There is only the passion of life.
—Federico Fellini

The author closes the book and carefully places it in the child's brown suitcase, which has been constantly near him all evening. He remains still for a minute, his back to the audience, his eyes fixed on the suitcase, his head lowered. Bringing his right hand to his lips, he takes a kiss and gently transfers it to the suitcase. He then takes off the captain's jacket, folds it lovingly and respectfully, and places it on the bench beside the suitcase. He removes his captain's hat as well and, with a sweeping gesture, places it with the rest of his belongings. Next, he turns to us, takes several steps forward, and now stands literally over our heads. His posture is forthright, the look on his face noble, and he has a generous smile for all of us. Whatever sorrow remains in his soul he has surely left on the bench with the rest of the items. He looks to right and left to make sure that his smile has been delivered to all corners of the hall. Removing the watch from his right wrist, he holds it up for all the audience to see. The complete silence of the last five minutes finally breaks with the words, "I am happy when I have something to give rather than take," and he continues to hold the watch out prominently in his outstretched right hand.

The giant screens show us a photo of Dr. Time, dressed in his surgical gown and with his stethoscope around his neck. It's the first time we have seen our doctor's face, and it is indeed a beautiful face with a beautiful smile. The author is also lost in Dr. Time's eyes for a moment; then he continues nostalgically.

"In order to have something to give, I need time to prepare my action. The birthday card took just five minutes to prepare, yet the pink magic stick continues to provide positive reaction to patients. The visit to my parents took a ten-minute drive and a two-hour chat, yet my parents' euphoria lasted for a week. The night out with my wife lasted for several hours, yet the positive reaction continued for a month. Action, reaction, satisfaction!

"Nevertheless, a bad action can bring about a fatal reaction. Leo's hasty action in crossing the junction on a red light triggered a fatal reaction, depriving him of the most precious thing in the world—his time! Time to live, time to give, time to take. The almighty time gives and takes at will before you learn how to manage it properly.

"To honor the first illustrious passenger in our wagon, our Dr. Time, I kindly ask you to stand up, remove the watch from your wrist, and hold it up as high as you can. Those of you who are not wearing a watch, take your cell phone instead. Hold it up until your hand goes numb, until you can't hold it any longer.

"Excellent job! The panoramic view from where I stand is so moving! I can see each of you with camera-lens clarity. I see your faces shining like stars in the Sky. We have to create a nuclear fusion in the core of a star to make it shine bright. We must generate massive nuclear energy for the light to travel from the star to our planet. It looks like we've done an excellent job; our collective fusion and energy has just caused a star to explode, giving birth to a supernova that is billions of times brighter than the sun. Well done!

"Hold on for just a little longer. Yes, I am sure you can! You have the strength within you to make it happen! It's your choice not to let time hurt you or dictate to you. You have the power to deal with the time and make it work to your advantage.

"Thank you very much! Please leave the watch or phone in your pocket or your bag for the remaining time we have left together. I, in turn, will put my watch in my right pocket. Stay on your feet so that we can do something different now. Let's go and close our eyes while raising our hands without holding the weight of time. Let's go and remember Leo, who is left out of time, and memorialize all those who lost the battle with time. Let's go and close our five fingers into our palms and form a powerful fist. Let's go and send our power to Aria and positive thoughts to all victims of time.

"We have the power needed to light a candle in every home, in every state, in every country; to illuminate our brothers and sisters with the knowledge that the most precious thing in the world is time! One more hour, one more day, one more year.

"Let's slowly open our eyes and realize that we are still standing; we are still here in the Sky. We have the power to say the words 'Let's go' and travel at supersonic speed across the planet. Say the words 'Let's go' and travel through time and space. We have the power to visit our past for supplies and continue into the future with hope. Yesterday's memories are the fuel that will take us to tomorrow's stations. So here we go. Let's go. Let's go and live right. Let's go and live well! Let's go and have a choiceful journey to a successful life—a full life! What a wonderful blessing!

"Thank you very much for following my instructions. Please take your seats again because the train will now continue on its course. The train never stops! Our choiceful journey continues! But don't forget to find a way, each and every one of you, to remember that the most precious thing in the world is *time!* I, for example, have laminated my doctor's note, and I see it on my desk every day. You can also see it now on the big screens. Whenever I read it, again and again, I always remember my goal: *by conserving my time, I am saving my let's go.* That's how I keep going! What are you going to do about your time?

"It looks like the Sky has bright stars tonight, so let's do another exercise, with the help of our second illustrious passenger, my old friend. Just have a look at his bright smile, his luminous spirit projected on the giant screens, and immerse yourselves in his eyes for a moment. Then recall his journey—*from painful to painless with the right choices!* Let's try to feel it too. Let's go and locate the two tireless workers in our chests that ensure our every breath—our lungs. Let's bring our two palms to our chests, as I do, and by closing our eyes, try to trace the life that lies within. Every breath, as our chests move up and down, gives us another moment in time.

"Every breath, up and down, gives us another second.

"Every breath, up and down, gives us another minute.

"Every breath, up and down, gives us another hour.

"Every breath, up and down, gives us another day.

"Every breath, up and down, is a tide of emotions.

"Every breath, up and down, is our goodness that wants to come out.

"No one in this world, no matter how strong the love is, could offer us another breath. Only our lungs can perform this duty.

"As we have our eyes closed, we exhale and inhale goodness. As we do this, think of a person you have in your life who needs another breath. Who has a need for a kind word, a thank-you, an apology, or a simple, 'Hey, I want to spend some time with you.'

"Now, open your eyes and your mobile phones. Write a message to the person who first came to your mind and press SEND without thinking twice! Do it now, right now. Now, not in a while. Now, not tomorrow. Now, before the red light comes up and stops your flow. Now, when my shot of goodness has overcome your judgment and your mind. Now, when you have the blessing of finding that contact on your phone. The reason we call them *contacts* is precisely because they need frequent and quality contacts—through loving messages, beautiful conversations, and warm hugs. As long as you have contactless relationships in your life, you will remain carrying heavy luggage.

"I am so happy to see you all typing your messages *right now.* Even as I continue with my chatter, you are anxiously typing your messages, *right now*! I am so happy to see you ignoring my chattering while you deal with a more urgent and important matter *right now*! I don't know if it's the bright screen on your phone or if it's something magical here in our Sky that's happening *right now*! From where I stand and look at you, I see you all with bright faces *right now*! Like stars in the real sky. I am so happy to spot some of you talking over the phone *right now*—in the middle of my speech—assuring your contacts that all is just fine. We're not wearing our watches, so we don't care if it's already midnight. However, no one is complaining about receiving your messages or calls *right now*. Some are obviously worried or surprised by what you're doing, as it's been a long time since you last played such a lovely trick on them, especially if they have been contactless luggage! Oh, and don't forget to mention that you are taking them to their favorite restaurant this week. And don't hesitate to stay there as long as possible. Make them discreetly send you away by bringing the bill. Don't forget to clink your glasses loudly for that wonderful moment—*right now*—when the time is *right* and is right *now*!

"Thank you so much for following my instructions once again. Leave your phones in silent mode and your contacts in the right mode—in good mood! Don't forget to find a way, each and every one of you, to remember that the most precious thing in the world is *perseverance!* Remember all those heroes who never give up and who stop at nothing—heroes who take a step forward, even though their legs are broken. Heroes who choose to leave a breath of hope in a book, rather than on the asphalt. Heroes who landed their two feet on the moon! Heroes like Odysseus. Heroes who survived their personal odyssey and continue their journey. Everyday heroes like you! I have my old friend's first-edition book on my desk, on my left, where the boat *Family and Friends* is, to remind me daily of the intensity I need to have in my every effort. The intensity of my actions. The intensity of my breathing. Because only I can breathe for myself. What are you going to do about your perseverance?

"With such an amazing class, I suggest we continue our exercises. Try to recall Grandpa Takis's statement: 'If you stop eating, the body will starve. If you stop reading, your mind will starve, and if you stop playing, your soul will also starve.' It is now time to thank our lovely hosts and sponsors for the treats they offered us tonight, so we've eaten! And then thank all of you, my lovely audience, for your love of reading, for loving my book, and for coming to this station tonight, so we have read! We can therefore assume that we've done well with eating and reading! I, consequently, take full responsibility for not having played as much as we should. So, let's go and have another play!

"Remain seated, and offer your right hand to the person sitting on your right and your left hand to the person sitting on your left. Keep your hands linked as genially as you can. No need for an assertive grab, just a genuine handshake to keep you warm.

"Well done! Now, let's go and exhale and inhale goodness. If you want a good outcome or if you need help, delegate this *action* to the person sitting beside you who truly cares about you. If you want a good *reaction*, then you must learn to ask for help and, thereafter, accept help. And then, you must learn to give help in return without expecting any gratuity. Once you feel the *satisfaction* coming from another person's help—a surgeon who saves your life, a lawyer who saves your reputation, an accountant who protects your property, a writer who inspires your spirit—then you will understand the greatness that lies in *giving*. Action, reaction, satisfaction!

"Now, close your eyes once more, and as you have your hands linked—right and left, like boats in a harbor—ask yourself what kind of transaction is taking place right now.

"Do I give or take?

"Is it something good or bad?

"Do I give goodness, or do I receive it at the same time?

"Do I leave something good, or do I accept it as well?

"Do I make a spiritual deposit or withdrawal right now?

"Is my luggage getting heavier or lighter right now?

"None of us can divide goodness into parts or distinguish giving from receiving good. Good is one and inseparable. Good has no size, no unit of measurement, and it cannot be broken down. Good has only one worth, and those who are not kind are simply not worth it; they become unworthy.

"From the bottom of my heart, I thank you for following my instructions once again. Please take your hands back and bring your palms together in the posture of prayer. You have the right to believe in whatever God your heart and mind loves. Whatever you call Him, I am absolutely certain that your God also rewards goodness, as our illustrious teacher was rewarded! Find a way or include in your night's prayer a wish to never forget that the most precious thing in the world is *giving*! I keep a copy of the best teacher in the world's letter on the desktop of my laptop, so that every time I open it to write another word of my new book, it will always be associated with giving. Take a look at the screens to read her letter with your own eyes and contemplate. What are you going to do about giving?

"We have eaten, read, and played. Maybe it is time to tell the rest! To have a happy life, I have to make the right choices. Happiness in life is as personal as your own breath. No one can breathe for you, no matter how much they love you; no one can make you happy, no matter how hard they try; no one can make you unhappy, unless you let them. You can only create your own happiness by creating happy thoughts. As only you can breathe for yourself, happiness is entirely a personal choice.

"My grandfather, my doctor, my friend, my teacher, my family, my publishing partners, my business partners, all those who choose me as their coach, and all the people I meet daily are all passengers on my train. Some are permanent, some are temporary, and some are just passing by. But they are not scattered throughout the many carriages of a random train. They are all gathered and neatly seated in one big carriage of my train.

"And if I speak to you in fairy tales and parables, it's because it's easier for you to listen. My life is a train that carries wagons full of people. I travel with a specific mission—to find luminous people in every corner of the planet and ask them, 'What is the most precious thing in the world?'

"Sometimes, I get tired and stop to refuel. When I reach a station, my wagon doors open automatically, and I am very happy to welcome new passengers into my life. I always stand formally dressed and wear a big smile. At this station today, I feel blessed to have my doors open and to welcome all of you aboard. You are now in my life, and I am in your life. We are fellow passengers!

"I am overjoyed when I welcome people and crushed when I say goodbye.

"In March 2012, at an emergency stop I had to make, the door of my carriage opened, and my most distinguished passenger got off.

"My son got off the train. My dear son, Arsenios.

"He left holding his small brown suitcase, into which he had just about managed to place all the love we gave him in the little time he was with us. On that day, I agonizingly watch him in the left-hand outside mirror of my cockpit, unable to do anything to convince him to board again, he turns his little head to me and sends me a flying kiss with his palm. The second-to-last warning siren for departure rips my heart, while Arsenios sits on the station bench, opens his bag, and pulls out a screwdriver. He bends down and finds the bolt that had come loose, which is causing the bench to creak and wobble. With his little strength and his immense persistence, he manages to tighten the loose bolt. Then he gives me another fleeting glance. This time, he is not looking at me with a sad face. He is proud of everything he's accomplished so far. And he is proud of what he is leaving behind. Holding his suitcase tight, he lifts his head up to read the station's sign. He wants to be sure that he got off at the right station. He chose the station called Ten Lanterns as his final destination and seems quite excited to count ten lanterns under the station roof. With his right foot in the sky and his left still on the concrete pavement, he takes a brave last breath and blows with all his strength toward the lamp above his head. A loud explosion shatters the glass lamp into a million pieces, and the station becomes a little darker. The station remains with only nine lanterns. And the station clock has stopped at exactly seven o'clock.

"No matter how much I protest to the station master, no matter how much money I pledge to the ticket agent, no matter how much I weep beneath the broken lamp, my son is unable to return to the train for us to continue our journey together. I have no choice but to stay at the station with him. The last siren warns of the three minutes that remain before the train resumes its journey. Nothing can keep a train from its course.

"I am desperately looking for help to my left and right, but it seems I am hopelessly alone.

"No one will be able to replace the lamp and fix the damage!" I cry aloud. I pick up the fragments of what remains of my life, yet pieces of glass remain on the floor. As I hold some in my hands, I cannot decide whether I should throw them away or keep them close.

"Suddenly, the girl with the violin appears. I am curious why she is not holding her violin as she approaches.

"I come to say goodbye and give you a warm hug."

"Where's your violin?"

"My mission has just been completed, and my Father is waiting for me inside. I gave my violin to the next angel who has just arrived to replace me. He's around here somewhere—a beautiful little boy with a brown suitcase."

As I abandon my weak body into her little arms, she says tenderly, "Please do not delay any longer at this station. The train waits for no one. As soon as the clock hands start moving again, the train will be eager to leave and continue its course, exactly like the impatience of the four seasons, waiting to come back into our lives. I will not let you miss your train! However, I will let you cry every March, and I will pray to our Father to bless you with happiness for the remaining eleven months of each year. But there is one condition: look at your watch every time it reads seven, and look for the amazing opportunity that's hidden in your life. Now, please run, as you only have a few minutes left."

I watch her bright, happy pace as she walks away. A sudden gentle touch on my back makes me turn around. An old man has appeared out of nowhere. He's dressed in a janitor's uniform, even though it's two sizes too big. The sleeves almost hide the palms of his hands, and the trousers droop over his gray military boots. He wears a baseball cap in shades of white and black—a mixture of dirt and work. The hat does not promote a baseball team but has instead the inscription BELIEVE IN ME printed in red capital letters. Beneath the hat, I can see long white hair that has become almost one with his white beard. Under the shadow created by the hat, I notice the wrinkles on his face, which confirm his old age. He couldn't be the station janitor despite the fact that he wears the uniform with all the appropriate insignia. The hat, the long hair, the beard, and especially his age are totally incompatible with the role, and I am now quite weary of this man!

Suddenly, his face is illuminated by the lantern as he raises his head to look me in the eye. He scans my face and cracks a smile, tilting his head to the right. He continues to stare at me, tilting his head once to the right and once to the left, as art critics do when they stare for hours at a precious work of art hanging on the wall of a gallery. I remain skeptical and in no mood for a conversation. But if he is really the station's foreman, then I have the opportunity to ask him to repair the damage.

"Are you the station foreman?"

"I have been for many, many years now. Bless the station master for letting me still wear the uniform they gave me the very first day I started working here. My soul is bound to this station with a golden chain. No matter how far I go during the day, the golden chain pulls me back to this station every night. Bless the station master for letting me walk here at night when the station is closed. He has a bodyguard on his team for free. Bless the station master. Bless him."

"Can you fix the damage, then?"

"It will take a miracle for my old body to do such a demanding job. It has been done many times in the past, but I'm afraid it needs a special emissary for this delicate work."

"If you just lend me a ladder and give me a lamp, I'm sure I can manage just fine."

"You ask me for the impossible, young man! Everything you need right now for such a complex task is locked in the Great Warehouse, and the key is held by the Big Boss."

"The station master, you mean?"

"Yes! Bless the station master who still tolerates me and keeps me in his employment. As I previously mentioned, for free."

"And what are we going to do about this dark corner of the station?"

"It's no good calling our station Ten Lanterns when one of them is smashed, right?"

"Exactly. At last, we've come to an understanding! What can we do about it?"

"Tonight, I am sorry to say, absolutely nothing. But don't you worry at all. Even if only temporarily, we'll have light from the other nine lanterns."

"But you can't call yourself Ten Lanterns Station and have only nine lanterns! You said so yourself. It's like saying your name is Mr. Best, and you're the clumsiest football player in the world! Imagine the commentator saying, 'Ladies and gentlemen, another huge blunder by Best! Alone with the net, and he's kicked the ball out!' This is crazy."

"Bless you, young man. You've got me laughing."

"Stop laughing, please, and tell me what you're going to do about it."

"Listen to me carefully. This is just temporary damage. If you cling to it, or even worse, if you don't have the instructions on how to fix it, then I'm afraid you'll be *burned*. Not to mention that you'll miss your train."

"Fine, what are we going to do, then? So I miss the train because we were chatting! Not that I really care."

"You must care, young man! You will leave all your anger and sadness with me, and you will continue your journey. Please, don't be angry when I call you *young man*, and don't be sorry for something that can't be fixed, at least for the time being. Your train is leaving in one minute. You'll have to make your final choice."

"What about the broken lantern?"

"It will forever remain broken in your heart, but look at your wrists. The station master handed you the same gold chain as mine. This means that you can return to this station any time you like, exactly as I do, especially in the evenings, when all is quiet and souls are strolling without a care. With just a thought, you will be here at supersonic speed."

"Then why should I leave in the first place, if I want to return to this station where I lost everything; where my most distinguished passenger abandoned me?"

"You didn't lose everything, and no one has abandoned you. Give me a chance to explain. You still have nine lanterns to show you the way and a train full of people who love you and care for you. Our lives are full of stations. We take a break, observe, evaluate, and move on. Until the next station. The train never stops. In order to have good progress, look outside the windows of your wagon, looking up to find the stars and not down to find mud or scattered glass. By looking up, we learn from the stars we have in our family, at our work, and in our world. These stars are not to be envied or undermined but only to be admired for how hard they work to be as bright as they are. This is how you can become a star as well. Would you like to accept some advice from an old traveler like me, who has traveled the world and always faithfully returns to his station every night?"

"Do I have a choice?"

"Plenty of choices, young man. Here's another one. I have a new path for you that takes just four steps!

"First step: the nine lanterns are enough to show the way and help you continue your journey. They will safely take you to your desired destination. As soon as you reach that station, you will be able to finally light the tenth lantern and complete your mission, to some extent.

"Second step: return to Ten Lanterns Station only when you have gathered all the knowledge and experience you possibly can from your journey. Only then will the station master hand you the keys to the Great Warehouse. Inside, you will find much more than a ladder and a lamp.

"Third step: accept that your distinguished passenger has chosen to get off at this station to continue his own mission, assigned to him by the station master. Once he has completed it, he and his Father will be reunited. No one abandons anyone."

"Why will my mission be only a partial success? What else will it take?"

"Fourth and last step: you will need to pass on your knowledge and experience to the whole world. Once you have restored all the lanterns, you will possess the most precious knowledge in the world: *the Ten Lanterns!* You will thereafter have the wisdom to create your own lanterns or complement the existing ones. Don't leave a single word behind. Do not let the stowaways or the confidence thieves discourage you and convince you to do otherwise. Especially do not let the *master thief*—that is you—look at you in the mirror every morning and convince you to do nothing. Do not let anyone stop you! Generously share your story with the whole world. I want you to know that I've been traveling and stargazing for centuries, and I still haven't been able to get out of the mud. But I don't give up because when I raise my head up, my lanterns light my face. I still have many miles to go. And so do you! Move forward without looking back.

Choose to have good life.

"Having a life is a gift you cannot return; having a good life is a choice! I will now leave you to make your last choice. Choose to have a good life. Make it worthwhile."

I close my eyes and lie down on the concrete pavement. I can't decide, regardless of the diligent efforts of the perennial foreman and the girl with the violin. Suddenly, a powerful force—some strong hands on my right and some on my left—lifts me up against my will and puts me back on the train. I keep my eyes and ears closed as we leave the station. I want neither to see nor hear anything.

● ● ●

"And my heart remained sealed throughout the years that followed. March will always be a torturous month, but I have found the courage and the strength to open my eyes, my ears, and finally my heart. When I am in despair, I look up to find the stars, I listen to my favorite songs to find comfort, and I allow the other eleven months to warm my heart. I can see, hear, and feel again. And thankfully, I still have the two boats, on my left and right, to protect me from any harm.

"During the years when my soul remained buried in the dark, my life's train was on the move. Even though my eyes were closed, the train made no exception. Even though my ears were closed, the train was streaming music to all wagons and continuing its course. Even though my heart was sealed, my train was speeding along, leaving me breathless. I have been blessed to have other people behind my steering wheel, even if they do not have a captain's license.

"They have managed to take me to the next station. And station by station, step by step, breath by breath, I have finally begun to resume my duties. My second captains, who helped me leave behind the ruins of my life and continue on my journey, are my beloved Dr. Time, my old friend, and the best teacher in the world, as well as the boats at my sides: my family and friends on my left, and my God on my right. They all have had the patience to tolerate my worst version of myself.

"The love of my mother, the strength of my father, the kindness of my sister, the companionship of my friends, the kindness of my associates, the gratitude of my clients, and the endurance of Grandpa's Ten Lanterns have been more than enough to light my first candle. What a blessing!

"My eyes opened for the first time when I tried to lighten my pain by lighting the first lantern: I choose to have good company.

"I accept the presence of pain, but as soon as I invite others and have *good company*, I am not alone and helpless anymore. This accomplishment—lighten my pain by having good company—is not a personal victory but a collective triumph brought about by the inexhaustible efforts of a team of people.

"Through their undying will, not to let my *time* go to waste; through their *perseverance*, not to let my eyes close; through their *giving*, not to let my heart be sealed; not to let the last burning flame inside me be extinguished.

"They safeguarded my hope! If hope means offering your time, your dedication, and your tenderness, then *hope* is enough for me to survive and live another day. If hope is provided by those who truly love us, then *love* is enough for me to survive, live another day, and to make some new choices. If my new choices have helped me endure an unspeakable tragedy, then my heritage—the Ten Lanterns—has been my guide in how to light my way and lighten my pain. In mastering this skill—to lighten my pain—then I am finally painless; I am free! Free to continue my journey. A choiceful journey for a successful life!

"I can either move forward or backward but never stand still, even if I want to. Others will pass me by, thus sending me farther back, but life is never stagnant. Everything flows! My train will never stop!

"My journey became lighter when I tried to lighten the pain by lighting the second lantern: I choose to have good mood.

"Good company and good mood widened my eyes even more, and, bit by bit, my heart began beating faster.

"There is no doubt that a piece of my heart will forever be of stone for my distinguished passenger, for every March, for every year. However, I am not blaming anyone for my life's outcome. I now travel my uphill and downhill path in kindness. I now have luggage as light as a feather. One by one, I offered my heartfelt apologies, my gratitude, my love, my time, my patience, and my help, and my journey has no more heavy burdens.

"I have forgiven and forgotten those responsible for the disembarkation of my distinguished passenger, and my heart has become as light as a feather, and my mind is at ease. I continue my journey free of heavy loads. My train will never stop!

"The third lantern was lit to help me lighten the pain once again: I choose to have good manners.

"My life was changing! Good company, good mood, and good manners helped me escape from my mental inertia. My life was profoundly improved when I learned to use three words: I need help. Once I did that, the response came almost at supersonic speed, like the one Grandpa used when visiting me in my darkest hour: *My chosen boy, good food at a good price equals kindness. A good man with good values equals gentleness. You should always be a dignified, honorable, gentle man. See to it that you distinguish yourself by having good intentions.* My grandfather's words are like the station's warning siren, reminding me to get on board and never give up. My train will never stop!

"My path became even more clear with the lighting of the fourth lantern, aiding me to lighten my pain much more easily: I choose to have good intentions.

"Four lanterns are almost enough to transform a muddy, crawling larva into a butterfly. Having good company makes me useful, having good mood makes me cheerful, having good manners makes me respectful, and having good intentions makes me faithful. A total transformation! The butterfly makes its first altruistic flight. It is exciting and fun! Almost perfect! However, the flight to the sky has no limits, and there are many miles still to go. Nevertheless, a small miracle has happened—a crawling caterpillar is transformed into a butterfly. From the mud to the sky; that's progress. Progress means advancement. Advance your path to something higher. That's what the caterpillar achieves. Stop crawling and choose to fly. The journey continues. My train will never stop!

"The fifth lantern was finally on, and the flight has become emotionally bearable whenever I manage to lighten my pain: I choose to have good progress.

"I now have five choices to aid my endeavors. Immutable, unstoppable, and powerful choices. Not one by one, but all together at all times. Five constant, inseparable, and solid choices, like the fist made by my five fingers. If I want my fist to be effective, capable of knocking down a mighty oak with a single blow, then the five choices must be infinite and indestructible. To make this viable, I have learned how to live with them and live by them and, most importantly, to have the ability to be perfectly in tune and in sync with all five of them: good company, good mood, good manners, good intentions, and good progress. I can adjust the flow of all five elements so that they are in perfect harmony. This musical harmony from five different musical instruments reaches the ears and the hearts of other people and soothes their souls. Everyone needs an old friend who is useful, cheerful, respectful, faithful, and resourceful. My train will never stop!

"I eventually managed to ignite the sixth lantern, making it even simpler to lighten the pain: I choose to have good timing.

"The sixth lantern made me mindful. The ability to adjust my spiritual compass and follow my spiritual map, using carefully synchronized actions, brings positive reactions and gets me closer to my final destination: action, reaction, satisfaction. My mindset has constructed small but decisive steps to help me advance on an uphill or downhill path. But I am not stagnated. March uphills are still hopelessly difficult to overcome, but I am never alone. I have two boats that hold me tight and eleven more months. I have my spiritual life jackets. I still experience great fear when I need to stop at the train station for refueling, but I can't help it, and stopping and refueling is an unavoidable daily task. However, I will never get used to parting with my passengers. Nonetheless, no matter how dark it gets, I now have six lanterns to light my way. I am not wasting a moment on grumbling, blaming, or complaining. All I need to do is have a break, take a deep breath, refuel, and continue the journey, even if the clock still shows seven o'clock. My life is full of stations. I therefore take a break, observe, evaluate, and move on—until the next station. My train will never stop!

"The real break comes by activating the seventh lantern, to lighten my pain at will: I choose to have good memories.

"My Sunday feasts with Grandpa, my first day at school, my family's Easter tree, my mother's letters, my carefree dances with my beloved sister, my first car ride, all my creative moments at work, and all the wonderful moments of my life are my eternal fuel. What a wonderful blessing to have had them and what a blessing to be able to create more of them, all captured by a camera's click. And then, they are carefully selected and arranged in my life's album so they will endure in time, in mind, and in my heart, with a single click. I click, I recall, and I count my blessings. I have eyes capable of understanding, ears willing to realize, lungs eager to take another breath, and a heart ready to forgive, forget, and go forward. I have feet for another step, arms for another hug, and a mouth trained to offer kindness: *I love you, I miss you, I forgive you, I apologize, thank you for everything*, and most importantly, *I need help*. Under the warm light of the seventh lantern, I once took a piece of paper and wrote down all my blessings. A single page was not enough to list them all, so I started drafting my book. Finally, my good memories made me grateful. And my train will never stop!

"Oh, my dear God, what more could I possibly ask from You? Nothing at all! My physical and spiritual health is more than enough to arm my will and march toward more accomplishments. It's now crystal clear that to continue the journey and reach the desired destination, I have to pay the fare. I have the ticket in my hand, and I wait for the train attendant to escort me to my seat. Everyone is entitled to a seat, but not all seats are the same. Only distinguished passengers are entitled to sit in the front seats. Those who trusted, tutored, and finally took the triptych knowledge from the doctor, the old friend, and the great teacher—never waste your time, never give up, and never stop giving—are now traveling in VIP seats.

"I have done everything with reverent precision, and I am ready to claim my distinguished place. The usher is standing right across from me, waiting to check my ticket. My heart is about to burst as I give it to him. He swipes the ticket through his machine, and the seat is automatically calculated, based on my achievements to date. The screen reads, "useful, cheerful, respectful, faithful, resourceful, mindful, and grateful passenger." It then determines my seat and informs the usher accordingly. He nods to me in a serious manner, and I follow him to my place. Something deep inside is boiling and upsetting me. Perhaps my total harvest will not be enough to feed the guest at my Sunday table.

"I follow with rapid steps and am glad that at least we have passed by the last wagon. We are now leaving behind the economy seats, and my spirit is somehow lifted. We need just one more step to enter the business-class wagon. And yet, just one row from it, he stops and shows me my seat! I am left staring at him with knitted eyebrows, longing for the front carriage. I'm just one step away! I don't know what else I need to do in my life to be entitled to claim a better seat. I'm already tired and overwhelmed. I urgently need a break to catch my breath. I need a stop. I have a seat to rest, yet I feel like it's not enough. I feel like my mission is unfinished. I will get some rest, but I will not get too comfortable! I'm going to continue my journey. My train will never stop!

"Once more, my train has the answer I was looking for. The solution is in front of my eyes. I see the magazine, the *Sunray*, which is in the net case in front of my seat. The cover has a picture of a well-groomed gentleman and is captioned, 'The millionaire who gave it all away.' As I have all the time in the world, I decide to stop fretting about my current seat and read the story of the Egyptian businessman who, at forty-five years old, decided to donate his entire fortune to charities around the world.

The skillful journalist had left the important question to the end, holding the reader's interest until the last moment.

"Mr. Akins, what prompted you to donate millions to charity?"

"I had to honor my name and my tradition. Akins in Egypt means brave. After arming myself with all the necessary bravery that such an action requires, I was able to create the reaction that I wanted."

"And what is the tradition all about?"

"The ancient Egyptians believed that once the body dies, the soul continues its own journey. The first one they would meet would be their god, Osiris. He would ask the soul two questions. If the first one is answered correctly, then Osiris moves on to the second question. The answers would determine whether the soul's journey would continue or not. The first question was, 'Did you offer joy?' and the second question was, 'Did you find joy?' These two goals are our sacred duty in life and the only way to eternal happiness."

"I close the magazine, as it has just done the job! I glance out the window. Despite the heavy rain and lightning strikes out there, inside my wagon another luminous person has shown me the way and put me back on track.

"All that I have courageously accomplished up to this moment—remarkably, admirably, and against all odds—will never have substance if I do not generously *donate* them to the whole world. Not just to my family and friends, not just to my city and country but literally to the whole world.

"As the usher returns from the first carriage, I grab his left arm and thank him for putting me in the right place. I turn my eyes out of the window once again. I have the choice to look at the mud or to lift my gaze to the sky. As I watch the black clouds, a tiny gap appears in the sky, big enough for a single ray of light to pass through at supersonic speed and illuminate my soul.

"The ray of light activates the eighth lantern, lighting up another blind spot and giving me the courage to lighten my pain: I choose to have goodness.

"Goodness is a deep desire to contribute to other people's happiness, even if you don't know them or will never meet them. When I grabbed the usher's left arm with the need to thank him for putting me in my place, I became truly *thoughtful* for the first time! I don't know how soon I will have the opportunity to meet my dear foreman at Ten Lanterns Station, but I have a feeling that I am getting closer and closer. As soon as I find him again, I will say a big thank-you to him as well. The foreman, God bless his soul, helped me to take the first decisive step while I was spiritually handicapped. And he was absolutely right after all. Nine lanterns are more than enough to keep me going on this journey. My train has not stopped since then!

"The ninth lantern is now on, and I can testify that I can lighten the pain whenever necessary: I choose to have good purpose.

"Tonight, as I stand before you in humility, consider me to be just another witness; living evidence. Living a miracle taught me how to live a life of miracles.

"Living a miracle refers to all the acts that I've experienced. In small portions, like my grandfather's meze; otherwise, it would have been impossible to digest in a single bite. I took off my coach's hat, captain's hat, director's hat, partner's hat, speaker's hat, and writer's hat, and I put on my student's hat, with a strong will to learn. Whenever the student wears his hat, the master mysteriously appears. Feel free to browse my life's chapters to find again all the knowledge offered to me. And I will remain here, waiting to put you in your place. In your rightful place! Turn back to remember all the great masters I have had in my life—the cook, the king, the doctor, the old friend, the teacher, the foreman, the usher, my grandfather, and my mother, all with a spiritual lesson.

"Living a life of miracles refers to all my efforts to light my way and lighten my pain. I have the Ten Lanterns engraved on the stony part of my heart. They give me hope and light my way, as I cannot erase the terrifying nights in the hospital that are also engraved on my heart. I cannot say, nor do I want to say, a last and final goodbye to my son. Thankfully, he is also etched into my heart and soul. My greatest accomplishment, perhaps my most precious achievement, is that I continue to find the heavily disguised opportunity hidden behind every problem and grab it by the hair. Then, I kick Mr. Pain from my life. Let pain come but not be welcome. I now have plenty of *choices* for every occasion!

"If I live a life of miracles, then you can make it too—no matter how heavy your luggage is, no matter how difficult your journey seems to be. Count your illuminated lanterns and continue your quest until you have managed to light them all—until you make your own miracle. Your train will continue its journey until it reaches the next station. One day, it will stop at its final destination. What would you like to find at your last station?

"There is one last thing left, one last visit I must make on my journey to Ten Lanterns Station. I travel first thing in the morning, as Grandpa taught me, and I have in my ears the Greek folk songs he liked so much. I weep again with the song that speaks about traveling the oceans. As I listen to it after all these years, I finally understand how prophetic the lyrics were when I first heard it at the tender age of sixteen. It was alerting me that someday I would lose all my harbors, but I must stay strong.

Oh, Sea, my sea, what have you done to me! I lost
every port for you. And I am since then a sailor and
tomorrow I set sail again alone.

"I was hearing the lyrics with my ears, but my soul was catching a deeper meaning. That's why my eyes filled with tears. I was too young to believe it. I didn't want to believe it, and I didn't want to lose my faith—the faith in You, the faith in me, and the hope for a good life.

"I don't have time to listen to the whole song, as I arrive at the station. It is still daytime, and I will not have the chance to meet my eternal foreman, as his visits are only during the night. Besides, I am seeking the station master to ask for the key to the Great Warehouse. In it, I will find the ladder and the lamp I need to fix the last dark part of my life, to light up the tenth lantern.

"I stand in front of the main entrance and bring to mind three people: my son, the girl with the violin, and the foreman. I am entering the station building and heading to the inner staircase, following the signs on the walls for the Station Master's Office. I end up in a long, dark corridor on the third floor. I am now passing several closed office doors, left and right, and I am very near to the end of the corridor. I politely knock on the door and set my ear to hear the approval to enter. The only sound that comes to my ear is a rock ballad playing inside the office. I slowly and politely open the door, and the music spills out into the hallway. The song is now recognizable: "Send Me an Angel" by Scorpions. I enter the office just as the lyrics say, "Here I am; will you send me an angel?"

"My legs can't hold me upright due to the tide of emotions, and I collapse on the couch behind me. I manage to have a quick look around the office, and I am in shock! How is it ever possible to be here? Again? Inside the same office, listening to rock music on the stereo?

"I am completely alone and subconsciously waiting for my old friend to come out from the bathroom or for Aria to knock on my door. However, there is no door next to the bookshelf, my old friend is not the station master of this station, and Aria is now a busy judge! I focus my eyes on the table in front of me that my knees are almost touching and realize that there is an envelope with my name written on it.

"Taking the envelope in my hands, I take another look around the room. I step out into the hallway again and confirm that there is not another soul in the building. I walk back into the office and close the door behind me. For some strange reason, even though I am completely alone in a huge train station, I am not overcome by fear.

My ears catch the angels' lyrics that send a subliminal message that all is well.

"I need oxygen and head for the window on my right. I open it and see a beautiful green park in front of me, identical to the one the judge saw every day from his window. How is it ever possible to be here? I am in the same office of the district courts, and I am listening to rock music on the stereo. I close my eyes and hear Aria saying, *Your coffee is on your desk, Judge.* I open my eyes again, and there is no coffee, yet the aroma of an Arabica blend penetrates my soul.

"The song of the angels is finished, and absolute silence spreads through the room. I don't have time to gather and organize my thoughts. I hear the second-to-last warning siren, and I have five minutes left to exit a three-story building and catch my train. I have almost the same feeling as I had in 2012. I don't want to leave, but this time, the feeling is much different. Back then, it was cold, and I was desperate, while now, it's warm and intoxicating. I'm drawn to it like a magnet. I want to crawl in and get comfy on the black leather couch—just relax and enjoy my letter. Nothing else matters.

"*Oh my God, I wonder who left this letter for me.* I sit on the couch and slowly peruse the mysterious envelope when I know I should be running to catch the train. I bring the envelope close to my nose and inhale deeply. I close my eyes and feel all my senses being stimulated by lavender, jasmine, and sandalwood. A prolonged exhalation follows, with my decision to stay here forever. I then open my eyes and take another breath. This time, the combination of vanilla and eucalyptus takes me like a spring breeze to Grandpa's mountain mansion. I'm under the giant oak tree that covers half of the roof, its long, velvety leaves hugging the entire west side of the house. On each branch, a small flower, a sheath containing many tiny seeds. When the seeds finally decide to sprout, they join together to form a small container that looks like a tiny pot. I bend down and pick up a dried acorn shell, and again, my senses are excited by smells and memories. Grandpa was gathering the acorns and using them to make his afternoon tea.

"The final warning siren forces my eyes to open and brings me back to the station office. A stone bangs against the window shutter, while the other half is still open. I get up to take a look. Below the window, the foreman is smiling and throwing pebbles to get my attention.

"'What are you doing here? I thought that your visits are overnight.'

"'That's right, but an emergency task came up, and my golden chains immediately dragged me here. What are you doing in there?'

"I do not have an answer to give, and I unconsciously bring the acorn shell close to my nose again. The foreman will complete his emergency task, judging by the confident tone in his voice.

"'Heaven, my dear child, smells much better, and I assure you that you will not find it in that office.'

"I close the window and gather all my strength in order to catch both the train and the foreman. I owe him a big thank-you and a warm hug. Clutching the last manuscript tightly in my hands, I take one last fleeting glance at this great office, from which all my good masters used to work—the good banker, the good trainer, the good coach, the good counselor, the good partner, and the good speaker. They have all accomplished their tasks. There is one task that remains unfulfilled—an order from 1470. For this emergency task, I must return to my new office and continue my journey. This time, I will try to become a good writer!

"I'll have to pay the price for it, so I give ten pounds of gold to the ticket agent and put the last manuscript in my leather bag before I leave the station for good. With my right foot on the train and my left foot at Ten Lanterns Station, I have one last chance to look at this place. It is seven o'clock on the dot, and the window on the third floor seems to be too high and too far away from me.

"*Perhaps it is not yet ready to accommodate me forever,* I reflect. I leave my dear boy, my son Arsenios, with the angels and return to the driver's seat. Before I leave the station for good, I count the ten lanterns, inhale deeply, and give my last exhaled breath to the last lantern; it now flashes along with the rest.

"The only thing I miss doing is thanking my dear foreman. I have my captain's hat on and wait for the station master to give me the green light. The clock is ticking, and finally, it is past seven after so many years of waiting! This time, I have a new mission—to deliver the most precious thing in the world to everyone.

"My train made a stop here at your station tonight. This is my story, or if you prefer, this is my fairy tale. My life is a nonstop train that carries the most precious thing in the world. For as long as I am blessed to have my captain's hat on and passengers in my carriage, we will all be traveling first class—not economy, not business, only first class! This is my final message that I bring to you tonight, while wishing you all the best and thanking you for traveling with me.

I will never stop broadcasting my message until my last breath:

> Be *first* in everything you do and *class* with everyone
> you meet. Always be a *first-class* traveler!

"And if I speak to you in fairy tales and parables, it's because it's easier for you to listen. And if you have been touched by my story, the Sky will become brighter with your applause. And they lived happily ever after!"

• • •

The lights are on and the Sky is indeed bright! Cries of joy, tears of happiness, applause, and cries of admiration are all dedicated to this man who has managed to deliver his message across the world: *From painful to painless with the right choices!*

A man struggled with pain for many years until he finally found the way to lighten the pain—the physical pain that consumed his lungs and the mental pain that turned a part of his heart to stone. Nevertheless, he managed to light his way and lighten his pain. He now stands proud and—most importantly—free on stage. Free from the nightmare of the disease waiting for him at the next station and free from the nightmare that every parent dreads. He has managed to miraculously bury the pain and resurrect his soul. He now travels to all destinations—and what a blessing it is to have him here tonight to wake us up with a fairy tale.

Our applause is overwhelming and unstoppable. The author of our hearts constantly bows to our ongoing applause, and we constantly bow to the greatness of his soul. After several minutes, a gentleman wearing a white suit and white tie, who has been sitting all night just five seats away from me, goes onstage and gives the author a prolonged hug. At the same time, a young lady appears from backstage bearing a bouquet of roses for our star in the Sky. She also hands a microphone to the gentleman in white, as we, at last, sit in silence.

"My captain, I have been blessed to have you in my life for some time now. You are a train captain, and I am a sea captain, but we are fellow passengers on the same road— the Great Road. Since the day I met you, God has given me nothing but fair winds to enjoy my journey. Since I have been blessed and my lockers are full, I never stop offering my help to all in need. Strangest of all, since the day I met you and changed course, I am constantly giving without expecting anything in return. How is it possible that my lockers are still full? How is it possible that my stock keeps increasing, even though I make only withdrawals? I will need your reply one day, as I suspect you are not just a train captain, but a life Captain—with a capital C. Thank you from the bottom of my heart for accepting my two invitations. The first one was many years ago, when you honored me with your presence at lunch with me in the marina. The second one is today, when you accepted my company's sponsorship for this event. I will close with a wish that changed my own life and, as a result, improved the lives of thousands of passengers in my shipping company: *I wish you a fair wind and smooth sailing until you reach the destination your Captain desires.* Thank you all for coming! A cocktail party will follow to honor our guest, and you are all welcome. Have a nice evening!"

As the audience resumes the applause, I look at my watch, which now reads one minute before midnight. After this magical experience, the only thing left to happen is to turn me into a pumpkin! The bodyguards of the gentleman in white, dressed in black, like ravens, set up a security perimeter behind the front row, where we are seated, and direct the audience toward the fire exits. They do not allow anyone in or out of this perimeter. The participants who are patient enough will have the chance to meet the author in person at the cocktail party to follow. Coach and I remain within the cordon, together with the shipowner's relatives and a dozen or so other distinguish guests. As the crowd reluctantly disperses, still gazing at the stage and enjoying the music, the *star* of the night is just an arm's length from us, chatting cordially with the shipowner's family members. Feeling a little uncomfortable—like stowaways who have been exposed—I turn to Coach, desperately trying to start a conversation. The giant screens are showing a video clip of the song "Amen"[6] by Enigma. Both the image and the lyrics draw me like a magnet.

> I am out on a new road in search of a land with no name! And I never look back 'cause I'm walking through sunshine and rain! I'm a man who lived in the tombs and who's broken the chain! I was blind and now I see. What I've got is not for me. And I know, it's time to go. Watch out—I feel the pain. Watch out—I'm alive again. The past is gone for good, it's time to say amen.

The clock now shows it's past midnight, and the miracle I have been waiting for happens before our eyes. No, we didn't turn into delicious pumpkins, but our protagonist is standing right in front of us. He is done talking with the rest, and it is now our turn.

"Here you are! Two more familiar faces in this lovely country!" He

---

[6] If you want to find us in the Asynchronous Zone of Today, search for the song on the internet, and enjoy it with us right now.

looks us in the eye with a huge smile. Then he extends his left hand to me and his right hand to Coach. We are holding hands and creating our own private perimeter. I feel numb, and the only thing my body can do is to remain standing as I shake my head and gaze at him like a puppy. Thankfully, Coach steps in and continues the conversation.

"We know you from your book, and we are fortunate to meet you in person tonight. How do you know us?"

He comes half a step closer to Coach, turning his ear to him because there is still a commotion in the theater. We can barely hear our own voices.

"I recognized you immediately. I could see you all night, enjoying the story, and my heart was gladdened. I feel proud for not letting you down. What do you think? Have we finally accomplished our mission?"

His use of the plural is incomprehensible, but extremely intoxicating, like all his previous spiritual shots. I feel like flying again; just as I flew when I was in the hospital, being administered the medical shots. I am gathering all my strength to take part in the conversation.

"But what do you mean by, 'Have we finally accomplished our mission'? You, my dear author, have done all the work. We were just spectators!"

I'm not sure if he has been able to hear me or has just ignored me, as the noise within the Sky is so loud. Maybe this is why he is giving us such bizarre responses.

"Oh, my young boy, I meant, have we made it? Have we accomplished our mission to deliver our message to the four corners of the room, not just up here in the front?"

Thank God that Coach has stayed tuned during this elusive conversation, when space and time are playing extrasensory games with us. He looks at the author and then right at me. He is looking at his future and his past, while we three are still holding hands tightly! He takes a brave breath, and with teary eyes, he replies, *"Yes, we did it!"*

The young boy, the coach, and the author—one inseparable, weightless, playful soul, flying in the Sky of the Asynchronous Zone of Today!

When we let our hands free, our soul is finally free to continue the journey, to return to the time and space it belongs to at supersonic speed.

The young boy returns to his space, back in his parents' house in Eantos Street.

The author returns to his time; after buying a shot of optimism, he flew forward.

The coach remains in the present—that's why it is called a "present." He finally honored his promise: "If the regressions from the back-and-forth journey make you dizzy or confused, please be patient until we reach the last station. There, I promise you, the last route will light the way, and all will become crystal clear."

First Chapter:
The Heavenly Directive

What is impossible with man is possible with God!
—Luke 18–27

October. Day One.

What a blessing!

"Evagoras, if you can hear me, please open your eyes. That's it, well done! Now, please squeeze my hand. A little harder, please. Very good! If my eyes are green, please blink your eyes three times. As you can see, I kept my promise. I was the last and the first person you see! That means everything went well. The doctor will visit later on.

"Oh no, my dear, please don't try to talk. Just listen to my voice and try to stay as calm as possible. You are still intubated in our ICU. We have you under sedation—let's call it artificial sleep—so as not to disturb the breathing tube in your throat and to rest your respiratory muscles. You finally have a chance to get some real rest yourself, right?

"Oh, dear, I've scared you with my medical jargon. Well, let me tell you what is really going on here. We love you so much, and we want to take care of you the best way we can. Just let us provide you with oxygen for a few days. As unreal as it may sound to you, we will breathe for you! If you understand what I'm saying, please close your eyes and relax. Everything is going to be just fine.

"Good night, and I will see you again tomorrow morning. This is a promise.

"Evagoras, close your eyes and don't give up hope."

Day Two

What a blessing!

"How is my friend doing today, Sister?"

"Somehow better, Doctor. He had hypoxemia last night. Arterial oxygen values were between 88 and 90 percent, and we had stage-one arterial hypertension; systolic pressure at 170 and diastolic at 110. As you can see on the monitor, the oxygen is better, and the hypertension has been controlled."

"Is he calm?"

"Yes. His technical sleep is constant."

"Good! We will continue administering analgesics until his systolic pressure drops to normal levels. We will reassess the situation tomorrow morning. We might also remove the tracheal tube tomorrow afternoon. I am quite sure his lung will respond well. Try to wake him up for a while, please."

"Evagoras, please open your eyes to see who is here! You have your first visitor. Open your eyes."

"Hello, Evagoras! You sleep like a baby! Your wife told me to keep you here for a month until you eventually change minds. I can't do much about your brain, but we've certainly fixed the lung! Everything went well. Forget the talk we had about a transplant. You have a perfectly able lung that is eager to get back to work as soon as possible. I want nothing but positive thoughts from now on. So try to stay calm, and I will come visit later on. I'll now leave you in the capable hands of Sister. Go back to sleep."

"Evagoras, close your eyes and don't give up hope."

Day Three

What a blessing!

"Evagoras, open your eyes."

"I can't. I'm under sedation."

"Not the eyes you have in your head; open your soul."

"You? Here? How did you manage that? I thought the gold chain limits your routes to the station only."

"The chain always takes me where I am needed, my dear coach!"

"But how can I even be conversing with you while my body is in this state? Oh my God, look at me covered in tubes and wires!"

"Whenever you are unwell, you choose to pull on my chain, and your old dog obeys you faithfully. Do I, at least, offer some comfort?"

"You do, and I want to thank you for all your help. Ideally, I would like to give you a warm hug, but look at me! Now that you are here with me, I'm not entirely sure if you really are an ordinary foreman."

"First of all, there are no ordinary foremen. There are competent, incompetent, and indifferent foremen. The third category is the worst. There is no excuse for a competent foreman who is not willing to help. It is shameful! *With our care, we make God rejoice for our lives. He then gives abundant blessings to His care-giving children.* To be a foreman, a caregiver, means you must take care of your task until you manage to complete it to the best of your ability. To a certain extent, I would say that even you are a caretaker."

"Could you please explain that a little better, partner?"

"I light their way with my spirit, and you light their way with your lanterns. You have already proved your care with your seminars, training sessions, and coaching. Whether you have conducted your task to perfection, allow me to have my doubts. Perhaps this is the reason I am still here! It seems that I have not been able to complete my mission either."

"What else do we need to do?"

"You should tell me that! All I know is that if you go to court and withhold information or knowledge that could potentially help solve a seemingly unsolvable case, then that makes you an accomplice, and you will be convicted. Withholding the truth is a potential lie. Denying important information is as reprehensible as lying. It may seem innocent, but in reality, it can be more destructive than the biggest lie. The honorable judge—the strict voice inside you—will not exonerate you this time. You are withholding information, and you will be convicted of indifference. So, as I said, it is shameful!"

"I see where this is going! The story of 'The King and the Cook'! I will not rest until I bring my story to light. What are my chances of success in such a mission?"

"What are the chances of you talking to me right now?"

"My mind says none whatsoever!"

"What does your heart say?"

"Don't lose hope!"

"Then it's your choice to whom you listen. You have had the same dilemma your whole life: listen to reason or listen to your heart. What has been your verdict each time?"

"I've always listened to what my heart was telling me to do. But how is it possible for you to know so many things about me?"

"Please close your mind and open your heart so that we can come to an understanding. I want you to realize that the effort needed to bring your heritage to light will be far less than the energy you have spent all these years to keep it in the dark! Do you remember the girl who played her violin at the station? I saw you two talking just before we first met. Do you want to tell me what you were talking about?"

"She was incredibly happy because she had finally carried out her mission. She then handed her violin to the following angel and left happily to meet her Father again."

"Tell me about your first meeting?"

"I first saw her at Time Station, playing her violin for passersby. She was performing Vivaldi's *The Four Seasons*, while everyone else at the station was having a cloudy day. I don't believe she got a hefty tip that day."

"Then you should know that the girl, just like me, works for the station master for free. Our reward is in what we give and not in what we get. What was your first impression of me?"

"The best!"

"You have a funny face when you try to hide the truth. You won't be able to convince any judge this time, so listen to me very carefully. My dear child, the first time we met, I saw and felt your pain. I held back my tears so as not to discourage you completely and smiled at you to give you strength! Do you remember?"

"Yes! You were looking at me while tilting your head to the right and to the left."

"At that moment, your brown eyes were staring at my wrinkled old face, and your mind raged with a thousand questions and assumptions in an effort to satisfy its curiosity. I let my disguise entertain your inquisitive mind for the time I needed to speak directly to your soul. At some point, the eyes of your soul opened, just for a second, but it was enough for us to communicate for the first time. Do you remember?"

"Help me better understand."

"I will remind you of what I whispered into your soul that night under the burning lantern:

> My dear soul,
>
> When a captain loses his way, the first thing he needs to do is consult his navigational instruments, compass and map. For this to be accomplished, I bless you with having *faith in yourself.*
>
> If not enough, then the second thing a captain needs to do is ask his team for help. For this to be accomplished, I bless you with the ability to say, *I need help.*
>
> With God's help, the captain and his team will get the ship back on course. For this to be accomplished, I bless you with having *inexhaustible perseverance.*

Occasionally, self-confidence, navigational instruments, and a capable team will not be enough to help the captain tame the raging ten-Beaufort sea. The storm will drive you off course again. To overcome this problem, I bless you with having *undying patience.*

On the way to the next port, you will find yourself again in the middle of the ocean, in the middle of nowhere, where no one sees you. "May you always have a clean shirt and a clear conscience," as they say in Scotland's harbor. This means that any of your rubbish on board, literally and metaphorically, stays on board! You do not throw them overboard. It is your duty to keep your ship and the sea clean. You keep your ship clean with fresh water, and you keep your sailors fresh with your good manners! For this to be accomplished, I bless you with the ability to show *absolute respect.*

If you ever lose your faith, perseverance, patience, and respect, you will have lost your way. Then all that will be left is prayer. For this to be accomplished, I bless you to possess *endless hope.*

And if you fail to count your blessings, you will eventually lose your orientation. If you lose your orientation, you will lose your direction and find yourself begging on the street. Leaving behind the sea to wander the streets means that you have lost your perseverance, and when the next storm comes you will be defeated by the very first wave because you have lost your patience as well. When you lose your respect at the very end, you will end up on the street, homeless and directionless. And I have no blessing for that!

My *chosen boy,*

If I have learned one thing from my travels across the seas, it is the power of "we": *We can do it!* Every captain needs the help of every sailor to tie the ship to a safe mooring.

If I have learned one thing from my travels to stations, it is the power of "I": *I can do it!* Every captain needs to have faith in himself and never give up.

The sea taught me the power of "we" and the tracks taught me the power of "me." That's why the sea is much more beautiful. That's why the sea still makes you cry! You must finally accept the tears of joy, and let your face shine like a lighthouse. If you can do it, then the rest will follow. Follow your light as you show others the way!

I bless you with fair wind and smooth sailing until you reach the destination your Captain desires!

"Unbelievable! You have just repeated verbatim the letter I found at the station. My mind wonders—story or fairy tale, truth or fantasy, possible or impossible?"

"And your heart replies, 'It doesn't matter!' What really matters is what has been awakened inside you. So, what are you going to do about it? When will you finally complete your mission? When will you offer your melody to the whole world? The violin has been in your hands for a long time!"

"Can you at least help me with a title?"

"This conversation is possible because your mind is closed, and you are finally calm. Your body is pain-free, and you are finally relaxed. When we lighten our pain, our souls can fly. This is how we've been able to meet and communicate today, when your mind, body, and pain have been released! Let me light your mind and body, while you do what is needed with the pain."

"Got it!"

"Well done, my child! Once you do it, you'll be an example for everyone else. Only then will you have accomplished your mission. Once that is done, then nothing will stand in the way of your reunion. Now I must let you rest."

"Just stay for a little longer, my wise elder! I have many things to ask you."

"The time we have is limited, and I know for a fact that you don't waste it on small talk when you meet your luminous passengers. I know the exact question that has plagued you from the first moment you met me. Well?"

"Why was my son only given so little time?"

"This is not a leading question. I was expecting a better one from an experienced coach. Ask the right way to get the right answer."

"I need help to understand why this tragic event has happened to my family."

"Try to remember another Father who also lost His Son. You gave him one last look from your left mirror, and He gave Him one last look from heaven. You wept for him with a river of tears, and He opened the heavens and poured a flood of tears. So, both of you, each in your own way, have mourned your loss and go on with your mission, as each destiny dictated. God wanted to save His Son from the cross, as you wanted to save your son at the crossover. God sacrificed His Son for all of us. How about you?

"Do you remember the interview you gave in that business magazine on November 2011? The last question put by the reporter was, 'What is the most valuable skill for a coach?' At the time, you answered, 'His perseverance! Never give up trying to help and improve the lives of others.' My dear coach, what about your life right now?

"Do I need to remind you how many supportive letters, messages, and positive feedback you received in your career as a coach and trainer—the desperate people who found hope, the lost who found their way, those in pain who found peace after your seminars and talks? What would you say to the suggestion of offering a book that can help ten or one hundred people, or one million lives? How about the chance to save someone else's child? The possibility of saving an entire generation of young people? What do you say?

"You say your son left you at the station, and I say that he took from his bag some of the immense love you gave him and sent you a kiss. He wanted to tell you, 'I love you!'

"You say your son left you at the station, and I say that he took his screwdriver from his bag and fixed the loose bolt. He wanted to tell you, 'Thank you for everything you taught me!'

"You say your son left you at the station, and I say that as soon as he repaired the bench, he looked at you and whispered to your soul, 'Daddy, be strong. Get your own screwdriver, and fix the *loose people* who have lost their hope!'

"You say your son left you at the station, and I say that he left you to all of us. He renounced his father to leave him to the whole world. Does that ring a bell? Does it remind you of someone who gave up a loved one for everyone else?

"Arsenios left you to all of us because he always knew the gifts you received from our Father. After all, he had seen them while selecting you at the well with the crystals.

"Arsenios left you to all of us because if he remained, you would've channeled all your energy and talents into his upbringing—as expected and as any proper father should do.

"Arsenios left you to all of us because he never lost his hope in you. He wanted to leave behind someone worthy. He wanted to share you with the rest of the world and not keep you to himself. Besides, he knows quite well that once the mission is fulfilled, the reunion will follow.

"Arsenios freed you from your priceless chains—parenting—to go and find your mission. 'So, if the Son sets you free, you will be free indeed' (John 8:36).

"You can be free to become a father to many. Deal with your pain, my dear coach, and then release your spiritual wealth to the whole world. So, why you are so quiet? Will you realize the Latin root of your name and the gifts you have generously received from our beloved Father? Do you understand that He patiently waits for you to honor your name and fulfill your purpose? Well, will you finally speak without fear?"

"Oh, my dear God! As Akins the Egyptian businessman did! He honored his name and then gave away his entire fortune. He offered and found joy."

"Praise the Lord, you have decided to speak, Evagoras! Your name has a dual meaning. The prefix *Ev*, which means 'good', and the ancient Greek word *Agorevo*, which means 'speak.' So, what does this give us?"

"The good speaker!"

"Exactly. And you've been doing it superbly for many years. The second meaning is quite remarkable as well. Once again, we have the prefix *Ev*, meaning 'good' and the Greek word *Agora*, which means 'market.' At the market, you have a variety of goods at your disposal to satisfy a particular need. In the very first chapter on economics, we learn the dual role of goods. The *economic goods*, which on the one hand are found in certain quantities, and on the other hand require effort, sacrifice, or a monetary price to acquire; and the *free goods*, offered in unlimited, in relation to our needs, quantities, such as the air we breathe, the sea, and the sun. Both categories fall under *giving*. For the sake of discussion, let's consider that humans can provide for the economic goods and our God provides for the free goods. Well, your book will be a category in itself. While it will be found in specific quantities with a small monetary price attached to it, once one reads it, understands it, and applies all the knowledge within, then the energy received will be as vital as the air and the sun. This book can become the oxygen and the light for millions of people, as long as they choose it from the millions of other books on the market, trust the knowledge with their hearts, and thereafter apply it faithfully until other people see their transformation."

"You are obviously referring to the Great Road, The Gardener's Five Rules, and the Ten Lanterns! The spiritual heritage of the Conali family. Right?"

"Exactly. The spiritual map and compass. You possess the spiritual ingredients that can form a powerful vaccine to cure a pandemic—the pandemic of pain. I must inform you that the spiritual rights are not exclusively yours; they are global. When will you finally honor your name and your son? When will you finally honor God for the gifts He has given you?"

"While my mind still experiences pain, my heart is now revived. While my mind wants to stay in the past, my heart now wants to live in the present. I will do what I always did. I will follow my heart once again."

"Thank God. Once you accept that the past cannot be changed, you will have the power to change the future. Don't forget to live in the present with three drops of hope—one for you, one for the others, and one for the almighty God. *Nothing occurs without God's providence, and where His providence occurs, however difficult, it will bring benefit to the soul!* This is your *personal resurrection*! Get out of bed and continue your mission."

"I promise on my royal honor, my wise foreman."

"The time has passed. The clock reads seven, and the station master will start looking for me. Your deepest thought honors me, but I'm going to disappoint you. I'm not Him. I told you before that I've been crawling in the mud for years, but I'll never give up. As soon as I complete my mission, I also will be reunited with my Father."

"Then who are you, my wise old man?"

"It doesn't matter who I am but what I am to you. You will always find me in my pearl of wisdom, when I still had oxygen in my lungs, many years ago: *'For as long as we live, we have the right to complete our spiritual examinations. There is no such thing as failing the exam. Let us strive to get at least a passing grade and get a pass into heaven!'*"

"What about the soul-whispering?"

"The Lord said to me: *'Go, chosen vessel of Mine, to bear My name before them!'* I, therefore, serve Him as a mail carrier, and I sometimes read the letters so that I learn and become better. I am also trying to get a passing grade for my spiritual exams. When you were studying for your spiritual exams twenty years ago, during your recovery after your third surgery, you underlined a single paragraph in Scott Peck's book, *The Road Less Traveled*. You singled out the following:

> Spiritually evolved people, by virtue of their discipline, mastery and love, are people of extraordinary competence, and in their competence they are called on to serve the world, and in their love they answer the call. They are inevitably, therefore, people of great power, although the world may generally behold them as quite ordinary people, since more often than not they will exercise their power in quiet or even hidden ways!

"Do you see more clearly now? Are you ordinary or extraordinary, my chosen boy? Therefore, exercise your power in quiet ways by serving you, serving others, and quietly serving our God."

"And because I will need all His power and blessings, will I see you again?"

"I very much doubt we will have to meet again at this station. My mission is over, and yours has just begun."

"How can you be so sure?"

"Just look at your wrists. The *golden chain* has disappeared from my wrists and is now on yours. You hold the heavenly directive. You can either use it to continue your journey or to reunite at once with our Father. But since we are associate foremen, allow me to give you one more piece of advice: '*Leave your last breath in your book and not in this hospital room!*' And don't ask me why or how, as we had this conversation many years ago! As one single thought is enough to set the coordinates for your next station, I have a parting message for you: *Go, chosen boy of mine, and be my vessel as you pass on your Great Road. Give your spiritual fruits to others as a good gardener, and finally set me free to reunite with our Father!*"

"And if I need your help again?"

"If you ever need anything, you will find me in the quotes left behind for a better world. Just repeat my final words: '*Thank you, my God, because this was needed for my salvation!*' Remember, my dear child, please leave your last breath in your book and not in this hospital room. Do you hear me?"

"So, this is goodbye?"

"Yes, for now. But before I leave you, could you please remind me of your great-great-grandfather's name?"

"Amadeo Conali."

"Has your grandfather Christakis explained the meaning?"

"Yes. Grandpa Takis told me that the Latin name Amadeo means 'the one who has God within.'"

"That's right! And what about his last name?"

"He hasn't told me anything about that."

"Then you should begin Italian lessons. The prefix *Con* means 'with', and the word *Ali* means 'wings.' Imagine this—a man who had God within him and who had wings!"

"An angel on earth. Oh my God!"

"You should have realized that the surname Evagorou is only temporary. When will you finally spread your wings and fly, *Evos Conali*? Here I am; will you send me an angel?"

"You now call me Evos Conali."

"I baptize you with it. You should reintroduce yourself to the whole world, provided they *detect and tell* the benefit of your spiritual legacy. Good night, my child, and may God be with you always. I'm leaving now to let the doctors do their job too, like good caretakers."

● ● ●

"Doctor, we have a pulse."

"We have got him back, Sister. Thank God."

"What is impossible with man is possible with God. God bless you, Doctor"

"Praise the Lord!"

First Meeting:
The Coaching Session

The mind is not a vessel to be filled
but a fire to be kindled.
—Plutarch

February. What a blessing!

Welcome! The time has come to finally introduce ourselves. I am Coach Evos, and I am a descendant of the Amadeo Conali family.

To be entitled to use my family's surname, I must first honor my name, unfold my tale like an orator, and awaken what is spiritually good for you. I must bequeath my spiritual heritage to the world and offer the spiritual good to future generations. You must thereafter *detect and tell* the benefit of the spiritual good, and honor me with your recognition—as the king honored the master, as the cook called his lodge Ten Candles, and as the customers labeled their favorite restaurant Ten Lanterns. Only you, the recipient, can rename me and put me in my rightful place in history. Only then will the fairy tale be transformed into a story and, while disguised as a butterfly, take flight to all four corners of the world. Only then will I be entitled to a distinguished place with the other nine recipients in heaven—a seat at the Conalis' Sunday table. Only you can give me the wings—conali—and reunite me with my family.

Today, I live on a beautiful Mediterranean island called Cyprus, bathed in light. All I need for yet another journey is an invitation to speak and a wagon full of people. I am willing to come to your station if my story and presence will be beneficial to just one person. I will take the stage and present the spiritual wealth I inherited from my family, offer the most precious thing in the world that I have discovered along the way, and describe my adventures on how I managed to light my way and lighten my pain.

Today, you understand me perfectly, even though I speak the Greek language. We appreciate each other because my words are humble and universal. What is happening right now is a small miracle—my coming into your home, as you chose me from millions of other options available in the market. I, therefore, will leave the great miracle of the transformation to you.

Today, communicating and appreciating each other means that you are sitting comfortably in your seat and holding my book in your hands. You are gratefully staring at the wagon's back seats that you left behind with your efforts and courage. You want to plan your next action, reaction, and satisfaction to reach the distinguished seat that you deserve. All I need to do is help you remember your own spiritual map, which is engraved in your heart and was drafted at preschool. Open your notebook, and you'll find it all inside. Otherwise, take some notes.

Today, I am unable to teach you anything new except to remind you of all the good things you have hidden inside, along with an urgent and important note: if you stop playing, your soul will starve. That's why, today, you must do the following:

» Hide your watch, and make time for someone important to you.
» Hold out your hand, and offer your help to someone in pain.
» Write a letter, and send it to a loved one.
» Feel your lungs, and then exhale goodness to the whole world.
» Give, right and left, without expecting a tip from anyone.
» Take your life's remote control, find a happy channel, and create another good memory.

These are your actions for today.
Today is a wonderful day!
Today is a blessing!

I have something extremely important to tell you. Please have a look at my photograph one more time. You'll find me at the end of the book, trying to encourage you to take another step forward. I am direct and do not exaggerate. If I've made it this far, then you can make it too. Since I didn't leave my last breath at the station and carried on, I won't let you waste a single breath of yours. I will give you all the available choices once again, and you can make your final decision. You will enter the coordinates into your control panel. You hold the remote control of your life. But if you believe in me—like a best friend from the old days would do—let me give your choices once again. If you agree to that, then let's sign the coaching contract and continue our session. Are you ready for a coaching session?

Allow me to start first, as I have a confession to make.
I needed and received help.
I needed help! I made the necessary journeys to discover my lost self. Although I was under the influence of strong analgesics, I made sure to set the right coordinates for journeys back and forth in time and in every direction in space. I am grateful because I met Young Evagoras, who won the battle and freed himself from depression, fear, and anger. I conversed with Coach Evagoras, who helped and guided thousands of people with his seminars and sessions. I admired and applauded Author Evagoras for passionately continuing his mission. I took a journey with Evagoras into the Asynchronous Zone of Today.

I received help! Young Evagoras reminded me of my perseverance to overcome four difficult surgeries and two stagnant years in my adolescent life. Coach Evagoras reminded me of my giving to my fellow passengers, and Author Evagoras reminded me that I have all the time in the world to accomplish my mission. At the same time, I was enjoying the greatest support from the luminous passengers on my train—the time-giver doctor, the persistence-giver old friend, and the hope-giver teacher. Gratefully, in my darkest hours, I met the help-giver girl with the violin and the care-giver foreman. Fortunately, even when I gave up, I had two boats, on my left and right, that kept my life steady during the storm.

All you need to do right now is close your eyes, make the same journey to the illuminating stations of your life, and find yourself. There, you will find your true self. There, you will meet once again all your *givers* in life. This is your first exercise to get our sessions off to a great start. We will open one lantern at a time, so you need to be patient. Your first exercise is to find yourself and all those who have helped you so far. Grab a paper and pen and get started! Are you ready to travel?

Allow me to continue. I've also managed to overcome the recent surgery that was necessary for me to continue my mission with robust breathing. Once I recouped my strength after my fifth surgery, I opened my laptop and wrote my first words to you. I had to type with my left hand, as my right held the tubes coming out of my chest. The slightest careless movement caused crushing pain, but I managed to write a whole page:

> I write to you every day. I write until my eyes get misty. I write until my hands are numb. I write to you as fast as I can because I have discovered that time is one of the most precious things in the world. To free your body and soul from pain requires a journey to the illuminating stations of your life. To do this, you must break the boundaries of time and space. If the regressions from the back-and-forth journey make you dizzy or confused, please be patient until we reach the last station. There, I promise you, the last route will light the way, and all will become crystal clear. I welcome you to the distinguished seats of the first carriage to continue the journey

of the quest together—the invitation is mine, and
the choice is yours. May the words infuse the spirit
and encourage the desperate, awaken the asleep,
welcome the lost, and, above all, comfort all those in
pain. May the journey provide each passenger with
inexhaustible strength for personal development
and transformation. May the luggage we carry be as
light as a feather. "Story or fairytale, truth or fantasy,
possible or impossible?" the mind asks curiously.
"What difference does it make? What really matters
is what has been awakened inside you and what you
are going to do about it," the heart replies. Enjoy our
choiceful journey to a successful life!

Was it helpful reading the 'Note to the Reader' for a second time?
Can you see the level of understanding and how differently you feel
right now by reading it again? How robust is the meaning behind each
word. How much understanding you want to give me.

You want to be useful because I need good company. You want
to be cheerful to elevate my good mood. You want to be respectful
so you choose to have good manners. You want to be faithful and
evaluate my story with good intentions. You want to be resourceful
so you accept the Ten Lanterns to help your good progress. You want
to be mindful because you appreciate the power of good timing for
a new life ahead. You want to be grateful so you browse your life's
album to be refueled by good memories. You want to be thoughtful
so you choose to exhale goodness to the world. You want to become
purposeful so you choose not to negotiate for your good purpose in
life. You want to become insightful because you have learned that you
are the architect of your good life.

We have just put the pieces together, and the mosaic of your life is
clearly visible before your eyes. The puzzle has been assembled; your life
has been composed. How glad I am that, on this trip, you were looking
up to the stars. How happy I am that the first page written in September

kicked off a beautiful y)k. How pleased I
am for finding you, and ess market. If you
feel sad or not ready to another quest for
you. Another adventur ourney?

Thank you for be ng my book, but I
am afraid you have rea ed from Station 10
and worked your way
"What practical t ourney?" the mind
asks curiously.
"What do space a e heart asks boldly.
If you want to fi ant to understand
me, if you really wan piritual good, then
you should start all o from Station 1, and
don't stop until you r), we will definitely
meet once again. Tak ke ten further so we
can meet again and f e distinguished seat
that you deserve. Do varm hug when you
find me again, instea ever, to see my smile
and recognize me on look up to the stars,
and never look down willing thereafter to
accept my goodness, ne for being so effuse.
It goes without sayi eek blood is boiling
inside, creating a tide n endless flow of love
for everyone and eve hat my heart tells me
to do, despite the li set. Squeeze me just
enough to keep fron iat you leave me with
the oxygen I need to n you can take all the
rest. Take as much a ontinue your journey
to the next station.
By starting your ng, from Station 1, you
will discover that th ife is your own life. It's
the first breath you efore you get your first
hug from your moth ion-to-station journey?

Light your way with the first lan

This gift of life, given by G not be digested in one bite. That's why rld, we do so with intense weeping. Pain ence in the first chapter of our lives, but ht after that—the warmest and most ove. Love, therefore, is the second feeling in makes us cry, and love makes us rejoice. mpany us in our journeys, like the warm hts. All you need to do, once you leave you ur first steps and enjoy your childhood. Th ur path to lighten your pain. Do you see it *life.*

Light your way with the second la

Grandpa Takis Conali's ins, read, and play is your only job. My job you're old enough!" Therefore, food wil arning will take care of your mind, and p r soul. Marshall McLuhan's instructions o tries to make a distinction between edu oesn't know the first thing about either." wisely said, "We don't stop playing because ecause we stop playing." Well, stop at no o stop you from learning and playing. Ju spicy condiments and new dishes occas palate because it's pointless to eat the sam s your favorite. Thus, your first steps, your nging for good life will take you to the nex ntern. The second lantern illuminates your o you see it? *It is your choice to have good pu*

Light your way with the third lantern

Every day when you wake up, eet on the ground, you should say, "Thank ng the

238

opportunity to be, to feel, to have, to hope, and to foresee. Be thankful for receiving an hour, a day, and a whole year ahead of you. Be thankful for having twenty-four hours available on a daily basis. And then pray to God to bless you with love so as to sow your love and to offer goodness so that you may receive it as well—goodness for you, for those you care about the most, for those who need it the most. Everyone needs love, and the whole world needs goodness—and, of course, a little help from our God. If you manage to stay loyal with goodness, then all the bad people will magically disappear from your path. Today, you argued with your colleague over a promotion, yelled at someone who had been gossiping behind your back, or argued with a driver who cut you off abruptly. Yesterday, you were insulted by your manager, and a week ago, you were searching for your lost self-esteem and confidence. On a daily basis, you dislike your reflection in the mirror. But where is everyone now? Where are your self-esteem thieves and your confidence master thief? You still see them every day, but they are not the same. You are not the same! The third lantern illuminates your path to lighten your pain. Do you see it? *It is your choice to have goodness.*

Light your way with the fourth lantern: *good memories.*

Since you have the right coordinates, you have arrived at a spotless station. A fair wind cools you down and offers an air of optimism and joy to your fellow travelers. It offers a holy day; a Sunday feast to fill all of you for the coming week. And then, you take your glass and clink it loudly with your good company to scare the pain away. This is how good memories are created, crafted by your positive attitude. You now possess the skill to choose colorful brushes and paint your own journey across the sea. Create your choiceful journey to a successful life. The journey of life continues, and now your strong steps leave footprints on the golden sandy beach. You are no longer small, despite the fact that you still enjoy your mother's hugs. You now take initiatives, make decisions, and influence your passengers with your choices. The fourth lantern illuminates your path to lighten your pain. Do you see it? *It's your choice to have good memories.*

Light your way with the fifth lantern: *good timing.*

You now have the ability to separate the important from the unimportant. You have the choice to invest your time in meaningful activities. You have the choice to regulate the flow, intensity, quality, and outcome of your actions. You have sole responsibility for the speed, safety, comfort and joy of all those on board your train. You take care of your fellow passengers' needs in a timely manner without expecting any gratuity. Your actions do not hurt other people; they only create a musical harmony that reaches their ears and their hearts, helping to soothe their souls. Just as you need care, love, and security, all living creatures on earth have the same need, whether they are reptiles, flies, insects, humans, or our planet. Every kind has its own rhythm, mission, and reason for existence. Every human being is born to accomplish its own greatness in its own time. Nevertheless, our behavior and actions should not offend or threaten the existence of others. There must be a flow of love and security for all living things. Create a harmonious cohabitation. And remember that there is no shortcut in the Great Road! You will need persistence for the implementation, patience for the recognition, and respect for all people and species. The fifth lantern illuminates your path to lighten your pain. Do you see it? *It's your choice to have good timing.*

Light your way with the sixth lantern: *good progress.*

The engines are hot, the tank is filled with fuel, and the correct coordinates are programmed into the navigational instruments. Your train is full of people. They have all paid for their tickets and are looking forward to having a nice trip. The penultimate siren is giving a little leeway to the latecomers, and the last siren is awakening the loafers. You have the green light from the control room, and all is set. You are set to go. You want to make your first big trip. You are driving your first mile behind the wheel, and you've got a carriage full of people. You now have all the responsibility in your hands. You are a fit and proper driver, and you will reach your first station and write your first chapter in gold letters. You want to make your passengers proud, especially those traveling in the first-class seats. However, you constantly encounter problems, obstacles, and difficulties that you have never faced before. You need help, and that's when you remember the words of Grandpa Takis Conali on synergy: "Operation acquires substance with cooperation; hence, the prefix *co*. Cooperation produces added value to operation!" Therefore, you learn to overcome the obstacles with other people's help and support. Don't forget, at the end of the day, to collect all the positives and forget all the negatives. What counts is what you bring to the table and what they bring to the table, so collect all the ingredients for a rich meal. There is no pride in those who reject help and support, only insanity. The sixth lantern illuminates your path to lighten your pain. Do you see it? *It is your choice to have good progress.*

Light your way with the seventh lantern: *good intentions.*

The right coordinates, a skilled captain, and a strong team are sometimes not enough to overtake the avalanche covering the rails. Difficulties will make you and your team even more experienced and come closer to each other. The simplest problems will be the mechanical ones. You'll take a screwdriver and fix the damage. If you don't have the skills to do it, then you need to have a good craftsman on board who is willing to help you and teach you how to fix it yourself. The same goes for health problems. You must never neglect your health care, and always have a first-aid kit equipped with all the necessities for treating minor abrasions and bumps. If you don't have the skills to fix a deep wound or repair a major injury, then you should have a doctor on board who is willing to help you. The most complicated problem you will encounter on board is managing your relationships with your passengers. How to handle the wicked, how to deal with the toxic, how to accept the diverse, how to handle the strong perceptions of others, how to resist malicious criticism, and how to utilize their feedback— these are the real problems, and they will be in your path daily. If you fail to turn on the seventh lantern—your good intentions—then you will steer in the dark. *Good intentions* are your heart's ability to override your mind's discriminating decisions and offer goodness to all. If you manage to have good intentions toward everyone and not at will, you will discover a tremendous power that exists within you called *forgive, forget, and forward!* With this power, all wicked and toxic people will stay at home. Things will get back on track, and the obstacles will become fewer and fewer. You will start to enjoy a downhill course in a positive way. You will save fuel, as you will no longer stress your engines. You will advance without much steering, effort, or contemplation. You won't even think about it, as your mind will work on autopilot. You will be respectful with all, unaffected by their own behaviors and attitudes. The seventh lantern illuminates your path to lighten your pain. Do you see it? *It is your choice to have good intentions.*

Light your way with the eighth lantern: *good manners.*

It sounds great, but it is extremely difficult to maintain. You need to set the right tone in every communication, and choose respectful words in every conversation. Every passionate relationship will stimulate your mind and soul. Since passion is highly contagious, you will pass it on to others. Seek to do good, and good will come to you! It is your choice to have good manners. Remember that good manners were, are, and will always be in fashion. You now hold eight illuminating lanterns, strong enough to light the way right to the end. The country road will disappear, and you will enjoy the city road that brings you safely and closer to your final destination—the Ten Lanterns restaurant. Upon your arrival, you will once again enjoy Grandpa's thirty-three divine delicacies. Those who make it to the city road will never miss their final destination. They will be spared the nagging of Grandma Vasia on the phone. Now, let me remind you of Grandpa Takis Conali's sign at the restaurant entrance: "Choose to have a good mood, or choose to leave right now!" I may have failed miserably to grasp the profound message when I was sixteen, but today, as I approach the fifth decade of my life, I can grasp exactly the value. The eighth lantern illuminates your path to lighten your pain. Do you see it? *It is your choice to have good manners.*

Light your way with the ninth lantern: *good mood.*

With the ninth lantern on, you will be blessed to enjoy the rest of your life. So what if the chef has overcooked the chicken wings? So what if I am recovering from a difficult surgery? So what if my son clumsily spills coffee on my clothes? So what if a hailstorm pours out of dark clouds when I'm enjoying my August vacation in Puerto Rico? I will say *thank you* for providing food on my table; *thank you* for blessing me to survive the operation; *thank you* for having my son in my life; *thank you* for having the opportunity to travel. Nothing can erase the smile from my face because after the dark clouds, a beautiful rainbow appears, and behind every problem, a wonderful opportunity hides. Do not let your emotions control you with an unexpected event. Nothing can impact your good mood because you control it yourself. Our lives are full of stations. We take a break, observe, evaluate, and move on—until the next station. The train never stops! The ninth lantern illuminates your path to lighten your pain. Do you see it? *It's your choice to have good mood.*

Our coaching session for today is almost finished, and I need your help to change the world, to leave a better world for our children, for all children in all four corners of the world—a legacy that will make our descendants proud for at least ten more generations. Nevertheless, if by 2500 we have failed to make our world a better place, then let us hope that the *twentieth recipient* will manage to change everything and start fresh, if it's not too late. And if we indeed fail our mission, then the paintings, sculptures, books, and great manuscripts we so carefully kept and preserved all these years will have to be burned once again in the central square of Florence, in the Fire of Perpetual Human Failure. Hopefully, we finally will write the proper manuscript that will redeem us, a spiritual guide that will take us to the wonderful world we deserve, to a world called Hope, with love as its only currency. It's a new world that values the spontaneity of the young and the wisdom of the old, accepts all skin colors and approves all good perceptions, and offers food to the hungry and unlimited riches to the poor. A new world with fresh air for our lungs, warm sunshine for our hearts, spring water for our trees, and vast, clean, blue oceans for our travels and adventures. A place that has children playing and laughing in every neighborhood, birds singing on every branch, and happy people free from pain. A world where every citizen will be proud. A world made up of the best version of everyone. One version—Uni Verse—one world!

Let us accept all the mistakes of the past with good intentions. If we finally accept that the past is impossible to change, we will gain the strength to create a better future. No one deserves an ending without the opportunity to answer both questions: "Did you offer joy, and did you find joy?"

Having said all that, let me tell you why I am not afraid for our future. It's because I have good company, and when we meet, we raise our glasses and clink them hard to drive pain away.

The tenth lantern is on: *good company.*

The tenth lantern is the most important of all, and thankfully, it's on and is warming our souls. I remind you to set your coordinates right from early morning. The execution of your day will be based on your morning order, and your day will unfold, based on your first choice. You should bring to the table your positive attitude ("Good morning to all. Today is a great day for all of us"), and you should leave the demoralizing one ("From where do you have that good mood? Today is a tough day") for Mr. Black and his miserable company. Choose carefully what to order because soon the kitchen will close, just like the lights will be turned off, and you'll be left alone on stage. Therefore, choose carefully how you want your day to be; choose carefully what you want your whole life to be like. If the Ten Lanterns have lit your day today, then they also will be able to light your month. If your month is successful, then the year will be fruitful as well. Year by year, day by day, step by step, breath by breath, you will build your castle and host all your good company, with a huge oak tree protecting its entire roof. The tenth lantern illuminates your path to lighten your pain. Do you see it? *It's your choice to have good company.*

What is left to explain is why the last lantern, good company, is the most crucial of all. After medical consultation and verification, I learned that prolonged unbearable pain is capable of exhausting even the most ferocious lion. I also learned about the last station called Time Zero. This is the time when science and medicine can offer no more help or relief. Well, now that we've grown up, it's time to tell the rest. It is the right time to reveal something very important. I want to explain how the pink magic stick works—when it works its magic and when it doesn't.

Dr. Time explained to me that there are numerous patients who have managed to live beyond the reasonable limits of time for only one specific reason. Patients with only one month left, laugh about it and fool the pain—and manage to live a whole year. Patients with only a few months to live, laugh about it and fool the pain—and manage to live a couple of years. Patients who have been told their disease is incurable, laugh about it and fool the pain—they somehow achieve a complete cure. These are real-case examples of patients who manage to fool the pain and time, who manage to fool life itself. How is this ever possible? Well, it's not a secret anymore. *We live because we have good company, and we die because we are alone.*

Since we've grown up and are driving our thousand horses on the highway, it's time to tell the rest. The instructions from Grandpa Amadeo were specific: "When you read it for the first time, you will assume it's a simple and an easy process. However, the application requires great effort and courage. It requires you to walk the long path of your transformation. This long path is called La Grande Strada— the Great Road—and it contains four stations. The first three stations complete your *application* phase, and the last station brings you ever closer to *recognition*. The four stations are *I choose, I dare, I become,* and *I am.*"

In order to complete the four stations, we need the guidance of the Ten Lanterns. Let's refresh our memories one more time and continue our choiceful journeys to a successful life.

> » I choose to have good company to become useful.
> » I choose to have good mood to become cheerful.
> » I choose to have good manners to become respectful.
> » I choose to have good intentions to become faithful.
> » I choose to have good progress to become resourceful.
> » I choose to have good timing to become mindful.
> » I choose to have good memories to become grateful.
> » I choose to have goodness to become thoughtful.
> » I choose to have good purpose to become purposeful.
> » I choose to have good life to become insightful.

A choiceful journey to a successful life indeed!

You must be particularly happy because you have made similar or exactly the same choices at some point in your life. Therefore, the Ten Lanterns have been in your life for some time now, since the time of elementary school. All we have accomplished together is to put them in order; yet again, the order doesn't really matter. What is important is how you feel about it right now. Anyway, let's get them in order.

The Great Road has a beginning. The execution will be based on your order. Your day will unfold, based on your choices. The hours will become days, the days will become months, and the years will pass by, so don't delay any longer. Your character will be sculpted by these choices. Your choices will be transformed into values. Your values will become the roots of your character, and you will shine with your personality. Are you ready to answer the question, "What is your character like, and what is your personality?"

The first station of the Great Road, "I choose," is possible. Are you ready to make the first of your choices?

The gifts of nature and the gardener's care transform a seed into a sapling. At first, it needs support to stay upright and nurturing for it to grow quickly and sturdily. In time, the oak spreads its branches to shelter and protect your entire house. The oak shields all inside the house who have helped it grow well and become the strongest tree on the mountain. The oak tree—to shed some light on this allegory—is your mind. It contains the fertile soil that received the seed, trusted the gardener to protect it from hardship, accepted the fertilizer to keep it strong, tolerated the spray to kill the weeds, enjoyed the clear water to irrigate its roots, and let the sun warm it and give the light to nurture it. And as a result, there are dry fruits to excite your senses with their scent in your tea and broad branches to protect your house. The mighty oak, our mind, protects you with the choices you make every day. Let the earthquake and the storm come; nothing will bring down a deep-rooted tree. You'll be ready for anything! Are you ready for the next station?

The second station of the Great Road, "I dare," is possible. Will you dare to continue?

This station has many stimuli from nature and the gardener. The gardener—to shed some light on this allegory too—is all the learning and guidance you have in your life. The environment you live in and the people who surround you are extremely important. Your sunny days and your goodness will sail you across windless seas, while your cloudy weather and discourtesy will drive you along rocky roads. Goodness is the major ingredient for the "power of we" and discourtesy for the "power of me." Which journey will you choose? Sailing calm seas or driving rocky roads? You already know my choice; you already know my favorite song, the lyrics of which still move me to this day.

Oh sea, my sea, what have you done to me?
I lost every port for you.

And I am since then a sailor and tomorrow I set sail
again alone.

Despite the fact that, at some point in my journey, I lost all my
harbors, I have been blessed with soul-whispering and finally found
my port. Did you find yours, or are you still looking for it?

The third station of the Great Road, "I become," is possible. What
do you want to be in life?

If you succeed in the first two stations, "I choose" and "I dare,"
then you will have in your possession a spiritual map and a compass
for the rest of the journey. Having a map and a compass is enough to
guide the treasure hunter right to his fortune. Your spiritual map—to
shed some light on this allegory—refers to the daily predetermined
and well-thought-out plans you must make to help you understand
and appreciate your own personal, unique entity and reality. This
clairvoyance—your insight—is the map you use to move in every
direction of space and time. If the map you hold is correct, then you
know where you were, where you are, and where you want to go.
Therefore, the mapping you do is crucial and requires a great deal
of effort to craft. Your spiritual compass, on the other hand, refers to
all the aids, tools, practices, values, and perceptions you will have at
your disposal to make your journey, safely and successfully. It will be
everything that will potentially get you back on track when you stray
off course—your personal lanterns showing the way of the Great Road.

Your daily choices should be based on and synchronized with
your spiritual map and compass. Your daily choices will be your daily
coordinates. The spiritual map and compass will show you, step by
step, the virtuous path, until you also find your port. The third and final
station of the application phase, "I become," is obviously the most time-
consuming and the most difficult stage. It's not a quick fix with your
screwdriver. If it was that simple, then all the luminous teachers I have
had in my good company already would have succeeded, through their
intellectual superpowers, in making the world a better place for all of us.

Who can doubt the wisdom that lies in the following books?:

» *The 7 Habits of Highly Effective People* by Dr. Stephen R. Covey
» *How to Win Friends and Influence People* by Dale Carnegie
» *The Road Less Traveled* by Scott Peck
» *Think and Grow Rich* by Napoleon Hill
» *Man's Search for Meaning* by Viktor Frankl
» *The Monk Who Sold His Ferrari* by Robin Sharma
» *Wishes Fulfilled: Mastering the Art of Manifesting* by Dr. Wayne W. Dyer
» *The Greatest Salesman in the World* by Og Mandino
» *Living Loving and Learning* by Leo Buscaglia

And my personal favorite,

» *You Can Heal Your Life* by Louise Hay

What did we do wrong?
Where does success lie?
To answer the first question, I will leave it to your judgment. It will need deep analysis and honest self-criticism to identify, diagnose the cause, and find your answer. Any comment or criticism from me is completely unnecessary. I will carry out my own introspection, and we will discuss our findings at the next coaching session. As far as the second question is concerned, I have already offered my opinion, my input, and my compass and map in this book. I have granted you my entire heritage—my spiritual wealth! In my mind, the procedure is simple. You need to pass the application phase, and the recognition phase will not be long in coming. This is a promise!

The fourth station of the Great Road, "I am," is possible. Where are you struggling, and where do you need my help?
Once you feel really proud of yourself for completing the application phase, I want you to stand in front of the mirror and give

credit to that person who went through so much hardship. You have made so many steps, so many changes, and so much progress. Then, shout out, "Well done," and be sure to celebrate that day as if it were your last. Thereafter, you will buy a gift for yourself to remind you of your transformation day—the day of your *personal resurrection!* You have been reborn, and you have changed your title—from pessimist to optimist, from disoriented to oriented, from useless to useful, from awful to wonderful, from painful to pain-free. You've done it, and congratulations are in order. You have managed to lighten the pain that was inside and that was preventing you from shining like a star—*from painful to painless with the right choices!*

Before we say goodbye, I will give you a soul-whispering: *Take your own time for your recognition, and don't expect a gratuity from anyone!*

If you rush to gain your recognition, it means that you are limiting your journey, and you are expecting a specific treasure at a certain station. Let's assume that you fail to find it, and as a result, you become disappointed and give up. Obviously, you are tired, overwhelmed, and exhausted from all the effort up to that point. You have arrived at the station, and you want a break, a breath, acknowledgment, and a distinguished seat. Let's once again assume that all your desired treasures—reward for your efforts and recognition of your choices—are to be found at the next station, just a few miles away. What a shame if you give up just before the end, just one station away.

If you expect a gratuity—a bonus or a compliment after every good deed—I am afraid you will live a life full of disappointments. With your first disappointment, because the gratuity was meager to zero, your own misery will leave the next well-meaning customer disappointed and starved; hence, you again will be without a tip. Having convinced yourself that you were right after all, you will unfortunately abandon all your good deeds and efforts. It goes without saying that you will eventually lose much more than the tip. What a shame if you become the victim of your self-fulfilling prophecy.

Your recognition will come, sooner or later. Every passenger has his own path and his own place with a personal timeline. Please stop reading other people's biographies in order to make a chronological comparison with your own life. There will always be someone who will sit one seat in front of you, whether that translates into having better health than you, living and working in a better country than yours, or simply experiencing stronger benefits than you have. It's perfectly normal to compare our lives with other people's lives, but it's absolutely absurd to keep score. The only score to keep track of is where you were yesterday, what you learned today, and how many steps you took toward a better tomorrow. Therefore, you should read other people's biographies only to fuel your desire, improve your plan, and take another step forward. *Learn from your experiences to become wise. Learn from others to become wiser. Ignore learning to remain a fool.*

Learn to live and enjoy your own timeline, your own space, and never stop learning from the stars. Never be jealous of them, but always try to be as bright. Some people's stars shine from early on; for some, it comes later; and for others, it sparkles just before the end. The important thing is to light your own star. Believe me, true recognition will come to all those able to live a spiritual life. And because you and I have been blessed for another hour, another day, holding our books, and nurturing our minds with positive thoughts, I am quite sure that both of us are close to our recognition. For your information, I still await your recognition with undying perseverance, patience, respect, passion, and hope. Once you recognize me, I would like to kindly ask you to call me by my new name: *Hello, Evos Conali!*

Thank you for keeping me good company. Companionship will make a difference throughout our lives and especially at Time Zero. We need people at our sides, illuminating our lives and helping us not to give up. Our family and friends—the boat on our left—are enough to extend our time, even if science has thrown in the towel. God, the boat always on our right, will obviously lend a hand. We will seek another hour, another day, another week, another month; we will make time, as much as it takes, to accomplish our mission fully—like good caretakers.

I bid you farewell, leaving you all the necessary notes on the following pages. You will find what you need, what to do, and how to do it, right after you refuel by counting your blessings.

I have left it for the end, even though it is in no way short of value. I leave you with a wish:

> May you have fair wind and smooth sailing until you reach the destination you desire. Take your time; it's all yours anyway. Just make sure that it will be good time. May you have a choiceful journey and a successful life!

With love,
Coach Conali

First Exercise:
Count Your Blessings

Always give without remembering and
always receive without forgetting.
—Bryan Tracy

March. What a blessing![7]

The month remains a torture, but the page never remains empty
because I have you.

---

[7] The best memorial for Arsenios Conali is to fill this page with all your
blessings.

First Experience: The Treasure Box

Constantly add some spicy condiments and new
dishes to stimulate your palate. It's senseless to eat
the same dish every day, even if it is your favorite.
—Evos Conali

Get ready to reap the harvest of your actions soon. You have just
counted your blessings, and you are ready for the next step. You will
find below (a) what you need, (b) what to do, and (c) how to do it.
With a request: it is urgent and important that you begin immediately.
Good luck—*In bocca al lupo.*

(a)   What You Need
(a1) A deep breath before you start—soul-whispering.
(a2) An aid to guide you on the journey—the Great Road.

(a1) *Sussurro dell'anima*—soul-whispering
My dear soul,
You are blessed to have faith in yourself, so when you lose your
way, you should check your compass, map, and coordinates. *Do not be
afraid to make the necessary corrections to get back on track!*

You are blessed to have substantial help, so when you lose your way, ask for help, and it will come at supersonic speed. *Do not hesitate to ask for support and guidance from other people!*

You are blessed to have inexhaustible perseverance, so turn a deaf ear to the pessimistic shouting, and stay true to your course. *Do not give up, no matter how difficult the obstacles!*

You are blessed to have plentiful patience, so take advantage of the storm to sail you to your destination sooner. *Do not lose your determination, no matter how little fuel you have left!*

You are blessed to have absolute respect, so live in harmony with all your cohabitants. *Do not take actions that would offend or threaten their existence!*

If you lose your faith, perseverance, patience, and respect, you will not lose your way because ...

You are blessed with endless hope, so say your prayers as you look up at the stars, and count your blessings. *Do not look down and extinguish the flame of hope within you!*

If you fail to count your blessings, you will lose your direction; if you lose your direction, you will lose your way; if you lose your way, you will end up on the street, homeless and directionless; and I have not blessed you for that.

My dear soul, my sea journeys have taught me the power of *we*, and my street journeys have taught me the power of *me*. That is why the sea is so beautiful. I bless you with fair winds and smooth sailing until you reach the destination you desire!

(a2) *La Grande Strada*—the Great Road

The application phase requires self-confidence and perseverance, and the recognition phase requires patience and respect. Your personal success requires you to go through the four stations of the Great Road. The first three stations will complete your application, and the last station will bring you close to your recognition.

I Choose

1. *Creation*: use your mind to invent your future. Visualize exactly what you want to be and where you want to go. Conceptualize your mission, and theorize your path.

"It doesn't matter how long you've been in the dark; a single match is enough to light up a dark room that hasn't seen light for years. The match (your thought) will fuel the branch, the branch (your mind) will ignite the log (action), the fire (reaction) will heat the room and our hearts (satisfaction)!"

I Dare

2. *Action:* bring your thoughts to life by putting in writing and in great detail a concrete plan of action. Keep it in a prominent place, study it daily, and let it stimulate your desire to take another decisive step.

"Plan accurately, and you will reach your chosen destination; plan inaccurately, and you will reach a destination you dislike; fail to plan, and the captain will take you wherever he likes!"

I Become

3. *Reaction:* safeguard your choices, thoughts, and actions, based on your spirituality. Enhance your mind with good studies, your body with quality food, and your soul with carefree play on a daily basis. Close your ears to those who want to steal your confidence.

"We all wish to find happiness at the next station or get to it as soon as possible. Some head in that direction on foot, some ride their bicycles, and some fly like the wind!"

I Am

4. *Satisfaction:* have fun with all your heart and congratulate the protagonist of your life for your personal transformation. Everyone

will now detect and tell your achievements, thereby confirming the success of your journey.

"Once we savor a good moment, we thereafter store it as a good memory. A good memory's aftertaste is so intense that it does not let us settle for anything less!"

The Great Road
I Choose—I Dare—I Become—I Am
Creation—Action—Reaction—Satisfaction
Tetragrammaton
YHVH

(b) What to Do
(b1) Prepare a clear plan to convert your good thoughts into definite actions—the Gardener's Five Rules.
(b2) Combine the elements that will make the difference and will set you apart—the Triptych of Success.

(b1) *Le Cinque Norma Di Un Giardiniere*—The Gardener's Five Rules

Whatever you want to do in your life, whatever you want to achieve, the Gardener's Five Rules will be the roots that will keep the mighty tree safe and strong. Let the earthquake and the storm come; nothing will bring down a deep-rooted tree.

Beginning

"Our life is full of stations. We stop, observe, evaluate, and move on, until the next station. The caravan never stops!"

The execution will be based on your order—execution upon request. Your day will evolve, based on your morning choices. Your week will be completed, based on your daily choices. The year will end, based on your collective choices. Choosing the green or red button is a daily matter. Your thoughts are the coordinates so be certain before you select them. You hold the remote control of your life.

Planning

"The sun gives us light, the spring gives us water, the tree gives us fruit, the book gives us knowledge; we have something to give back too!"

Your action plan must have well-thought-out steps that will give value. Don't let a single minute go to waste, even if you have to toil while everyone else is sleeping and resting. That's the only way to make up for lost ground. You are not a photovoltaic cell, doomed to have life only when it is sunny; you are not a wind turbine, doomed to have life only when there is wind. You are an all-weather living organism, blessed to produce energy around the clock, if you so desire—even in the dark of the night when everyone else is asleep, even when you are asleep.

Cooperating

"Operation acquires substance with cooperation; hence, the prefix *co*. Cooperation gives added value to operation!"

You want to reach your destination and write your chapter in gold letters. You want to make your passengers proud, especially those traveling in the first seats. You constantly encounter problems, obstacles, and difficulties that you have never had to handle before. You need help, and then you remember Grandpa's words about operating, cooperating, and added value. You realize that only with synergy will you manage to overcome the most difficult obstacles. It is insanity and not pride that makes you reject help and support from other people. Use your power of *forgive, forget,* and *forward*, and continue with an attitude of cooperation; at the end of the day, collect the positives, forget the negatives, forgive the mistakes, and move forward with your journey.

Desiring

"Every desire that is reinforced by passion, longing, intensity, and energy stimulates our minds and our souls. Once this irrepressible desire is born in your mind, you must immediately bring it into the light through your actions. Give flesh and blood to your noble and sincere desires!"

The results of your actions will surprise you, as the reactions of other people will be encouraging. It will have a positive effect on everyone. Your efforts will be appreciated by the young and the old, the knowledgeable and the ignorant, the happy and the doleful. The collective positive reaction will help all of you to make a wonderful journey happen. Everyone will be satisfied, and no one will blame your aspirations, as long as your desires are pure and your actions are passionate.

Respecting

"If you are always able to show good intentions toward everyone and not just at will, you discover a tremendous power that exists within you that is called forgive, forget, and forward!"

If your desires are pure and your actions are passionate, then the collective reaction is satisfaction. And remember the *detect and tell* requirement: if all recipients feel this positive feeling, then you are entitled to enjoy it too. Once the recipient benefits from it, the sender is then entitled to benefit from it as well. You have provided safety, comfort, and joy to everyone on board and have met their needs. You have performed your duty without expecting any gratuity; the bonus will come, sooner or later, and it will be the greatest in the world.

(b2) *Tre Ingredienti Del Successo*—The Triptych of Success

"Everyone is entitled to a seat, but not all seats are the same. Only distinguished passengers are entitled to sit in the front seats!"

Never waste your time, never give up, and never stop giving more than you get.

(c) How to Do It

Love the Ten Lanterns like a fairy tale, and
appreciate them as you would a heritage. I
promise that your life will be transformed. Can
you promise to try with all you've got?
—Takis Conali

It takes time and intensive effort to complete the application stage with the light from the Ten Lanterns. As soon as they are rooted in your heart, you will need to transmit them to all those in need. After all, this is a prerequisite and part of the recognition stage. As long as we keep them to ourselves alone, we violate their very nature. I urge you to follow the light of the Ten Lanterns and enlighten the rest of the passengers. Utilize your powers of perseverance, and apply them until they become self-existent in your soul.

The Ten Lanterns do not have riches and fame as an end result, but I assure you that their dedicated usage will lead you where your soul desires.

Some choose the spiritual realization as a final destination, some prefer to have professional success, and some even decide to take up monasticism. You have a list with limitless options. You can have one or as many wagons as your soul desires, so choose wisely. You are worthy of having it all!

Dieci Lanterne—Ten Lanterns
"To have a good ending, you must make good choices!"

First Lantern:
I choose to have good company, and I am useful.
Second Lantern:
I choose to have good mood, and I am cheerful.
Third Lantern:
I choose to have good manners, and I am respectful.
Fourth Lantern:
I choose to have good intentions, and I am faithful.
Fifth Lantern:
I choose to have good progress, and I am resourceful.
Sixth Lantern:
I choose to have good timing, and I am mindful.
Seventh Lantern:
I choose to have good memories, and I am grateful.
Eighth Lantern:
I choose to have goodness and I am thoughtful.
Ninth Lantern:
I choose to have good purpose, and I am purposeful.
Tenth Lantern:
I choose to have good life, and I am insightful.

Epilogue

The Epilogue of Pain

Don't wait for hope to fly in through the keyhole
of your door. Make sure you open all the windows
and all the doors for the sky to pour a rainstorm of
hope onto your doorstep. Just open your heart!
—Takis Conali

The long journey of my personal quest is over, as is the event. The lights have gone out, my audience has gone home, and I am left alone on the stage. I am at the bar, enjoying my cocktail and rejoicing at the outcome of the evening. I look at my watch, and it reads three o'clock, almost dawn. Despite the physical pain I feel from exhaustion, my mind torments me with one particular thought. It is so intense that I must deal with it immediately to calm myself down.

The long journey of my personal quest is over, but the journey of personal development continues uninterrupted. Despite the fact that I have made this journey hundreds of times, I still have an inexhaustible supply of curiosity to observe and search for that something new that I have not yet identified in the previous presentations. My undying curiosity is activated, my desire for good progress is ignited, and my innocent, childlike inquisitiveness returns to turn on yet another lantern.

The idea continues to dominate my thoughts as it grows gigantic in my mind. Even after an amazing and successful night, my mind wants to push me one seat farther up. I will need the pink magic stick to bring my audience back to Sky Hall for one more minute, one more night, since I owe them something.

The experience I gained over the years was not through experiment as I was alone in my lab; after all, I am not a chemist. It was not a painting as I sat alone in a country; after all, I'm not a painter. It was not a psychological support to a single patient; after all, I didn't become a psychologist. It wasn't philosophies and quotes that I wrote, alone in a closed office; after all, I am not a theorist. In any case, if I'm ever left alone, I'll wither and die. On this journey, I was constantly with other people—in seminars, workshops, coaching sessions, and lectures; teaching and being taught. I was traveling on a real caravan, as envisioned by Grandpa Amadeo half a century ago. Therefore, the knowledge within this book may have germinated from the seed of the Conali spiritual heritage, but the oak tree that stands tall is the result of a collective effort.

This journey contains a cluster of cognitive treasures awaiting recognition through transmission, until it arrives at every home, in every neighborhood, and in every city; until it eliminates as much pain as possible from every soul. After all, I am a writer, and I want to see my work do some work. I want my book to continue its journey and find its own fate. As much as I love it, I can't breathe for it so I will let it continue on its own. I release my book from any emotional shackles and offer it to you until it becomes your book. The contributors to its success cannot be mentioned in one tome. Among the protagonists, I will mention Amadeo Conali, who planted the seed, and all those who have safeguarded the century-old oak tree. Most important of all are all those who believed and ultimately transformed their lives with the spiritual fruits, the Ten Lanterns. Therefore, I release my family from any exclusive rights and invite all of you to claim them as your own. They are yours, but don't forget to give them to the rest of your fellow passengers. Despite the fact that this is a personal journey, the sea has taught us the power of "we," and the roads have taught us the power of "me." That's why the sea is so beautiful!

To win the war and eradicate the pandemic of pain, we need all capable fighters on our side. Since we are talking about battles and personal victories, and since everyone should be a master of himself, I will quote the words of a great Greek philosopher, Plato the Athenian, who said, "The first and greatest victory is to conquer yourself; to be conquered by yourself is of all things most shameful and vile!"

To defeat yourself is the first and best victory of all. This swirls around in my mind as the sun comes up. While most people are sleeping, my mind is still struggling with a huge worry. I have said goodbye to my audience before telling them about the most important discovery from my trip. That is why I want them back and light the stars in the Sky once more.

While I lose my reasoning, you must not lose your faith. Stay with me for a while so I can reveal my utmost wisdom to you. Since I didn't transmit it to my audience, I need your help. Please read about it, and learn about it. Once you make this philosophy yours, then convey it to the whole world. I feel uncomfortable because my audience bought a ticket for a distinguished seat, and the captain has left them at the second-to-last station. They bought a ticket to find out what is the most precious thing in the world, and they left without a clear answer. At least I offered them a compass and a map, and they are one breath away from the last station. They'll have to take one more step to slip in and be lost in a seductive world—the path of happiness!

I feel comfortable because you are still with me, and we will have the chance to enjoy the epilogue of pain together. Please forgive my capitalized words below; it's the only way I have to shout it out loud to you.

In my personal journey, I have followed the Ten Lanterns religiously, as I have been assured and promised that my good choices will lead to good life. So many philosophers and writers have dedicated their lives and work to persuade us that WE ARE OUR CHOICES, and I will never debate this. While learning about choices, however, and the power they have in our lives, I have discovered that CHOICES ARE NOT THE STARTING POINT!

They are, in fact, the second station. It is by far the biggest and most important station of all, yet IT IS NOT THE FIRST ONE. It is built of red brick and has large arched doors, and its wooden shutters and doors are olive-colored; it's impressive how clean and tidy the Choice Station is—almost spotless—but it's not the *beginning*. At this station, you will make all the decisions that will potentially affect the outcome of your life, but I repeat, something else must definitely come first— the most precious thing in the world must precede it.

Oh my God! As I type these words to you, a thought strikes me! I am writing my last chapter! My eyes are filled with tears of joy, and I can't focus on the computer screen to complete my thoughts. I pause and let my mind take a break to recollect. I wrote my first troubling thoughts in September 2021, and I write my last positive thoughts in February 2022, just before my cloudy March finds me. Seven months in quarantine away from my office, my colleagues, and my fellow passengers. If I have managed to overcome the fifth surgery and escape from my physical and mental quarantine, then you will make it too because you have in your possession the spiritual map and compass. In a few lines below, I will finally reveal to you the most precious thing in the world, if you haven't already discovered it, as it screams at you from the beginning.

My dear God, your foreman was absolutely right. He told me to continue my journey, and when I am ready, I will be able to light my own lantern. I am finally ready!

My journey was completed because my passengers never gave up on me. They chose to save up *time* for me, chose to open my eyes with their *perseverance*, and chose to open my heart with their *giving*. If hope means "giving time, having undying perseverance, and giving without expecting anything in return," then I admit that I have been rescued by *hope*. If hope is given by those who truly love me, then I admit that I have survived through *love*. If I have survived a horrendous tragedy, then love and hope have aided me to light my way and lighten my pain. With this illuminating knowledge, I can deal with the pain and be *free* to continue my life's journey, having gained the most valuable skill in the world. Our time, perseverance, giving, hope, love, and freedom are indeed so precious!

I am finally ready to light my own lantern because I have just discovered what is the most precious thing in the world.

The most precious thing in the world is our ... GOOD THOUGHTS.

It is perhaps our only asset that we can completely control, provided we are fully trained to do so. Unfortunately, some teachers in our children's schools have continued to make the same mistake, year after year, over and over again, for hundreds of years. They rely on their rudimentary understanding, and their teachings only touch the hearts of their students in superficial ways. They communicate to our bright saplings the theory of good company, good mood, good manners, good intentions, good progress, and good timing, but they do not teach them the most important thing. They tell them *what to do* and fail to teach them *what to be*. And *to be*, you must first think of it—visualize it, conjure it in your mind. This can only be done with GOOD THOUGHTS. And the fertilizer for these thoughts is good memories, goodness, good purpose, and the eternal desire for good life.

Oh, my dear Lord, our grandpa Amadeo has transmitted everything we need for a successful life—a full life!

GOOD THOUGHTS will be the spiritual wealth—the coordinates— and our GOOD ACTIONS will be the spiritual good—the result.

Oh, my dear reader, although I am tempted to ask you to become a judge and sentence to life imprisonment all those who poison your thoughts, I would rather give you again the same advice I gave you when we first met. Do not let the stowaways or the confidence thieves discourage you and convince you to stop your journey to cross the Great Road. You will need one thing: *blind faith in yourself*! You already know that the factories that produce our thoughts are our own minds. It is the most important tool in our lives because it is through its lenses that we perceive the world. Love, passion, aspirations, memories, knowledge, stimuli, perceptions, and everything that the mind captures, stores, and processes only makes sense when presented to us through its lenses. Since the mind is our window to the outside world, like the train's window, it is essential to keep it clean and transparent to enjoy every detail—to notice and capture each message like, "Make a stop, and let the deep green give you a deep breath!"

You might be unaware of your mind's favorite game: bras de fer. Your mind loves to have constant daily fights with you until one dominates forever. There is no such thing as a tie, nor is there such a thing as rotational domination. Enter the fight with one goal and one goal only—to master your mind in order to discipline yourself.

Personal discipline is a great virtue. Once you tame and take the wild horse under your control, then you will enjoy riding it in the green pastures. Once you manage to have your mind, yourself, your passions, your desires, and your pain under control, you will be able to enjoy the journey and reach the destination you desire. So, make sure you MASTER YOUR THOUGHTS. This can only be achieved in one way: replenishment, disclosure, and confession!

Replenish your mind with the Ten Lanterns, disclose your spiritual wealth to all, and confess your ultimate goal—to cross the Great Road, as many have accomplished over the past five hundred years and were blessed with enjoying the spiritual fruits and recognition.

Speaking of refueling, you should know that your mind is bigger than the station master's great warehouse, so make sure you stock it properly, and keep it complete and busy. To accomplish this, you must prepare a well-thought plan that will run like a Swiss watch. Leave your mind no room for negotiation, or don't allow your mind to fill in the blanks on its own.

Speaking of time, keep your mind alert, even when you are resting or sleeping. I remind you of the best way to utilize your mind while sleeping: you prepare and enjoy a light supper and then go to sleep, along with your idea or problem. You sleep on it! In the morning, you will find the solution you seek right there on your breakfast plate. I guarantee this is the most effective problem-solving process. As long as your thoughts are always pure, spiritual aid will come at supersonic speed.

At this point, I encourage you to remember the chapter of the *confession*. You will have to make the same journey and face your own courtroom. To free yourself from the shackles of pain and begin your journey with light luggage, you must become judge and jury, prosecutor and defense, innocent and guilty. Wear and throw off all hats until you face all your thieves that are running after your positive thinking. Be ready to silence the familiar and welcome the unfamiliar. To accomplish this, you should pause your *I-know-it-all* in your present, forget your *I've-learned-it-all* in your past, and lose your *I-want-it-all* from your future. Only then will you make some space to learn something new. Once you finish your confession, you finally will learn something new; you eventually will find yourself!

Do not lose faith if you eventually discover that your self-confidence thieves are some distinguished passengers. Above all, do not be afraid when you discover THAT YOUR SELF-CONFIDENCE MASTER THIEF IS YOURSELF! You will use your immense power: forgive, forget, and forward!

Grandpa Takis gave me a promise. He told me that once the Ten Lanterns are instilled in my soul, a guardian angel would be with me for the rest of my life. The day he told me this, as I was blessed to still have him in my life, I was under the impression that the guardian angel would be Amadeo Conali. After all, he had the name and grace—*a man of God with wings*!

Today, I realize that the guardian angel was, is, and will forever be my beloved Grandpa Takis. Every time I despair and I look up into the sky, once I relive the experiences and recall his words, he comes with supersonic speed back into my life. It doesn't matter how long I have been in the dark. He will light a single match. The match will fuel the branch, the branch will ignite the log, and the fire will heat my heart. After my guardian angel's visits, the thought factory reconstitutes itself and produces only good thoughts.

Finally, I may not have recouped my March 2012 lost treasure, but I found my path, myself, and my guardian angel. I found it all inside the great warehouse, once the station master gave me the key.

The key opened the mind, and the spiritual reserves empowered my good thinking.

Let's see what you found in our journey. In the previous chapter, you received all the knowledge, as I found it in the safe box, as the king discovered it in the cook's manuscript. Even if you believe you seemingly have lost everything in your own fairy tale, I urge you to remember two things: the flame of hope that smolders within you—that's why you bought this book—and the hope you can find in other people—that's why I'm still here, if you need me. I encourage you to recall the humble beggar who dared to ask the king for a coin to feed his children. Once the higher king gives him a shilling, then the king's blessing begins. If the beggar feeds his family with that shilling, then his own blessing begins as well. If he deceives the king and spends the shilling on alcohol, then his own sin begins. And it will be a sin if you throw away the *golden shilling* you hold right now!

If you choose the spiritual path, you will achieve your personal transformation, and universal recognition will follow. It will be your PERSONAL RESURRECTION. If you stay at the starting point with wishful thinking or if you stay in the middle of the road with your pretexts, or if you give up with various excuses, there will be no one to blame but you. You will sin, and you will have no justification. It will be your fault. If you remain oblivious of the fact that this is how your life is, or, even worse, you think that life owes you a great deal and should repay you as you sit comfortably on your throne, it will still be your fault. Retreating from the responsibility you have will make you temporarily feel somewhat better, but soon you will have to face the harsh reality. If you don't even do that, it's still your fault. That will be your greatest sin. Eldridge Cleaver rightly said, "If you are not part of the solution, you must be part of the problem!"

If I made it, then you can make it too. If Ten Lanterns disciples have succeeded, then you will too. When you have total faith in yourself, a little faith in me, and eternal faith in our Father, only then you will experience your transformation—grow your own wings and fly. BECOME A CONALI! Obviously, your own guardian angel will have a role to play as well, so make sure you find your angel along the way.

To sum up, I want to bid you farewell with Napoleon Hill's quote:

> "Life is a chessboard, and the player opposite you is Time. Your pieces will be wiped off the board if you hesitate before moving or neglect to move thoughtfully and decisively."

My chosen reader, you cannot afford to let an hour, a day, a week, a month, or a year go to waste. If you finally detect and tell the value of my heritage and offer me the recognition I've been awaiting for years, then Evos Conali makes you a promise:

> I will continue to talk about the *positive thinking power*, at the risk of being considered old-fashioned, as we live in an era where negative minds and negative thoughts are becoming increasingly fashionable. I will continue to honor the Conali credo: good manners were, are, and always will be in fashion! I will relentlessly continue to learn, explore, and contemplate until I introduce myself in my next book!

My chosen reader, for the time being, just grab a pen and fill the empty page that follows with your positive thoughts. Right now! And who knows? You might finally introduce yourself to us again with your own book. What a blessing!

Goodbye, my dear fellow passenger.

Our train will never stop!

The Author

Evagoras Evagorou is a PTP—Positive Thinking Power—master coach. He is a qualified trainer, certified by the Cyprus Human Resources Development Authority, with over ten thousand hours of training, coaching, and lecturing in Cyprus and abroad.

He is a brief coach, certified by Solution Surfers of Switzerland, and an executive coach, certified by the International Coach Federation of America. He also achieved University of Cambridge certification for the High Impact Leadership program.

Evagoras has twenty years of experience working in banking and human resources management. Since 2007, he has been exclusively involved in the design and implementation of training and development programs in the areas of positive communication, culture empowerment and resilience, time management, inspirational leadership, and achieving outstanding results. At the same time, he offers consulting services and personal coaching.

His partnership with Franklin Covey has been accompanied by his training and certification in the areas of change management, productivity, and the delivery of the world-renowned program, *The 7 Habits of Highly Effective People*.

This book, *Ten Lanterns*, is Evos's first work in the category of inspirational and self-help books. Although he is working on an authorial sequel, he remains an active partner and consultant on HR issues in many companies.

Today, as another wonderful day dawns, before I put my feet on the floor and take my first step, I will count my blessings, one by one. Once I have filled ten books of blessings, I will thank God, who is always by my side, for His goodness in granting me another twenty-four hours.

The End
or maybe the beginning of something better.

Printed in the USA
CPSIA information can be obtained
at www.ICGtesting.com
LVHW040835130823
754938LV00010B/227/J

9 798765 237281